More Advance Praise for Lawrence Scott Sheets's
EIGHT PIECES OF EMPIRE

"Dean of the Moscow press corps Lawrence Scott Sheets has been everywhere and seen it all. Funny, engaged, and humane, he is a matchless guide to the tattered remnants of the Soviet empire."

—Anna Reid, author of *Borderland* and *The Shaman's Coat*

"A smoothly written and sensitively drawn personal portrait of the people and places Lawrence Sheets meets during the roiling collapse of the Soviet Union, and the furtive, now two-decade-long struggle of the resulting fifteen states to construct something new. I have the feeling that people will be reading his account for a long time to come."

—Steve LeVine, contributing editor at *Foreign Policy* and adjunct professor, Security Studies Program, Georgetown University

"Beautifully wrought and executed with admirable clarity, Lawrence Sheets's gripping, intelligent, and compassionate account of the years following the Soviet empire's end is a must-read for anyone interested in the human cost of change."

—Vanora Bennett, journalist and author of *Portrait of an Unknown Woman* and *The Taste of Dreams*

"During his almost two decades living and reporting in several countries that are former Soviet Republics, Lawrence Sheets had a front-row seat to the human casualties and political fallout of the collapse of the Soviet empire. *Eight Pieces of Empire* vividly captures the lived experiences of people caught on the sweeping waves of politics and history with intimacy and insight."

—Robin Hessman, director/producer of *My Perestroika*

EIGHT PIECES OF EMPIRE

A 20-YEAR JOURNEY
THROUGH THE SOVIET COLLAPSE

LAWRENCE SCOTT SHEETS

Crown Publishers

NEW YORK

Library of Congress Cataloging-in-Publication Data
Sheets, Lawrence Scott.
    Eight pieces of empire : a 20-year journey through the Soviet collapse / Lawrence Scott
Sheets. — 1st ed.
        p. cm.
    Includes bibliographical references.
    1. Soviet Union—History—1985–1991. 2. Russia (Federation)—History—1991.
3. Social change—Soviet Union—History. 4. Social change—Russia (Federation)—
History. 5. Post-communism—Social aspects—Soviet Union—History. 6. Post-
communism—Social aspects—Russia (Federation)—History. 7. Sheets, Lawrence Scott—
Travel—Soviet Union. 8. Sheets, Lawrence Scott—Travel—Russia (Federation). 9. Soviet
Union—Description and travel. 10. Russia (Federation)—Description and travel. I. Title.
    DK286.S44 2011
    947.085'3—dc23

                                                                        2011023849

ISBN 978-0-307-39582-5
eISBN 978-0-307-88885-3

PRINTED IN THE UNITED STATES OF AMERICA

Map by Hadel Studio
Jacket design by Ben Gibson
Jacket photography Harald Sund/Getty Images

10   9   8   7   6   5   4   3   2   1

First Edition

Dedicated to my grandmother
Helen Elizabeth Burlingame Groh (1909–2008)
("I'm not going to sit around waiting to age 102 to
read that manuscript!"—you kept your promise on that,
but you came close)

and my mother,
Joyce Arden Groh Sheets (1935–1985)

Contents

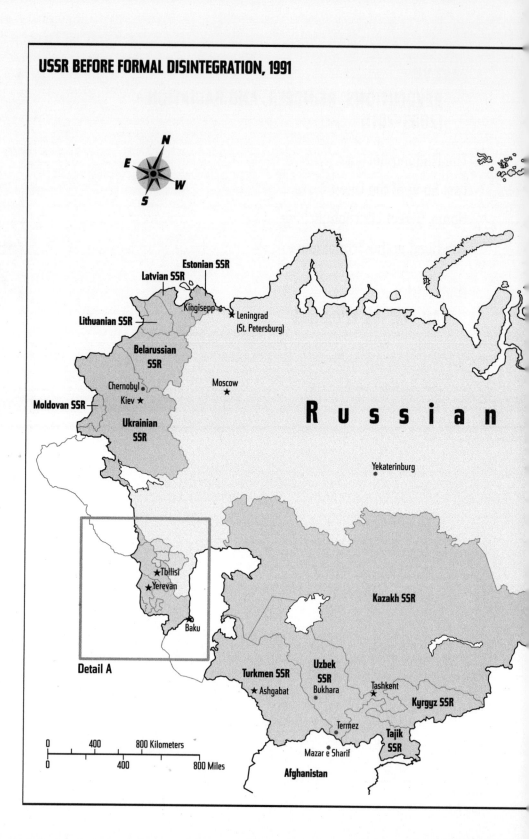

USSR BEFORE FORMAL DISINTEGRATION, 1991

N
E · W
S

Estonian SSR
Latvian SSR
Lithuanian SSR
Kingisepp
★ Leningrad
(St. Petersburg)
Belarussian
SSR
Chernobyl ●
Moscow
Kiev ★   ★
Moldovan SSR
Ukrainian
SSR

R u s s i a n

Yekaterinburg ●

★ Tbilisi
★ Yerevan

Kazakh SSR

● Baku

Detail A

Uzbek
SSR
Turkmen SSR   Tashkent
★ Ashgabat   Bukhara ●   ★   Kyrgyz SSR

Termez ●   Tajik
SSR

0   400   800 Kilometers
0   400   800 Miles

Mazar e Sharif ●
Afghanistan

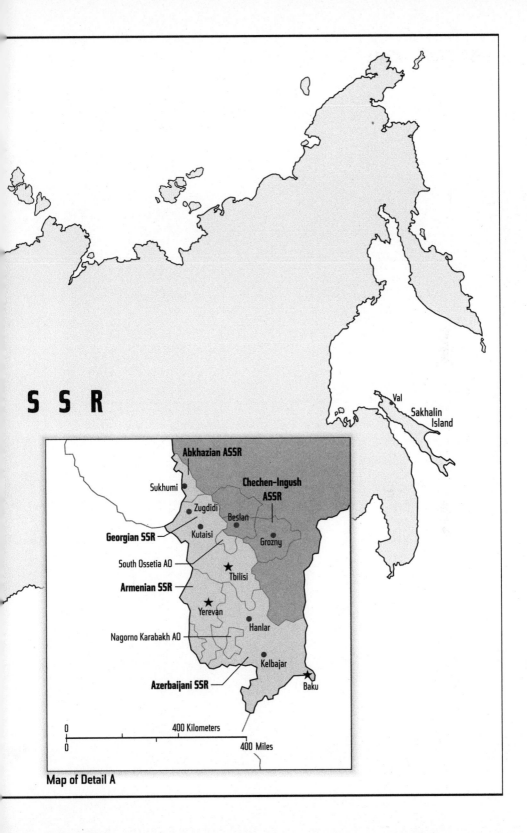

S S R

Val
Sakhalin
Island

Abkhazian ASSR

Sukhumi

Chechen-Ingush
ASSR

Zugdidi

Beslan

Georgian SSR

Kutaisi

Grozny

South Ossetia AO

Tbilisi

Armenian SSR

Yerevan

Hanlar

Nagorno Karabakh AO

Kelbajar

Azerbaijani SSR

Baku

0
400 Kilometers

0
400 Miles

Map of Detail A

LEGAL NOTE

In writing this book, I have relied chiefly on the nearly two thousand print and radio stories I filed over this period, as well as full notes and audio recordings taken over the roughly two decades of the book's narrative. In a few cases, namely the first part of the book (part I), I also relied on reconstructed memory, often with the help of people such as the former exiles Viktor and Mila; Pavel-the-once-Leningrad-button-maker; Ivan the journalist from Chechnya; Irina Mikhailova, formerly my producer at NPR Moscow; Zhorra Vardzelashvili, now a ghostwriter of novels in Georgia; and others to ensure accuracy.

The vast majority of the names of the individuals described are their actual legal names. In a few cases, however, I have omitted surnames at the request of my subjects. I have used pseudonyms for some first names at the specific requests of the persons in question and in reponse to their concerns for their own personal or family safety in some of the more insecure areas of the former USSR. I have not, however, employed pseudonyms to replace legal surnames. Nor have any persons of any major political or public profile been given a pseudonym; their names, surnames, and political or other profiles are stated as correct.

In a few other cases, I have made the decision to omit surnames or change the first names of my subjects; in these cases, the reasons are because I am no longer in touch with the individuals described and my efforts to find them have not borne fruit. In the event that any of these individuals are still alive, I wish to protect their identities, wherever they are today.

As for a few nicknames employed, most often these were not people I would have been asking for political information or other quotable advice, and in almost all these cases our interaction was fleeting. For example, the Preacher Man in part II was someone I found wandering around Abkhazia, and that is how we (journalists there at the time) referred to him, rather than by his given name.

Of the many colleagues or acquaintances whose fates sadly ended prematurely, I have not changed any first names or surnames. Included among these are: my friend and colleague the late journalist Adil Bunyatov in part III; and Galina Nizhelskaya, my friend who disappeared in Chechnya, in part IV.

AUTHOR'S NOTE

Those who read parts of this book before publication had vastly different feelings about its essential message. One friend described it as a book about *outcasts*. Existences were tossed upside down—in ways bad and good—by the Soviet collapse. Far-flung parts of the Soviet Empire struggled to find their own identities. Another reader called it a book about *death*.

I think both are correct—this is, of course, a book about an empire's death.

It is also about many of those who died as it fragmented violently in an extended, continuing process. I deliberately describe a variety of vignettes: a Russian acquaintance slipping into the world of extortion as the Union of Soviet Socialist Republics dissolved; a dissident poet locked away for years in prison in Uzbekistan; some of the flamboyant personalities involved in Georgia's armed conflicts of the early 1990s.

One might wonder how these various stories are related. The answer is that empires do not break down along nice clean lines. They fragment, and the dissolution of the USSR and of the personal lives and explosive situations affected by its fragmentation is the very subject of this book. The demise of such a monolith comes along with extraordinary rarity and produces completely unpredictable consequences. The Soviet Union was like an ill-fitting stained-glass mosaic, unsustainable and destined to shatter. Picking up and examining a few of those fragments is—for me—the only way to tell this story.

I observed the USSR's disintegration and its aftermath over roughly two decades. I was a student of the Russian language (in now again St. Petersburg) in 1987. I spent months in 1989 and 1990 as an interpreter and independent student in that city. In 1991, I arrived in Moscow as the empire entered the last months of its existence.

After 1991, I never really left the former Soviet Union again. I was bureau chief for Reuters in the turbulent Caucasus region of the former USSR from 1992 to 2000, and then worked for NPR (National Public Radio) from 2001 to 2008, including four years as NPR's Moscow bureau chief.

My early experiences in the late 1980s through nearly the end of 1991 allowed me the rare gift of immersing myself in the day-to-day life of the imploding empire. I lived it before I ever reported on it.

Even as a journalist, I was given a rich vantage point from which to view events: Being based for several years as a full-time correspondent in the Caucasus Mountains—the scene of violent conflicts in Georgia, Azerbaijan, Armenia, and Chechnya—freed me from much of the desk work and press conference–laden reporting that one encounters as a Moscow-based staff reporter. The dissolution of the Soviet Union took place among the spiral arms and fringes to which it was attached: in this case, now-former Soviet republics and far-flung parts of Russia itself. Conflicts erupted that few have heard of—such as those between the ethnic Ingush and Ossetians. New police states in Central Asian places like Uzbekistan emerged. Then there was the post-9/11 American war in Afghanistan, itself often called "The Graveyard of Empires." The miserable Soviet experience there helped lead to the USSR's demise.

As we mark twenty years of the empire's collapse, few speak about the USSR anymore or of what became of it. Westerners viewed it as a monolith. We largely failed to predict its demise—an object lesson about the ephemeral and perhaps our own sense of mortality, as nations and as human beings.

PART I
(1989–1991)

FAREWELL LENINGRAD,
FAREWELL EMPIRE

Aerial view of the Petrogradskaya Storona neighborhood of St. Petersburg (formerly Leningrad), Russia, in June 1990. The yellow cupolas of St. Vladimir's Cathedral are visible (*lower left*) and directly across (*lower center*) is the building housing the communal apartment where the author spent the summer of 1989 as the USSR began to disintegrate.

I n 1989, most Western Kremlinologists were still giddy with Soviet president Mikhail Gorbachev and his "reform" package to cure the ills of the Soviet Union. Known as "Glasnost and Perestroika" ("openness and restructuring"), the program was designed to bring the "Evil Empire" in from the cold (as it were). The prevailing view among the Western Kremlin watchers was that the Soviet Union was not destined for total collapse. Even after the end of that year, as Communist regimes in Czechoslovakia, Hungary, Bulgaria, East Germany, Romania, Poland, and even Maoist Albania had either fallen or were teetering, this view of the USSR as re-formable remained intact.

It was not just "Kremlinologists" who got it wrong. The notion of the Soviet Union going belly-up was incomprehensible to many Westerners. Empire is a seductive concept—reassuring, monolithic, predictable, and comforting—and we Americans (and they, the "Soviets") had cuddled up to the idea for about seven decades. During school drills, we'd huddled in fallout shelters with the telltale nuclear symbol, imagining our "foes" engaging in the same, predictable rite.

Waking up to find the Soviet Union gone was too mind-boggling to contemplate. If the society of our archenemy of the Cold War, the one we spent generations fearing, could collapse with such ease, what did that suggest about our own assumed immortality? Could not our American "empire" at some time unravel just as unexpectedly?

Those around me—in a once-posh but by then rundown Petrograd neighborhood—paid little attention to Gorbachev's long-winded speeches on state television. Some didn't care; others were oblivious. Most people were just too busy eking out a living. Yet in hindsight the empire's days were clearly numbered.

A CIVIL WAR OUTSIDE MY DOOR

I look though the smoky-colored windows of our communal apartment, toward St. Vladimir's Cathedral and its saffron-colored exterior. The empire is unraveling, and below, there are signs of the creeping chaos.

The scene around the cathedral is a source of practical information. Combatants converge around St. Vladimir's—on one side are the growing flocks of worshippers—on the other, the growing groups of drunks, whose numbers surge over the summer, proof that yet another Communist Party effort (spearheaded by Gorbachev himself) to battle Russians' love of the bottle is running dry. The image of drinking and of Russia may indeed be a Western stereotype. In fact, half the population imbibes little, if at all. Yet the drunks are there, right before my eyes.

The drunks favor the area for a simple reason: Out of spite or ignorance, the city authorities opened a skid row beer stand, or *pivnushka* (which in the official hierarchy of the Leningrad Municipal Department of Public Eating Places is literally at the bottom of the barrel—restaurants, cafés, and cafeterias rank higher), right next to St. Vladimir's, a cathedral sheltering one of Orthodoxy's most sacred icons.

Announced with a sloppily painted sign reading PIVO ("beer"), the *pivnushka* is just an open-air shack. There's no pretense here. The patrons, mostly bleary-eyed men who've seen better days, line up to get smashed—quickly and cheaply. Warm, brackish-tasting tap beer is poured into scratched-up mugs and passed into trembling hands.

By noon, drunken men are all around the beer stand. They spill into the street around St. Vladimir's and into its courtyard. They pass out on benches. They wave their drinking glasses. They spit, they shout.

Then the skirmishes commence—the pious, most of them women, scatter the drunks away from St. Vladimir's with raised hands, swinging purses. Many might be described as "babushkas." But "babushka" is another Western caricature—a balloon-cheeked granny in a multicolored scarf. These women are of all descriptions: gaunt, urban matrons with birdlike arms; college girls; wobbly, roly-poly peasant mothers, some of them with their grandchildren in tow to teach them to know their icons. This is new and daring. Two years previously, such catechism exposed oneself to the prying eyes of potentially informer priests.

The Saints usually win these daily conflagrations. With sweat popping off their foreheads, the Sinners retreat to their rear base down Talalikhina Lane near the *pivnushka*.

And in reality, both sides are winners, are they not?

For both, freedom has indeed been found! For the Saints, who now worship in public without looking over their shoulders. And for the drunks, who indeed would have been rounded up as parasites or miscreants just a few years back. They stand around, drinking and laughing and shouting in animated if inebriated conversation, oblivious to the robed priests and head-scarved women entering St. Vladimir's Cathedral, ironically in this year of 1989, the two hundredth anniversary of its consecration.

Yet to others, that freedom, the empire's demise, is a symbol of the impending anarchy, unpredictable and threatening.

A FEW STEPS separate St. Vladimir's Cathedral from our building's entrance at Talalikhina Lane 7/9.

Nina Nikolaevna and I pass through the entranceway, she making a deliberate attempt to ignore the loitering drunks. We slowly ascend to the fifth and final floor of the dark, winding staircase, stopping on almost every landing. Her legs are riddled with gout, victims of the

World War II Nazi blockade of the city, which killed nearly a million Leningraders—and barely spared Nina's life.

Our corner of the communal is the first room on the right. Privacy is a piece of cloth hung over a rope drawn across the middle. Nina Nikolaevna's bed occupies a sacred corner—the sheet of fabric serving as room divider is almost never pulled all the way back. I sleep on a small, hard divan near the door.

There is a black-and-white television set, a small table, a bookshelf. The tablecloth is pristine, the floor swept and scrubbed to a gloss. This is the inner sanctum, away from the shabby common areas in the hallway, toilet, and kitchen.

A ubiquitous "people's radio" is bolted to the wall, obligatory in any Soviet flat. It offers no choice of frequencies—just buttons to push for three government radio stations.

Interspersed with music, announcers read ominous-sounding Communist Party bulletins. The ring though the tinny speaker consists of stern warnings to the leaders of independence from the Baltic republics of Latvia, Lithuania, and Estonia who are already well on their way to seceding from the USSR.

NINA NIKOLAEVNA is sturdily built, with a wisp of grayish-white hair and warm but steely eyes that hint of a long, hard life. She makes the trip up and down the deep stairway several times a day on those gimpy legs. She might, one could presume, because of the exile of her daughter, or the hyperinflation devouring her pension, have less reason to defend the system than many other people. But that is not the case.

Nina is no Stalinist, not even a party member. Yet to her, imagining the demise of the empire is like imagining the sun won't come up tomorrow. She turns to the subject of the seceding Baltic republics, the first major crack in the empire. "The Balts are all full of empty talk." She waves her hand dismissively. "What's done has been done." In other words, the Baltic states will always be part of the Soyuz (Soviet Union) because they became a part of it (by whatever means) and were thus stuck being part of it for eternity, like it or not. Even at this terminal stage of the empire's existence, food stores emptier by the day and decent shoes scarce, Nina Nikolaevna is convinced that the Soyuz will survive.

I AM A *blockadnitsa*," says Nina Nikolaevna weightily. Her eyes glow in an extinguished sparkle, as if the phrase needs no elaboration. The experience of surviving the nine-hundred-day Nazi blockade defines the city's spirit, and makes any hardship a trifle by comparison.

"The siege is the most tragic in the city's history, and I think it was then the name Leningrad was finally adopted by the inhabitants who survived," wrote the celebrated poet Joseph Brodsky in his essay "Guide to a Renamed City" (1979). He was about three years old when it began.

Nina Nikolaevna was eighteen when the siege started on September 8, 1941, the date the Wehrmacht completely encircled the city. She was untold decades older when it was finally lifted on January 27, 1944, with the Nazis starting their retreat that would end with Hitler's suicide in his Führerbunker on April 30, 1945.

But that was later; that was victory.

Back in the autumn of 1941, then the spring of 1942, then the autumn of that year, and then all of 1943 into early 1944, defeat loomed over the city as it was pounded by German artillery and aircraft.

"It was not the sound of the bombs, but the silence on the streets in between the bombardments that was the most frightening thing," Nina Nikolaevna says.

Fuel had run out. What little remained was requisitioned by the army. No fuel meant no vehicles moving about—just the occasional sound of boots still healthy enough to hit the pavement.

Early on, the authorities began rationing food—canned goods from state stores, and then anything grown in garden plots: cabbage, onions, and carrots, mainly. When domesticated animals such as cows and sheep ran out, butchers turned to horses to make sausage, and then to cats, dogs, and rats.

"There was one case—they wrote about it in the newspaper—where a man came to his relatives and saw that their dog was still alive, even if just a bag of bones," Nina Nikolaevna recalls. They had already talked about the dog, about the fact he would have to be eaten. Then, when the man came to the apartment, the dog compliantly walked up to him as if completely cognizant of his final duty—to be someone's dinner.

Starvation finally arrived, and bodies piled up on the streets. Rumors abounded about human meat being hacked from the cadavers and hawked at the main bazaar.

"Eventually, they cut our rations to stale bread," she related. "Then a slice, then half a slice, soon half a slice of flour mixed with sawdust, and then sawdust mixed with crumbs and water."

NINA NIKOLAEVNA'S GRANDMOTHER was a well-known Leningrad museum curator, Darya Ivanovna Trufanova. The Leningrad authorities appointed Darya Ivanovna and other curators with the sacred task of hurriedly collecting masses of priceless art, icons, artifacts, and even imperial heirlooms—including Empress Catherine II's dresses—from museums and czarist summer residences, which were vulnerable to Nazi bombing runs.

It was often a dangerous job. Nazi troops were already within the outskirts of the city, where most of the former czarist estates were located. Darya Ivanovna was often accompanied by her daughter, Nina Nikolaevna's mother, Evgenia Timofeyevna Smirnova. "The last time my grandmother went to the outskirts of the city to collect more heirlooms, she heard voices speaking in German," Nina explains. Several of the palaces were later captured by the Nazis and destroyed before the art-gatherers got there. The Nazis shipped their contents to Germany before torching them.

Once collected, the icons and artwork had to be stored in places relatively safe from Nazi bombings. One was the massive St. Isaac's Cathedral in the city center, an edifice cut from incredibly thick granite and possessing a deep basement, rendering it practically bomb-proof. This gave the three—Grandmother Darya Ivanovna; her daughter Evgenia Timofeyevna, and the young Nina Nikolaevna—the privilege to dwell in that cathedral basement, safe at least from Nazi bombings.

But not safe from starvation. And so amid the collection of priceless luxuries and national heirlooms, the young Nina Nikolaevna withered away. She lay on a cot in the basement of St. Isaac's, too weak and hungry to walk, as the sawdust-bread rations grew smaller.

So Nina Nikolaevna lay away on her cot starving amid the empire's riches. Now she was within days or at most a couple of weeks of death.

But then there appeared that miraculous gift of sustenance from no-where—or rather, from the Leningrad Zoo. After all the other animals had long been devoured, there remained two once-playful seals. That they would ultimately be slaughtered was not in doubt; there was no food or fish left to feed them. The dilemma was not this, but rather whom the seals would save with their ultimate sacrifice. Who would be the chosen ones, those to receive precious bits of fat-rich seal blubber?

How would this momentous decision be taken? After all, it was a zero-sum question. That couldn't be denied. A lucky few would be se-lected. The seal blubber might bring them back from death's doorstep. Certainly there were scores—no, hundreds—of others whose lives would *not* be spared by the ultimate choice.

A family friend knew one of the zookeepers. A hunk of the seal blub-ber would be Nina's; the difference between life and death.

More than forty-five years after the end of the blockade, Nina de-scribes the sensation fully, as if the taste of seal blubber is returning to her parched lips and tongue. She describes how a man, a family acquain-tance, slipped into the basement of St. Isaac's Cathedral and handed the chunk of seal fat to her mother, who gently placed it in Nina's mouth. Nina chewed the fatty seal blubber slowly in that basement room stuffed with icons, washing it down with a bit of sawdust-bread and rainwater, waiting for the magic effect to set in, druglike, until the next day the swelling in her legs began to ease. She gradually got up and stood on her own two feet again.

The Leningrad Blockade may be a miracle of survival for some, but tales of surviving it are rarely paraded about. Even today, the subject is spoken of in whispers and serious conversations. Images of it are so harrowing that they are usually absent even in the bravado of Soviet World War II films. Along the city's main Nevsky Prospekt, I notice a plaque or two dedicated to the victims, and there are monuments here and there, but far fewer than one would expect of such a brutal experience. Nina's survival story is so gruesome, the knowledge that hundreds of other Leningraders were not the lucky ones saved by the magical slaughtered zoo seals, that she reveals the details reluctantly. She confesses she has never even told her own daughter, the exile Mila, the full story of the seals, a fact Mila later confirms to me.

BUILDINGS LEVELED BY artillery shells, carpet bombings, and whole districts engulfed in an inferno of flames—these are physical inflictions triumphantly rebuilt in defiance and victory. But the famine left no visible destruction. Perhaps that explains the reticence of survivors like Nina. A city being rebuilt after a pummeling to the ground is heady with a sense of renewal. Workers scurrying about, repairing bomb holes and collapsed walls. A sense of having prevailed!

Yet it's harder to know how to impart triumph into honoring a dead man, his hands out in his last moments, or mouth open, taking in those breaths, as he slowly starves to death. Even a man whose country was eventually miraculously victorious.

Perhaps that is why Nina insists the Soviet Union will survive—for she has survived. The country won "The Great Patriotic War," World War II. She has endured the privations, the exile of her dissident daughter, and despite a respectable career as a lawyer, she is confined to her crumbling communal. How can the Soviet Empire *not* survive?

OUR COMMUNAL

The communal is a place where perfect strangers are forced into an uneasy common existence, where even all whispers are audible. These total strangers inhabit a perpetually cramped virtual elevator. Every imaginable slice of Soviet society tossed together. Teetotaling gold-toothed engineers from Central Asia across the hall from beer-guzzling Siberians. Bespectacled spinsters with icons hidden under their beds treated to the nightly arias of the rail station whore next door. Notions of personal property blurred beyond recognition. Everyone "borrows" everything from everyone else, from sugar to socks, from tram tickets to tea. Everyone, from (former) royalty to (former) black-earth serfs, obliged to spit their words through the same brown-stained telephone receiver, line up outside the one toilet-for-all, and wait for someone else to replace the burnt-out lightbulb in the foyer.

"They—or rather 'we'—all lived in communal apartments. Four or more people in one room, often with three generations all together, sleeping in shifts, drinking like sharks, brawling with each other or with neighbors in the communal kitchen or in a morning line before the communal john, beating their women with a moribund determination, crying openly when Stalin dropped dead, or at the movies, and cursing with such frequency that a normal word, like 'airplane,' would strike a passerby as something elaborately obscene," wrote Brodsky in 1976.

There is a solitary doorbell, as the apartment was once the property of some baron and his family. Now, the once-stately spread is divided into five individual rooms. There's a makeshift system to keep up with socialist reality, with each of the five rooms in our communal having its set designated number of bell rings.

For Nina Nikolaevna, it's two turns of the old bell. It resembles the gentle "I'm behind you!" warning bell on the handlebar of children's bikes that you ring with your thumb.

Caution is advised in ringing the communal bell, because if you ratchet the dial a touch too fast, a third or fourth ring is emitted, rousing an annoyed neighbor who mistakenly thinks the ring is for him. But don't be too gentle—for if you stop at one ring, an equally perplexed resident is produced, thinking he is the subject of the summons.

There is a single telephone in the hallway placed next to a bench. Our number is 233-4832. Only two cities in the USSR of 1989 have seven-digit numbers—Leningrad and Moscow. The elite seven-digit designation is a source of pride. As for using the phone, the cardinal rule is that no one is allowed to monopolize it for more than a few minutes at a time. That's usually not a problem. Where the problem arises is that there are *two* Nina Nikolaevnas in our communal—my host, Nina Nikolaevna Slotina, and the Widow Nina (whom I will henceforth refer to only as "The Widow") across the hall, some twenty-five years younger, and whose patronymic is also Nikolaevna. Some callers use the surname of the Nina Nikolaevna they want to converse with to ease the confusion, but not all. Cases of calling the wrong Nina Nikolaevna to the phone can be humorous during the day, but seldom at night or toward dawn.

In addition to the five one-room apartments that make up our communal, there are also common areas. If residents do not really "own" their apartments, then no one "owns" the common areas, which in reality means that no one has any motivation to take care of them.

Down the hallway, for example, is the communal toilet. To get there, you must negotiate your way by the dim glow of a single, dust-encrusted orb. The wallpaper is stained and falling away in places. The floorboards have been sopped with dozens of coats of paint over the decades—dark reds and greens, mostly—that have been chipped and gouged and worn into grooves by the contact of a million heels.

There is one toilet for everyone, with no permanent seat. Rather, each room or family possesses its own personal wooden perch. Five of the wooden contraptions adorn the wall of the WC, hanging on long nails driven into the wall. Once, I used the wrong seat. Worse, I left it on the toilet, rather than hanging it back up on the wall. I won't describe the scandal that ensued—suffice it to say that if a long incarceration were a legal remedy for this crime, the offended would have demanded its swift application.

There is a large, dark kitchen with two ancient cast-iron gas stoves. Twinning them are two loudly snoring thirty-year-old refrigerators. Cooking is done in shifts; first come, first served. A constant smell of reused lard, potatoes, and onions (the mainstay of my diet during that summer of '89) wafts about, some of the few groceries possible to procure without waiting in long lines.

The Petrogradskaya Storona (the Petrograd Side), our district, is one of Leningrad's most beautiful, and that's no easy feat. We live in sight of the glassy Neva River, on one of the 101 islands that the city and its endless run of neoclassical facades are built upon. "Reflected every second by thousands of square feet of running silver amalgam, it's as if the city were constantly being filmed by the river . . . no wonder that sometimes this city gives the impression of an utter egoist preoccupied solely with its own appearance," wrote Brodsky in "Guide to a Renamed City." (The erstwhile imperial city smells of faded elegance and expropriated fortunes—a result of its status as a former haunt of the czarist empire's wealthiest citizens.)

Some owned ten-room spreads on two floors, replete with servants' quarters, dwarfing my imaginary baron's five-room spread on the fifth floor across from St. Vladimir's. Then came the February 1917 overthrow of the Romanovs, followed by the Bolshevik Revolution of November that same year, and everything changed.

With Russia facing a massive housing shortage after World War I, the Bolsheviks summarily relieved many previous owners of everything save a single room in their own mansions. Paper-thin walls—often only sheets or canvas strung from ceiling molds—slashed grand dining rooms of classic dimensions into weirdly shaped (and cramped) living shafts of two and three and even four units, now home to refugees and indigents.

Communist Party ideologists concocted theories about the communal as a quintessentially "socialist" concept: "consolidation"—the intentional comingling of former class enemies—served to break down social barriers.

In reality, the communal was a strictly utilitarian invention: You could pack more people into a small space if you gave it the right kind of name.

My communal neighbors, in addition to Nina Nikolaevna, include her husband, Igor. He is so quiet and overshadowed by her forceful presence as to be virtually invisible, and thus easy to forget. Is he a failure? Does he regard himself as one? With the entire Soviet system stacked up against anyone trying to get ahead (the Communist Party elite *"nomenklatura"* excepted, of course) and forced to live like laboratory rats in tiny Ferris-wheel cages, it is little wonder so many men turn to drink and women to religion. What would I do if this were *really* my life?

Other neighbors include a young man nicknamed "The Colonel," who occasionally mutters from behind his door about very dark things. I repeatedly turn down joining some dreamy scheme he rattles on about: smuggling rare Alexandrite gemstones out of the USSR, getting us both filthy rich.

There is also a quiet older man down the hall—another drinker—who rarely emerges, and an owlish old woman and her middle-aged son, who live next to the bathroom and tend to avoid me, the whispered reason being that a close relative works at a "secret" munitions factory.

Finally, there is the Widow. She's about forty, with a head of long black curly hair. The Widow exudes a frantic air of unrealized eroticism. She has two puberty-age sons. They take turns stomping in the hallway, ravenously laughing and explaining they are playing hide-and-seek with hamsters living under the floorboards—usually when I want to sleep. The Widow spends hours helping me practice my Russian late into the night and often, after her boys are asleep in the same room, tells me about every problem she has or is likely to have in the future. It seems that she thinks I might be part of the solution of relieving her of some of that burden, or banishing it altogether.

Each of the neighbors befriends me in their own way—even the folks with kin working at the munitions factory come around. One takes me to the traditional Russian *banya,* or bathhouse, across the street, where I receive my first beating with birch branches to open my pores to sweat and sweat and sweat. The grime-covered shower in our communal is not for the fainthearted. In stark contrast to—or perhaps because of— the decrepitude of the communal hallway, toilet, and kitchen, Nina Nikolaevna's room is fastidiously clean. She is always on guard against anyone entering without the little slippers known as *topochki* that are de rigueur in a Russian household. No matter how ill fitting, no matter how tattered, they must be worn. Eschewing them is tantamount to shaking hands with someone over the threshold of a doorway—a deadly omen that most Russians avoid by ripping their hands away if a foreigner makes the mistake of proffering his.

Nina sometimes laments the state of our building and the selection of goods available in the stores, which is dwindling by the day.

Somehow the subject of Stalin comes up, responsible for as many Soviet deaths during his thirty-year reign as the number who died in the Great Patriotic War fighting Hitler.

"Yes, people were executed under Stalin," Nina Nikolaevna says gravely but matter-of-factly. "But average folks were not generally harmed. Mostly, they repressed people connected to power in some way."

She says this as if political engagement is itself a type of guilt, and that innocence can only be found in passive acquiescence to authority.

Yes, admits Nina, the empire is capable of punishment, vindictiveness, and revenge. "But you have to remember that we lived rather well under Stalin," she adds. "There was food on the table. He won the war over the Nazis. We survived the blockade."

A long pause, and then:

"Our people need a bit of the Iron Hand," says Nina Nikolaevna, obliquely referring to the gathering chaos in the disintegrating empire, from the drunks down the street to the imploding planned economy. I will hear the same thing from other ordinary Russians for years to come.

In Nina's own eyes, the empire is also responsible for great feats. For her *the empire itself* was the mysterious hand that put that precious piece of seal blubber to her lips during the starvation of the Leningrad Blockade, giving her a second lease on life.

TEARS OF A KGB MAN

Nina Nikolaevna's crash course in the ways of the communal was reaching an end. I nodded knowingly at her entreaties about whom to avoid (the Colonel, for one) and who to turn to in need of help (the Widow). I had passed the communal home economics section as well. In addition to having learned to use the right wooden toilet seat, I could now distinguish between our grease-coated fry pan and the almost identical others, and I no longer used someone else's towels. One skill was pretending to lock the door with an ancient key. It looked like something pilfered from the antiquities section of the Hermitage Museum. (The locking ritual was an act of willing self-deception: Locked or not, the door often flung open when given a good shove.)

Satisfied with my progress, Nina Nikolaevna announced that the time had come for me to fend for myself. She and Igor had for many summers retired to a bucolic dacha outside Leningrad, and the time to return to some facsimile of their Russian peasant roots was at hand. (In reality, the "dacha" was a bare-bones rented room with no plumbing, but at least it was in the countryside.)

She pulled a tattered suitcase from under her bed, and I watched her gather a few blouses and a dress and fold them inside. Igor added a pair of old pants and a shirt and some socks, and a whole summer's laundry was ready to go. A second contraption—a duffel bag on a metal frame with vinyl wheels—represented the portable kitchen and was stocked with rice, sugar, and other staples hard to get outside the city. There were a couple of plates and bowls and a tarnished silverware set. (Igor tossed in a few packs of acrid unfiltered cigarettes).

Like a dutiful son, I helped them carry the luggage downstairs and to an overcrowded trolleybus that stopped in front of St. Vladimir's Cathedral. The trolleybus was sweltering hot and packed to the transoms with bleary-eyed men fresh from knocking 'em back at the beer stand; Nina Nikolaevna pretended not to notice them. We deboarded at Finland Station, where Lenin made his triumphant return to Russia in 1917 disguised as a locomotive worker, an event marked by an enormous statue of Vladimir Ilyich standing atop an armored vehicle that dominated the station yard. After the purchase of two tickets on the rickety if reliable electric suburban trains, we walked in the shadow of the statue among the human hustle and bustle of the platform, the bittersweet smell of burning locomotive engine coal staining the air with a sense of impending departure, while Nina Nikolaevna issued last-minute edicts about the rule of law in the communal.

"No drunks inside—especially the Colonel."

"Understood."

"Always lock the door, and if it doesn't work, don't leave until it's fixed."

"Yes, ma'am."

"And never, ever leave or go to sleep with the television on."

"Never."

This was an oath not to incinerate the communal in her absence; Soviet televisions were known to overheat and explode if the power cord was left in the wall.

Nina Nikolaevna and her Igor ascended the steps to their carriage, and she continued to issue last-minute directives while holding her cane like a scepter. Her pose vaguely resembled the nearby bronze statue of a triumphant Lenin thrusting his arm into the sky, and I almost felt that I was vowing to join the vanguard of the 1917 revolution against Denikin's Whites and other class enemies of the Great Socialist Experiment.

But it was 1989, and the only vigilance I was being drafted into was to be on guard against diabolical saboteur appliances and counter-revolutionary drunks. I promised that I would try.

Then the electric train silently pulled out of the station, and I was alone in Leningrad.

Or almost alone. Before leaving the United States, my Russian teacher, Viktor, and Nina Nikolaevna's exiled daughter, Mila, had given me some addresses of friends left behind in Leningrad. One was Lyona Shakhnazarova, an ethnic Armenian woman who had recently fled the Azerbaijani capital Baku; anti-Armenian riots had erupted there in one of the first spasms of interethnic unrest that would soon almost engulf the empire. There were whispers of dark forces being behind the violence.

Lyona was staying in a room on the first floor of a building near Bolshoi Prospekt, a fifteen-minute walk from our communal. Her first-hand experience of the ethnic supernova expanding across the empire informed her view of its future. She was convinced that there was none.

Lyona was well educated and from an intelligentsia family and was thus connected to the upper echelons of the Communist Party. But if she ever had any sympathy for the disintegrating system, it had turned to antipathy. Over thimblelike cups of Turkish coffee, Lyona hinted darkly about KGB practices—and that I should "watch out."

I chalked it up to paranoia—this was, after all, the era of Mikhail Gorbachev's declared *glasnost i perestroika* that were supposed to repre-sent a sort of Soviet "sunshine" clause on society. All the paranoid cloak-and-dagger stuff of the Cold War past was banished, forever!

"Be careful," she reiterated. "I know how they work."

I asked her to explain.

"Your apartment, for example," she said flatly, referring to the com-munal.

I was all ears as Lyona pointed out that only recently had foreign visitors been allowed to stay in private apartments—until then, guests such as me from the nonsocialist world had been confined to hotels or dorms. And as for gaining permission to stay in a communal like ours—especially one linked to forcibly exiled dissidents like Nina Niko-laevna's daughter, Mila, and her husband, Viktor—well, it was simply unheard of.

Indeed, the local visa office had initially told Nina Nikolaevna that I could not stay with her. Then, inexplicably, they changed their minds.

"You see," said Lorna darkly, winning a point.

"Why then," I asked, "did they issue me a visa at all?"

"Because they probably thought it would be more interesting if you did come than if you didn't," she said, giving the third-person pronoun an odd twist of ominous emphasis. "They probably want to find out what you're up to."

"What I'm up to?"

"Yes. The purpose of your visit."

"To work on my Russian, of course."

"Yes." Lyona smiled. "Of course."

ALL FOREIGNERS WERE required to register with the local registration office, known as the Otdel Viz i Registratsii, or Department of Visas and Reg-istration, referred to by all by its acronym, OVIR.

Call it an oversight; call it foolishness; call it exuberant forgetful-ness; call it deliberately courting doom (which it was not), but the fact remained that I was vaguely aware that I should have checked in with the OVIR authorities the day after my arrival, and I had not. To assist me in talking my way out of trouble, the Widow offered to accompany me to the OVIR, and I gladly accepted.

The walk to the OVIR led along the picturesque bank of the Neva River near the Peter and Paul Fortress (where notables from Dos-toyevsky to Tito had spent time locked up) and skirted the Gorky Metro station and a small amusement park, as well as an iconic old ice-cream café. It was a pleasure to be outside on that cloudless day, walking with the Widow.

At OVIR, I joined an orderly line of Russians waiting to obtain permission to travel abroad; the authorities widely started to allow this about a year earlier, as part of the gradual opening of the system. When my turn came, I handed my passport and visa to a clerk who, after a quick glance at the data, told me to wait.

Then she disappeared down a hallway into an office, reemerging a couple of minutes later and beckoning me to enter. The Widow followed, whispering that she was acting as my "translator," although she spoke not a word of English.

Behind a gray metallic bureaucratic desk sat a gray, metallic-looking midlevel bureaucrat, or *chinovnik,* who looked up at me with a gray, metallic look of shock and horror straight from central casting.

"This is very serious," growled the bureaucrat, pushing his body away from the desk. "You are two days late for your registration, according to Soviet law governing foreign residence in the USSR!"

His name was Comrade Shchemyakin, and his face was so severely cratered by smallpox or some other youthful disease that it looked like a kilo of frozen hamburger after a hatchet attack.* A taciturn bureaucrat, right out of Gogol. A live literary archetype, almost too good to be true.

"There will be a penalty!" announced Shchemyakin. "And you are obliged to leave your passport here while we determine the proper sanctions!"

The Widow swooned and pleaded with Shchemyakin in rapid-fire Russian, indicating that the situation was grave, very grave.

"Nado zhe!" implored the Widow. "Oh my!"

But Scar-face Shchemyakin only shook his head in the negative.

We exited the OVIR office in a despondent haze; for my part, I was kicking myself for having dropped the ball on the well-known registration business and saw my late Soviet adventure going up in smoke—or

---

* Those with a grasp of Russian phonology will appreciate the onomatopoeic sound of "Sh-che-MYAK-in." It emits a grating melody akin to the yap of a small dog or an old woman's scold.

more accurately, going up in the air on a twelve-hour flight back to the United States, with a Persona Non Grata stamp in my passport.

"We need to bring him a present," hissed the teary-eyed widow. "You know, an *Amerikanskii podarok*!"

An American present. *Palm greasers,* she meant—a bribe.

We practically sprinted back to the communal and up the stairs to the fifth floor and the other Nina Nikolaevna abode, where I tore through my bags for some potentially appropriate gift, settling on a couple of packs of Marlboros and a twenty-dollar bill. Then we headed back to the OVIR. We jumped the line of Soviet citizens trying to get out of the country that I wanted to stay in, and made a dash to Shchemyakin's door before the secretary could stop us. Once inside, the Widow Nina unceremoniously plopped two packages of Marlboro Reds on Shchemyakin's desk along with the twenty-dollar bill.

"What is this?" Shchemyakin sneered dismissively, in a tone that conveyed neither acceptance nor rejection of the paltry haul.

"It's not about that," he snarled, referring to the "gifts." "I'll call you once we get everything figured out. Now get out of here!"

Notably, he did not shove the gifts back across the desk before we cleared the door.

It was a long night spent fretting and worrying, with a good amount of self-recrimination and anger mixed with despair. I couldn't sleep until toward daylight, and woke to the grating sound of the communal telephone in the hallway ringing off the hook. I tried to ignore it, thereby saving myself the trouble of trying to decipher which Nina Nikolaevna the caller wanted—my absent landlady, or the Widow, who had retired in a fit of distress at my apparent fate. Let someone else answer, I said to myself, covering my ears with a pillow. But no one else seemed to be around. Finally I forced myself to my feet, headed into the hallway, and snatched the receiver in irritation, demanding who the caller was and with which Nina Nikolaevna he wished to speak.

I immediately recognized his voice. It was Shchemyakin. But instead of declaring me Persona Non Grata with twelve hours to leave the USSR, he almost beamed friendship through the receiver—and it was rather clear that our newfound camaraderie was not due to two packs of smokes and twenty bucks.

"Could you come to the OVIR office at eighteen hundred hours—six p.m.?" he asked politely.

"Of course I will," I replied.

Glasnost and Perestroika had apparently won the day.

Heading to Shchemyakin's office alone that evening, it occurred to me that the timing of our rendezvous was unusual. All Soviet offices strictly observed *priyom,* or reception times, typically 10 to 12 in the morning, and 2 to 4 in the afternoon. Before, between, or after those hours, the bureaucratic state was in lockdown; 6 p.m. thus seemed like a very odd rendezvous time.

My confusion deepened when I got to the OVIR. The main entrance was locked, and there was no one outside. I rang a bell. A well-dressed secretary popped her head out. She invited me inside—a little too warmly—and sat me down in the reception area. Then she and another pretty bureaucrat hurriedly packed their purses and rushed out the door as if late for their own weddings.

A few more moments passed in silence, and then I heard a distant door open and shut and the pitter-patter of footfalls approaching.

"Lavrernce!" said the voice in Russian.

It was Shchemyakin, wearing a smile so forced that it seemed to cause him pain.

He moved uneasily, stiffly, like a rusted robot, as he led me down the hall and into a comfortable room with leather sofas. There was also a coffee table carefully laid out with coveted "Misha the Intoed Bear" chocolates from the Red October factory, sundry cookies imported from abroad, Beluga caviar in a crystal bowl, and a bottle of Ararat "export" cognac from Soviet Armenia. Shchemyakin motioned to me to sit down, sat down himself, and handed me my passport and visa with a smile.

"Everything's fine with your documents," he cooed, as if being two days in "major violation" of the Soviet Foreign Registration Law had been a joke.

"Spasibo," I said, standing. "Thanks."

"But before you go, there is someone who wants to meet you."

THE AMERICAN IMAGE of Soviet KGB officers was reinforced by dozens of late-Communist-period B films made by, of course, Americans. Usually, the pristine Yanqui is snapped off the streets of the USSR and flung into the Gulag as if it's just for sport. The physical appearance of the KGB man was a constant as well: KGB men were almost invariably portrayed as sadistic, shabbily dressed, and paranoid, and as projecting zero humanity, whether feigned or otherwise.

In reality, most Russians knew the MO of the *chekist,* especially middle- and higher-ranking ones, to have been different, at least in the post-Stalin era, when there was less bloodletting. A solid career in the KGB was among the more prestigious Soviet occupations, like it or not.

AN ATHLETIC-LOOKING MAN of about fifty years of age entered the room and strode toward me with hand outstretched to clasp mine.

He was gracious, almost glib, and introduced himself as "Valery," though I have no idea if that was his real name. He acted like a stage actor emoting at a theater-in-the-parks summer fest, where you had to belt out every consonant and vowel. He wore a black leather jacket of high quality, a stereotypical KGB getup.

"Tak!" exclaimed my new friend, uncorking the bottle of export cognac and pouring us out two shots; Scar-face Shchemyakin hovered in the background, timidly following along with the ritual.

The first toast was to my arrival in the USSR. The second was a throwaway about the *druzhba narodov,* a standard trope about the supposed "friendship among nations" of the USSR, or in this case between the USSR and the USA. After some more chitchat about the need for international understanding and other gracious goo, Valery poured a third toast and dedicated it to "our work." This seemed odd, but I downed it anyway and was preparing to make my own when Valery put down his *ryumochka,* or shot glass, and looked straight into my eyes.

"So," he asked, without a hint of a blink of his steely eyes, but with a face still glowingly warm and smiling. "Who sent you?"

"Sent me?"

"Yes." He grinned. "What is the purpose of your visit?"

I must have looked dumb. I didn't know what Valery was talking about and said so.

"I have no purpose," I responded, using the Russian *"U menya net tseli"* and sounding far too existential. Valery rolled his eyes slightly, and Shchemyakin's pasted-on grin started to fade.

"I mean, I've come to improve my Russian. To see friends."

"And why is it you've chosen to study Russian?"

I'd heard this question dozens of times, from Americans as often as Russians. Many Russians assumed there was something innately dubious and possibly nefarious about foreigners wanting to learn the language of Pushkin. Many Americans, by contrast, automatically assumed students of Russian to be Commie sympathizers or wannabe spies for the CIA, thus reinforcing the Soviet assumption.

"But Russian is a beautiful language," I said.

"But there are many beautiful languages," countered Valery. "What about Italian? What about French or German?"

Then for some reason Lenin popped into my head, specifically a flashback from the monument at Finland Station, where I had seen off Nina Nikolaevna.

"But look at Lenin—he knew so many languages . . . ," I said.

Valery rolled his eyes again and poured us another cognac.

"Yes, languages are important," he reflected.

"But tell me," he said after a slight pause. "It must be quite uncomfortable for you to live in that communal apartment. I mean, to my knowledge Americans aren't used to such conditions."

I replied that I found the experience interesting, and that, at any rate,

I had no money for anything more luxurious. I was a student, in other words. I had saved up for the airfare while working as a waiter and also studying at university, and was not paying a cent to stay at Nina Niko-laevna's (unless you consider "rent" the two tins of hard-to-find cinnamon and some other simple gifts brought from the United States). Food and other staples in 1989 Leningrad were dirt cheap by Western standards. In other words, I could probably live more economically in the USSR (including airfare) for a summer doing nothing than working and renting a flat in the States doing some summer job.

"Perhaps we could help you?" smiled Valery. "I mean, it is very expensive to visit the USSR. Perhaps next summer, you could work with us? You could even work here, in the OVIR office?"

I stammered something incoherent, wanting to disbelieve what was happening. Valery the KGB man, who insinuated that I was on some deep-cover mission posing as an indigent American student without the brains to register his residency on time, was now trying to recruit me as a double-agent mole, implausible as it was. Or at least he believed I was valuable enough to recruit as a KGB mole, though I could offer nothing in the way of information or contacts. I was dressed in sneakers and had no job and not much money. I was living in a rundown communal, and not out of some hippie let's-all-be-poor wish. I had no connections, no ties to any government, real or imagined. The whole scene was too ridiculous to be true. I pinched myself, hoping that it was just the cognac, gone to my head.

It wasn't. I was being interviewed by a suave Soviet state security man who, after befuddling my brain, was now getting down to the real point.

"Tell us about the exiles," Valery gently prodded. "You know, the daughter and son-in-law of the woman you are staying with."

"Who?"

"Aw, you know!" exclaimed Valery with a smile. "Viktor and Mila, your teachers in the United States. "How are they? What do they say about the Soviet Union these days?"

I could not deny that I knew them—it was Mila who had arranged for me to stay in her mother's communal room.

"They recall with pleasure their days in the Soviet Union," I blurted, sounding ridiculous even to myself. The sentence was as clumsily bookish as it was absurd. Eight years after being exiled, Viktor only mentioned Communists in tandem with expletives.

"Really, with pleasure?" said Valery with a knowing smile, while twisting his shot glass slowly with his fingertips. "This is odd, because as you must know, their departure from here was rather . . . bitter."

BITTER? THE SELF-DESTRUCTIVE dissident Viktor had to be practically pried out of the empire because he refused to leave the same place that many other dissidents were desperate to get out of. One day in 1981, Viktor and Mila were summoned to the same OVIR office, where a lady clerk handed them a stack of forms.

"Your poor auntie in Israel is sick. Of course, you need to go help your poor auntie in Israel," said the clerk. "We are going to arrange exit visas for you both at once." Viktor shook his head in the negative. "We don't have any relatives in Israel." He laughed at the incredulous clerk, who acted like she was speaking to a man turning down a winning lottery jackpot.

"You're the first ones to laugh about this," remarked the clerk.

"Just fill out the paperwork and get it back to us by tomorrow," she insisted, shoving the forms at Viktor.

Once they arrived back at the communal, Viktor realized that he didn't even have the name of his nonexistent Israeli "auntie." He had the gall to ring the clerk up on the telephone.

"*Devushka* [young lady], what's the name of our Israeli auntie?" he asked.

"Are you screwing around, fool?" came the clerk's response.

"Well maybe we won't be going to Israel after all . . . ," answered Viktor laconically.

"Ummm . . . Just bring the damn documents yourselves. We'll take care of your aunt's name ourselves," came the clerk's irritated reply.

FOR WHAT SEEMED like an eternity, I pretended to be fascinated with staring at a nondescript office clock mounted on a wall.

"Well," I said at last, breaking the silence about Viktor and Mila's present attitudes about the USSR.

"Last we spoke, they said that they were really excited about Gorbachev's Glasnost and Perestroika reforms," I told the KGB man.

This was either a pathetic faux pas or my saving grace, because few words uttered by Americans evoked more nausea from KGB-type Russians. Our naive smiles and adoration of Gorbachev, a man at best grudgingly tolerated by most Russians at the time, evoked a sensation similar to the regurgitation of curdled milk among many of them. It wasn't that they were against reform, but Gorbachev's Communist-style vernacular led many to doubt his sincerity.

"Glasnost and Perestroika, yes," Valery said, still smiling but barely able to contain himself. "Interesting, of course. Tell me, is there anything else that Americans can discuss about Russia other than Glasnost and Perestroika?"

I did not need to answer but tried to make a rational assessment of my situation and found it wanting, pathetic.

Fact: I was drinking cognac and eating caviar after business hours with a KGB man who wanted information about my Russian teachers-in-exile Viktor and Mila. Both were acid-tongued critics of the Soviet regime. Before his exile, Viktor was so reckless in his denunciations of the party that some of his closest friends thought he might have even been KGB himself, acting as an agent provocateur. He had been a contributor to a well-known underground (*samizdat*) publication, *Tridtsat-Sem* ("Thirty-Seven"). (Or *Tridtsat Semitov,* meaning "Thirty Semites," as Viktor jokingly referred to it.) Mila, meanwhile, was in with a dissident women's group and trade union activists, which the KGB was particularly nervous about in light of the "Solidarity" events in Poland. Even eight years after their departure, when Communism, if not the empire itself, was clearly collapsing, the KGB man was still following them. Valery had personally handled their expulsion from the Soviet Union in 1981, a fact Viktor confirmed when I described Valery to him. Possibly there had been some internal squabble over whether a labor camp or exile fit their crimes. Perhaps Valery had come down on the losing side of the argument and was still bitter; who knew?

Second stupid fact: I had dredged up the already worn-out "Glasnost and Perestroika" theme. Even ordinary Russians were often disgusted by Americans' naiveté, assuming that reforming the USSR would be a painless matter of injecting a little democracy. It must have been especially galling for a KGB type like Valery to have to listen to twaddle coming from the toothy smile of a silly American who in his estimation didn't understand a thing about the consequences of an imploding empire.

Last and most embarrassing fact: I had failed to react to Valery's recruitment offer, if indeed the offer made to a clueless American kid in battered sneakers who was living in a communal associated with unspeakable dissidents had been made in earnest at all.

Another uncomfortable pause descended on us, which was finally broken by Valery.

"Tell me, my young American friend," he asked rhetorically. "Do you know what it is to spend your entire life building a house, just to watch a gang of vandals come and try to tear it down?"

I listened to his bitter soliloquy.

"Let us presume that the house wasn't a perfect house. Some of the beams were weak. Many mistakes were made in building this house. A fool designed the fireplace; it fills the rooms with smoke sometimes. A relative got electrocuted rigging up the electricity. But gradually, we learn. Yes, the house is not perfect. It leans to one side. But we live in this house, you see. It is our house."

I said nothing. Nothing needed to be said.

"Is it better to let the vandals tear it down with a bulldozer and kill all the inhabitants? Or is it better to move some of the bricks gradually, fix the beams one by one, rebuild the fireplace while keeping a kettle of soup on a little stove nearby?"

Valery's voice trailed off, and his glibness took on a paler hue. His eyes remained fixed and steely, but his lips turned up at a slightly weaker angle.

The tears of a KGB man.

A BIGAMIST BANDIT
AND A BUTTON MAKER

Leading a life of crime isn't easy." Vova laughed slightly at his self-evaluation. It was part justification, and part plea for sympathy.

We were just emerging from a brief and thankfully bloodless altercation with two men on a small bridge near the Kirov Theater. They had been walking toward us and slowed as Vova and I approached. It was just after dusk on a foggy evening. The combination of darkness and mist produced a disorienting effect, reducing real visibility to a few yards. Vova and the two men recognized each others' faces with difficulty. Once they did, all three pranced like nervous cats circling for a scrap. There was a long pause while menacing glances were exchanged, followed by a string of profanities uttered in quick, quiet succession. One of the men spit forcefully into the ground and muttered something to the other. Then the pair swaggered on into the gloom, as if they'd just benevolently granted us a stay of execution.

"*Da*," whispered Vladimir Kovannikov, aka Vova. "*Vsyo-taki ne legko vesti zhizn prestupnosti. . . .*"

"Living a life of crime really isn't easy . . . but it beats being a slave. . . ."

This was, in a way, the mantra of the Vor v Zakone, or at least the modified modern version of the "Thief in Law" credo that dominated the late Soviet criminal underground. Vova was my guide in trying to discover what it really meant.

$\bullet \quad \bullet \quad \bullet$

WE MET IN 1987 during my first visit to the USSR as a student at Leningrad State University. Vova was then "officially" working as a factory laborer in a clothing button factory. But with the Soviet economy already teetering, he'd taken to supplementing his wages by becoming a private entrepreneur—a capitalist—which was an economic crime against the state. At first it was harmless if still illegal stuff, such as buying name-brand wristwatches from tourists along Nevsky Prospekt and then hawking them to fellow Soviets for a markup.

That was the story of our first encounter: My roommate Jared was walking along Nevsky Prospekt when a lanky, loud, gregarious kid with a big head of frizzy hair going off in all directions, as if he used lye for a hair conditioner, approached and tried, in broken German, to buy Jared's Timex.

"*Spasibo,*" Jared had curtly replied when offered a week's worth of prorated ruble wages for the timepiece. "Thanks, but no thanks."

The offer was then doubled, but Jared still turned it down. Jared explained he wasn't interested in selling his wristwatch. Over the semester, we would often run into Vova on Nevsky Prospekt, and we gradually became acquaintances.

When he wasn't using his gutter German to score watches from surprised Swiss tourists, Vova gave us impromptu tours of what passed for Leningrad's underground hippie scene, and in between shifts at the clothing button factory (aptly named the "Button Factory") where he worked, he took us on expeditions to little-known former czarist castles and even organized shish kebab cookouts in the Russian woods for his two new American friends. Petty street black marketers like Vova were reviled as slime by many Russians of the time. Yet while some of my Russian "intelligentsia" friends ended up having ulterior motives in pursuing my "friendship," Vova never asked me for a dime or even a small favor.

A couple of years later, Soviet society began its critical meltdown. Words like *reket* (racket, as in criminal), *keelir* (killer), and *mafia* singed themselves into the vernacular. In fact, many Leningraders seemed to take a dark, Dostoyevskian pride in playing up their city's apocalyptic atmosphere, even if its outward reputation as being one big mafia operation was exaggerated. Most ordinary people were not personally affected by the growing mob. At least Vova wasn't, because he had become part of it.

ON THIS PARTICULAR day, we had agreed to meet at the Petrogradsky Metro stop. As usual, Vova was a few minutes late.

I didn't mind. Petrogradsky had always been one of my favorite Metro stations. The entrance had extremely heavy metal doors that were impossible to push or pull fully open. I couldn't understand if this was a deliberate design defect to save on hinge repairs, or some sort of sadistic ploy. One had to sort of prop the door open and squeeze through before releasing it, and the door would often swing violently backwards and lash the next poor soul in line in the face. Across the street from the station, there was a store selling posters emblazoned with Soviet-style propaganda exhortations. I remembered it as two years earlier having been full of classic Communist, anti-American bombast, such as a lithograph of a US missile with a picture of Ronald Reagan's head in the form of an atomic warhead. But Glasnost and Perestroika had taken their artistic toll during the ensuing years, and most of the more hilarious, rabidly anti-Western pictorial rants had been replaced by posters promoting sobriety, advocating ecological consciousness or, even more surprising, preaching touchy-feely peacenik stuff.

As I gazed into the shop window, I saw a shadow growing larger in the glass. I turned around without recognizing the man in the glass. It wasn't until he flashed his fossilized smile that I knew it was Vova. He'd shaved his head, revealing nicks, cuts, and divots around the perimeter of his tightly wrapped skull. His hands were stuffed into the pockets of an oversize, crème-colored trench coat. He looked menacing.

We exchanged a hug. I asked some requisite questions about his family and work, including the Button Factory. Vova screwed up his face.

"I don't work at the Button Factory," he snarled, waving his hand as if to swat away a mosquito. "I've got a new job now." Then he flashed a grin so wide that the brown rot between his gums shone like shiny bits of rust.

"Let's go," said Vova, grabbing me by the arm and leading me toward the street. We stopped a Lada-1—a Soviet knockoff of an early-1970s Fiat—and climbed in. "Kupchino," Vova told the driver, the name of a grimy expanse of factories and faceless apartment blocks in the south of the city.

"Why aren't we taking the Metro?" I asked. "It's faster—and cheaper."

"The Metro? What for?" countered Vova, as if the notion of a subway were suddenly beneath his dignity. "Kupchino!" he told the driver again. Then he turned and spoke to me in a conspiratorial whisper, just loud enough for the taxi driver to hear.

"You see, I've got a new system," hissed Vova. "I just wait until the driver approaches a red light where there's a lot of traffic. I tell him to get in the left lane."

"So?" I ask.

"Then, when the traffic starts to move, I jump out, slam the door, and run away!" snickered Vova. "The taxi driver is stuck. He can't get out and chase me with cars behind him. If he does, his car might get ripped off. He can't get over into the right lane either, because it's blocked with moving traffic. By then, I'm long gone."

I saw the driver jerk his neck slightly as Vova explained his fare policy for cabbies. Maybe the driver thought it was just a joke from a shaven-headed thug in a trench coat.

We sped south, over the elegant iron drawbridges across the Neva River. We had a perfect view of both banks, clad in granite block. The baroque and neoclassical buildings, without a space between them and none higher than the Winter Palace, seemed bathed in a kaleidoscope of fading pastels. Against the setting sun I could see St. Isaac's Cathedral. Half the city seemed to be in scaffolding, a Soviet hallmark.

As we passed south across Nevsky Prospekt, we began moving away from the city's heart and into areas dominated by the stolid structures associated with Stalin-era buildings, and then finally into the outskirts of the city, where the "functional" buildings of the Khrushchev era reigned supreme. While most were only twenty or thirty years old, the "suburbs of the future" were already crumbling, battered, cookie-cutter-identical high-rises. This was Kupchino, a formerly pristine (if swampy) forested area that was now a socialist-style ghetto of battered buildings, state-run factory behemoths, and gangland turf battles. It was a world away from my communal and Nina Nikolaevna's Petrograd district of cathedrals, czarist haunts, and long avenues of worn-down but warm coffee shops.

Kupchino's miles of apartment blocks were of such a uniform design as to be virtually indistinguishable from one another. The streets were laid out in a rectangular monotone. Humidity discolored the sides of the prefab buildings, leaving black sootlike lines that adorned the exteriors in abstract maps. This proved to be a godsend, for the soot murals made it possible to tell one identical building from another. Otherwise, it was easy to get lost in the Orwellian maze, possibly the work of a dissident urban planner bent on architectural sabotage. It reminded me of the crumbling housing projects in the south side of Chicago.

Kupchino may have had its aesthetic shortcomings. But from a sociological perspective, it was a hotbed of life as the Soviet Empire was collapsing. Among the endless stretches of crumbling residential blocks buzzed a beehive of fledgling extortionists and shady businessmen. They hung out in acrid-smoke-filled "billiard clubs" and slimy disco bars. All around were smoke-belching, state-owned factories waiting to be taken over in sham privatization schemes.

OUR OLD LADA rattled to a halt in front of a nondescript storefront. When Vova asked how much we owed for the ride, the driver shrugged. This was unusual, since Soviet gypsy cabdrivers—like cabbies everywhere—had a habit of overcharging anyone stupid enough not to negotiate the price beforehand. "Oh, it's up to you guys," said the driver, faking a smile. Vova handed him a wad of rubles as we got out of the car. The driver didn't bother to count them and looked relieved as we disembarked, as if he'd dumped off a pair of lepers.

There was a long queue in front of the store. People were grumbling.

Some were arguing. At first I thought the line was for vodka or milk. But there were no drunks hanging around, and no one coming out with bags of groceries.

Two tough-looking men greeted Vova. One was short and skinny. He had on acid-washed jeans and a shiny, synthetic-looking leather jacket. The other was taller and balding. He wore a tracksuit. Under the top half he wore a sweater. Vova and the men discussed something and we moved on toward the shop. The two men led us to the front of the line. I thought we'd evoke hostility for cutting in front, but no one uttered a word—or even gave us a dirty look.

A man in a slightly too-tight sport jacket and tie propped open the door and let us in. The number of customers was tightly controlled—there weren't more than a dozen inside. Several times more waited in line on the street.

An overly deferential managerlike man was there to meet Vova and his two "business associates." All four of them then shuffled away to a back room; Vova smiled and gestured that I should wait where I was standing, and maybe take a look around.

I did so, then realized with a jolt that we were in a state-run jewelry store. There were gold bands and neck chains, rings with small diamonds, and other items made from precious metals and stones. Customers were huddled over the few display cases. Most seemed less concerned with the aesthetics of the goods than with their practical qualities, such as grams and karats. One squat, middle-aged man with thick, pharmacy-style glasses purchased some sapphire earrings and two gaudy women's rings with completely different band sizes. I wondered whether he was making a foray into cross-dressing or just had a lot of paramours to please.

It wasn't that everyone had struck it rich and had started buying up baubles in the midst of an economic collapse. Prices for gold and stones had been set artificially low by the state, much lower than on world markets. Buying and then reselling to middlemen could be lucrative—like swapping a ten-dollar bill for a twenty. The shoppers would then go on to sell to other middlemen or take the loot out to Western countries and hawk the items for hard currency.

Vova and his lot were middlemen too, after a fashion. They controlled access to the store, taking payoffs from the people in line, who anted up for prime positions and rights to buy from "special" collections of goods. The gang then shared the payoffs with the store managers; the managers then used the proceeds to secure more jewels and gold from state suppliers, and so on. And Vova's guys also provided "insurance," as he put it. The "insurance" bit was obligatory, obviously.

Yet the gig wasn't a *reket* in the full sense of the word. Vova scolded me for misunderstanding the difference: A racket, he explained, was a simple, one-off extortion, with the extorters threatening to kill or maim the owners of a budding small-business cooperative (or actually killing or maiming them) unless they handed over cash on demand. Vova was adamant that this sort of crude shakedown had no resemblance whatsoever to his "respectable" line of business. His vocation had important sorts of "moral underpinnings," as Vova reasoned, because he and his associates provided actual protection for their clients, who might otherwise be molested by "real racketeers" or, worse, by corrupt Soviet police or bureaucrats, who could either extort money themselves or simply shut down the operation—and no one wanted that, did they?

Vova acted as if he were the only thing standing between the workers of the jewelry shop and chaos.

"We keep an eye on them so they don't get kicked around," he said. "You see, the people we protect would rather deal with us than the cops. Why? With the cops they might have to pay bribes, or they might end up tossed into the clink for no real reason. The cops could end up running the store, or the cops and some bureaucrat might close it down. So the workers prefer to deal with us."

It helped that everyone was part of the racket: the state suppliers who dealt the cut-rate goods for bribes, the store managers who took and gave payoffs, even the customers who bought purely for speculative profit. And, of course, Vova and his "business partners." They were the most parasitic on the food chain, but the fact that everyone in the entire game was corrupt helped calm his conscience.

• • •

BARDAK!" VOVA EXCLAIMED once we were back in another taxi and heading away from the jewelry store. "Whorehouse!"

This was Vova's one-word postulate about the nature of the crumbling Soviet system and usually signaled the beginning of one of his out-of-the-blue inexplicable rants.

The word *bardak* can literally mean "whorehouse" in Russian, but colloquially, it is something closer to "chaos" or "mess." It lacks the vulgarity connoted in English, and in the language of Pushkin, it is employed with great frequency. Still, I could not get over the curiousness of hearing "Whorehouse!" several times a day from the lips of average Russians whenever the slightest injustice befell them. In Vova's case, it sounded more like an explanation of the untenable social order that demanded his racketeering activities than a justification of the same.

"My father is a fucking Communist," Vova began. "He still believes in that nonsense, or at least he thinks he believes in it. I tell him he is a fool. The simple truth is that this is anarchy. And anarchy doesn't respect fools. . . ."

We drove on. Vova became silent. I said nothing. It started raining. The monochrome landscape blurred. We were now deep in the heart of Kupchino. Vova piped up, noting we were near the Button Factory he'd quit. And it was for those who continued to toil there that Vova reserved his most potent venom.

"*Whorehouse!*" Vova sputtered, shaking his head. This time the word served not only as an empty exclamation. "A bunch of fucking whores, that's what they are. Mentally ill people! I just can't understand why those workers keep degrading themselves. They are slaves. What's more, they enslave themselves to rottenness. And what is the only thing worse than a slave? A slave unwilling to liberate himself. He willingly submits to a state of enchainment. He works blindly in the name of a monstrous force."

Here Vova's monologue turned from the gutter-level Russian I was used to from him into a literary bloom of rich verbs. But the point was pretty simple. In a world of scoundrels and baseness, it is better to be evil and free than decent but enchained.

Vova suggested we stop off to see Pavel, a mutual friend and fellow watch-hawker I had met during the good old days of making barbecue in the Leningrad forest. Pavel also lived in Kupchino. The pair had met at the Button Factory, where Pavel still worked the night shift, a fact that Vova ridiculed. We turned onto Budapest Street and got out of the taxi, paid the fare, and entered another cookie-cutter-looking building. We climbed several flights of stairs—the elevator was out. The hallway smelled of sweet and sour garbage and urine. I slipped on what felt like some vomit on the floor and barely avoided tumbling head over heels down the stairs. We reached an upper floor and knocked on a door. A woman clad in a bathrobe with a faded purple-flower print—Pavel's wife, Sveta—opened the door cautiously and then began to smile.

"Vova!" Beaming, she eagerly invited us inside.

She led us into a tiny kitchen, where we found Pavel eating a bowl of noodle soup. Pavel embraced us warmly, and we took a seat. Sveta sat down and resumed the activity she had been pursuing when we interrupted her—twisting bits of cotton into small, compact pads. I asked her what she was making. She looked at me as if I were an idiot. Through an elliptical description, she explained that the rectangular cotton cutouts were, in fact, makeshift feminine sanitary pads—tampons were in short supply.

Pavel's mother-in-law walked in, a stout matriarch with a military bearing. She smiled and put her arms around me. Then she glared at Vova and grunted a hello. It was obvious the two were not on good terms.

"How are things, Vova? What are you up to these days?" she asked. "Oh, you know, just business," came the terse reply. The room became eerily quiet, save for the duet of Sveta's ripping her fluffs of cotton into sanitary pads and Pavel's soupspoon making regular contact with the bottom of a porcelain bowl.

Tenseness overtook the air. Vova quickly made up an excuse about having "affairs to attend to." Since we hadn't seen each other in a long time, Pavel convinced me to stay for a while. We saw Vova off, and he promised to call me soon.

Pavel was smallish, cautious, and quiet to the point of being meek. With no higher education, he nonetheless exuded a professor's aura. Perhaps he would have become one had he not done a short prison stint. A few years back, a friend had smashed a store window and stolen a pack of audiocassette tapes. Pavel had known about the theft. He hadn't taken part but was prosecuted under a Soviet statute making it a crime for not reporting the information to the police. That slipup, along with another friend's confinement in a psychiatric hospital for trying to emigrate from the USSR, had deepened his cynicism—and caution.

The Soviet breakdown was forcing Pavel and Vova to make major forced choices about their respective life paths. Vova obviously felt he had little to lose joining the expanding racketeering underworld. Pavel's situation was different. He had an infant son, who made his father more concerned with staying out of trouble than grinding axes over the affairs of state. Vova had tried to convince Pavel to join in his racketeering operation, but Pavel had refused, and things hadn't been quite the same between them since.

Pavel admitted the work at the Button Factory was grueling, monotonous, and poorly paid. The monthly three-hundred-ruble salary was once considered decent, but inflation had eaten into it. "It's enough to buy bread and cottage cheese for my son, basic things," he said. "Of course I'd like to do something else. I know Vova thinks that I'm degrading myself by working at the Button Factory. But what Vova is doing is really dangerous. I don't need any more trouble."

VOVA AND I met a few days later, this time on Vasilyevsky Island, connected to the rest of the city by bridges and the subway. Vova said he had a "surprise" for me, and we hopped into a taxi.

"How many times have you read *Master and Margarita?*" Vova asked. I replied that I'd read the Bulgakov classic tale of good and evil once.

"Only once? Do you know how many times I've read that book? Seventeen fucking times," said Vova.

He started to ramble on about the Master, a writer who together with his mistress Margarita makes a pact with Satan. In an antithetical slap to Stalinist orthodoxy, the devil then visits Moscow, wreaking havoc in an effort to prove the existence of hell. Vova digressed into a half-coherent speech about the essence of good and evil, and how, in Vova's estimation, the two concepts can be flipped upside down.

Given his choice of conversation, I thought perhaps that Vova was taking me to some new alternative production of *Master and Margarita*. But when the taxi pulled up to our destination, I knew it could not be so: Although the building resembled a cinema or theater, the folks gathered outside did not look like the average literati crowd waiting for a weekday matinee. Rather, the sidewalk was crowded with men in black leather jackets, waiting impatiently to get inside while circling one another like famished wolves. Most fit the same general description as Vova's thug partners at the jewelry shop.

Vova thrust two tickets into a window, and we entered a dank hallway. A concession stand sold slices of white bread with lumps of fatty sausage, chocolate bars, and bottles of champagne and vodka. Vova ordered us two cups of black tea and some biscuits—I rarely saw him drink alcohol. Surly ushers then opened the door to the main hall, and a fetid odor of stale sweat flowed out while the crowd of several hundred men began pushing to get in.

"*Kik-boks*," smiled Vova, ushering me to a squeaky red vinyl chair in the front of a boxing mat and ring.

Kickboxing.

I'd heard of the sport in the United States. But in Vova's world, the combination of martial arts and gratuitous violence was on a meteoric rise.

There were several warm-up bouts that served as a sort of school-for-savagery for me, with Vova helpfully noting the finer points of the art form. Wild applause erupted when it was announced the main fight would soon get under way. A loud gong sounded, and two fighters got onto the mat and began warming up with a series of hand thrusts and foot jabs into the air. One was an ethnic Kyrgyz, from Central Asia, whose name elicited some applause but mainly a chorus of whistles and derisive shouts. Then his opponent was introduced, and to thundering applause. An ethnic Russian, he was clearly the hometown favorite.

I still didn't understand much about the rules, but as far as I could tell, one wasn't supposed to kick one's opponent in the genitals. It happened repeatedly, eliciting a collective groan of agony mixed with approval from the throng.

The Kyrgyz was at a disadvantage with the crowd. Whenever he landed a good shot, you could hear "Kyrgyz, Kyrgyz" echo through the hall in hushed tones, as if it were surprising and scandalous. But when the Russian landed his blows, cheers rang out. Two truths occurred to me as I watched the gladiators in action. The first was that ethnic and geographic designations—whether Russian, Tartar, or Chechen—played an important role in Leningrad's pecking order of organized crime groups. The second was that this was manifest in sports, too. Tough, physically fit former athletes were some of the first to start protection rackets when capitalism crept into the crumbling USSR. Martial arts enthusiasts made good enforcers. Satisfied with this new knowledge, I grew bored with the contest and spent much of the time checking out some of the mugs in attendance for this cutting-edge Leningrad spectator sport. Then, with a fast fist-kick combo delivered by the Russian to his opponent's head and ribs, the Kyrgyz collapsed in a heap and it was over.

"The Kyrgyz got in some good shots, though," muttered Vova, giving credit where it was due as we left the fetid arena.

WE HEADED BACK away from Vasilyevsky Island toward Nevsky Prospekt, where Vova said we were to meet someone at the "Saigon" Café, an "alternative" haunt at the other end of Nevsky Prospekt and several kilometers away. For some reason, Vova set us off walking while he seamlessly returned to the life lessons to be gleaned from Bulgakov's *Master and Margarita*. In his estimation, the author had succeeded in portraying the

Soviet Union as Satan personified, a world where evil had become good, and good evil.

"Don't you see, the part played by the devil . . ."

Vova seemed to be living inside the book, tormented by the value inversions that had become his existence. Indeed, his life had in effect become a form of rebellion against the dying Soviet system, which he so railed against—and yet was so much a part of. For Vova, morality no longer existed. Perhaps from a distant perspective, this sort of relativistic thinking is easy to condemn. But in a collapsing society whose rules are quickly being rewritten, it becomes more comprehensible. Was it admirable to toil in a button factory where the workers were being ripped off by hyperinflation, corrupt asset-stripping managers, and predatory bureaucrats? Was it "moral" to be one of those managers or state officials? Was it less moral to run a "protection service" or to be a corrupt cop hitting businesses for shakedowns? The twilight of the Soviet Empire reflected into a crooked mirror, where dark shaded into light, heaven was a sham—and hell was visible all around.

Vova didn't stop his literary exegesis until we reached the Saigon Café. I'd been there once before but had forgotten how ill-matched the name was to the place. One naturally assumed to find a Vietnamese theme, however marginal, in food or decor. Instead, the Saigon was a run-of-the-mill Soviet-style cafeteria where the patrons stood up because there weren't many chairs. Vova again ordered tea.

No sooner were we sipping from banged-up plastic cups than an old woman hobbled in and accosted us. She was wearing a dirty overcoat and eyeglasses held together at the nose with transparent adhesive tape. She snickered loudly, mumbling something incomprehensible. The woman pointed with one hand at Vova, leaning on a cane with the other. He did his best to ignore her. I tried to make out what she was saying.

"I think she wants twenty kopecks," I told Vova, about a nickel at the time. Vova by this time was rattled by the bag lady's taunts, which she for no discernible reason aimed solely at him and not a single other patron.

"Granny, do you want twenty kopecks?" Vova asked her, gritting together what remained of his teeth. The street lady, deranged but with lucid eyes, seethed, launching into a tirade against Vova. "No, I don't want your twenty kopecks," she hissed. She rambled and waved her finger at him, mocking his facial expression.

The old woman maintained this enraged state for several minutes. Eventually she ambled back out onto Nevsky Prospekt. The episode spooked Vova. He'd just been talking nonstop about *Master and Margarita*, which for Vova served to soothe the contradictions of his guilt-ridden criminal life. To him, the unhinged bag lady was an apparition dispatched to expose his sins.

VOVA SOON RELAXED, however. A beautiful specimen of the emerging genetic strain of soon-to-be-post-Soviet womanhood, with light auburn hair that came down to her waist and warm, knowledgeable eyes, emerged, covering his eyes from behind. She was stuffed into an above-market skirt and expensive shoes. I didn't have to ask who was paying the tailor.

"Guess who?" she cooed.

Vova smiled and pretended not to know who it was.

Her name was Ellie, and she was a nineteen-year-old student from the local economics institute. She had come to Leningrad from Kingisepp, a town on the Estonian border about a hundred miles to the west. I learned all this as she took each of us by one arm, Russian style, and marched us out of the café, turning toward the landmark Kazan Cathedral before arriving in front of a much smarter-looking establishment that met the full "restaurant" classification (rather than the "café" class that the Saigon fit into or the low-rung beer stand across from my communal at St. Vladimir's).

It was obvious Vova was not there for the first time. The waiters, slouched around in dark cotton vests, scattered as we entered the dining room, obviously in no hurry to come into contact with him. Vova and Ellie sat down across from me. She summoned one of the food servers and ordered a bottle of the still-cheap Soviet champagne, along with some baked mushroom julienne with cheese—a Russian specialty—and some tough meat of an indiscernible variety.

Ellie spoke as if defending a philosophy dissertation. She began ruminating about the sorry state of the empire. Each sentence was prefaced by the somewhat pretentious words *predpolozhim* ("let us assume") or *dopustim* ("let us allow"). They sounded appropriate on her lips, along with the metaphysical terms she used while trying to divine the future in a country where the past was constantly being redefined.

"Let us allow for the fact that Russia may completely cease to exist," she began.

"You mean the Soviet Union?" I interjected.

"No, I mean Russia," Ellie continued. "I mean we have to be prepared for the fact that it may simply cease to exist."

Through the Armageddon-tinged pessimism that reigned as the Soviet Empire crumbled, Ellie's own mind was actually contemplating Russia literally sliding off the world map in a puff. Ellie imagined a great void taking over in the place where Russia was. Today, it is nearly impossible to understand the cataclysmic emptiness underlying this type of thinking. But in those days, it was not uncommon to hear from ordinary Russians.

I asked her how she and Vova had met. Her eyes darted around the room, and she blushed slightly. "Oh, we just met." Continuing with time-filling small talk, I asked her where she lived.

"At home, of course . . . with Vova, my husband."

This seemed strange, as I distinctly remembered Vova saying that he was living with his wife, Lena, whom I'd met many times. True, I hadn't seen her recently.

Later I would learn that there was a lot more to the story.

Vova suggested going to his father's dacha outside Leningrad for an early-summer outing. A couple of weeks later, on a Saturday, Vova and Ellie picked me up in a taxi. The day was unusually bright and warm for the time of year, and we headed out of the city in high spirits.

We passed small villages, where people from the city were tending their gardens in a get-back-to-the-land ritual as old as urbanization in Russia itself. Turning down a dusty road, we eventually pulled up to a nondescript but cozy-looking two-story wooden cottage and piled out of the taxi. Vova's father was outside, working the garden. He stood and silently scowled at us like interlopers to be barely tolerated. His facial expression gave away his thoughts: "Here comes trouble—my criminal son and his unsanctioned foreigner in tow to visit me, a Communist factory manager, here, at my getaway dacha. What's next?"

Vova shed his shirt, revealing a sinewy physique dotted with tattoos. He got out a slab of meat he'd brought for the occasion, and began chopping it into small pieces before putting the chunks into a metal canister, letting them marinate in vinegar and herbs. In the meanwhile, we were dispatched into a nearby wood to gather kindling for a fire. Vova relished the feeling of being in control, entertaining his guests.

He nursed the fire slowly until red-hot embers emerged. We stuffed ourselves with bread and pickles until Vova instructed us to start putting the meat onto skewers. He carefully turned each over the hot coals, making sure the proper degree of cooking was attained. Then we sat down to eat at a picniclike table, Vova's father grudgingly joining us, poking the shish kebab with his fork and chewing, a silence looming between father and son.

Vova eyed a bowl full of sugar for making tea, and the conversation turned to the price. Riding out in the taxi, a woman on the especially conservative Mayak (Lighthouse) radio station had been literally weeping through the car's speaker over the alleged lack of sugar in the stores. Vova mocked her, and especially the radio station, which he accused of deliberately using old audio clips in an effort to discredit economic reforms.

"There's been plenty of sugar in the stores for at least two months now," Vova sneered. His father countered that perhaps there was sugar for sale, but that after the latest round of price increases, it was expensive.

"The price is fine," snapped Vova. "But Communists always want something for nothing," he said, referring to his father.

Vova's father glared.

"So, Vladimir, when are you going to start working?" he pointedly asked.

Vova murmured something, and Ellie giggled. We finished the meal in an awkward silence.

I wondered what was going through the mind of Vova's father. The talk in Leningrad—some of it imagined and some of it real—was all about bandits, mafia, killers, and the like. Yet it was as if people were talking about mysterious creatures existing only in speech and print. Bandits and killers, after all, had parents, families; some had children. I doubted that Vova's father, when asked what his son did for a living, answered, "My son is a racketeer" or "My son is mafia." I wondered if he thought about it at all. Whatever he thought, his drooping shoulders betrayed a deep disappointment with the road his son was on.

After lunch, Vova's father went back to silently tending his garden, distracting his thoughts from the chagrin caused by his progeny while the rest of us lounged around. The sun approached its peak in the sky. The world was quiet. I watched Ellie tease Vova, sprinkling him with a garden hose. I wondered what exactly attracted her to him. I thought it must have to do with having a kind of status, or some promise of future wealth—or maybe the hope of meeting someone connected to Vova who could provide both in greater measure than he could. One thing was evident, however: Ellie was clearly not in love; she was merely passing time.

DESPITE ALL THE crock imagery of endless suitcases full of dollar bills associated with the "mafia," not everyone in racketeering-type activities was getting rich, including Vova. There was little romance to his "profession." True, he always anted up at restaurants and had enough cash to keep Ellie in nice threads. But he didn't even own a car, let alone one with a driver. Accordingly, our return to Leningrad was aboard one of the notoriously rickety, smoke-belching Ukrainian-made Lvov buses. It must have been manufactured not long after Stalin's death. We sat on the back bench, sprawled out, enjoying the rays of sun through the dirty window glass of the clunker. Back in central Leningrad, we took a short taxi ride to an old building near the Kirov Theater. We climbed up to the second floor of a decrepit corridor and turned right. It was another communal apartment.

Vova, having forgotten his key, knocked on the door; on the other side, I could hear a lock turn. The door opened, and there stood Lena, Vova's first wife. At this point, the mystery of what had happened to her became clear; they were still living "together" in the same communal, another prerevolutionary rundown wreck. They had two of the five or six rooms, one where Lena slept and another next door for Vova and Ellie, wife number two, their headboard directly touching the wall against hers.

Lena smiled at me and shrugged, describing the unorthodox situation without words.

After a few minutes of awkwardness, we all sat down in Lena's room—a down-at-the-heels rectangle with enough room for a bed, a couple of chairs, and a nightstand covered with some cheap cosmetics and old magazines. Vova opened some down-market Georgian wine with a flip-off plastic cap. For the first time, I watched him get drunk—and in front of his two wives, who seemed to be on good terms, more so in fact than with their "husband."

Vova drifted off into more banter about the rottenness of late-Soviet life, and his "delusional"—as he saw it—Communist father. He started in again about Pavel and his "degrading" work at the Button Factory, getting up to dial his phone number, 184-8488, only to be told by Pavel that he was leaving for the night shift at the Button Factory.

Vova instantaneously suggested we go visit Pavel at the factory. The two wives, sensing a possible scandal abrew, wisely declined to join us, and we were quickly out the door. "I'll show you a real Soviet factory and how those workers humiliate themselves," he snarled.

We grabbed a taxi and within minutes were at the side door to the Button Factory. Vova knew the place well, having worked there previously. A night watchman recognized him. "What the hell are you up to?" he asked. "This is an official excursion for our foreign delegation (me)," Vova responded, lying.

The watchman relented and we sprinted up a flight of stairs. I worried that Vova was there to stir up some sort of scandal with Pavel in admonishment for his continued "degrading" manual labor.

We ended up on an enormous factory floor where dozens of automated machines whirled away. Inside each were thousands of plastic buttons of all shapes and sizes, tumbling their way to a fine gloss.

Pavel appeared in a work apron, dragging a huge, heavy bag of buttons behind him. He looked proud, not degraded. Then a small group of workers, men and women of all ages and description dressed in work overalls, latched on to us, each trying to outdo the other in terms of hospitality. Several recognized Vova, the camaraderie temporarily turning his despisal for the "degradation" of the Soviet factory into smiles.

A foreman barked. He ordered one of the enormous tumblers, which sounded like little cement mixers, shut off, mentioning proudly that they were Italian made. He opened a panel on one machine and told me to stick my hands inside, like a pirate's chest. I pulled open my palms to reveal dozens of multicolored buttons. Some had two holes, some three, some four. Some were orange, some white or red. I went home with my pockets filled with the loot. Then he showed us around the facility, including a "rest area" with several showers. A few emptied bottles of cheap Soviet sparkling wine adorned a table. It was obvious the work breaks included more than coffee; a middle-aged man and woman were just emerging with wet hair with wide grins pasted on their faces. We parted ways with Pavel, the foreman proudly pushing more souvenir buttons into my hands.

Ellie and Lena were waiting for us when we returned to their communal. Vova again picked up his rant about the sorry state of the empire, reading jokes from a newspaper. Self-deprecating ones, expressing the misguided perception of the time of America-as-paradise.

Vova read aloud: "An American and a Russian are talking to each other. The American says: 'I have three cars. One I drive to work, the other I drive to my summer house. And the third I take with me when I go to Europe.'

"The Russian says: 'To go to work I take the tram. I go to my summer house in a bus.'

"'And how do you get to Europe?' asks the American.

"'To go to Europe I ride a tank,' says the Russian."

After he caught his breath following another convulsion of cackling, Vova sighed and offered to take me downstairs and hail a taxi. It was late, almost 4 a.m.

But Lena would have none of it. "Why, Vova, it's so late. There's plenty of room here. My bed is big. He can sleep on the other side." Vova sized up Lena quizzically. Lena was warmhearted, but I sensed an elaborate game of innuendo and revenge from her. Vova grumbled something and Lena pulled the door shut, with Vova and Ellie on one side of the wall, Lena and I on the other. As I lay on one side of the bed and Lena on the other, paranoid thoughts crossed my mind of Vova's losing it in an act of uncontrollable rage or suspicion, bursting through the door to strangle both of us to death.

Instead, I heard only what must have been a nightly ritual: a girlish voice from a Russian border town rejecting Vova's sexual advances. Next to me Lena lay in silence, still awake and listening to it all, no doubt contemplating her unusual fate.

The next morning, Vova was less than his cheerful self. Lena made no attempt to tease him or suggest anything improper had transpired, but he was circumspect with me. After a perfunctory tea for breakfast, we went downstairs to the street.

Then Vova, the former Button Factory worker turned black marketer turned Leningrad midlevel mafia enforcer with two wives and an uncertain future, gave me a perfunctory *"Poka!"* (See you later!).

VOVA DID, HOWEVER, accomplish one of his goals: "liberating" Pavel from himself. The day after our night visit to the Button Factory, the management summarily fired Pavel on the grounds that he'd shown a foreigner an "industrial facility with potential military applications."

Less than a year later, Pavel called me and said he had saved enough money to visit the United States, which he had always dreamed about. He asked if he could come to Chicago, where I was staying at the time, adding that he planned on being there for "two or three weeks."

Pavel's two- to three-week Windy City stay turned into two months. Then two years. Then twenty. He left his family behind, first working illegally at a junkyard owned by a Ukrainian slave-driver owner. He soon moved up, landing a gig as a busboy. Pavel developed a cocaine habit, was robbed on the Chicago elevated train (twice), married a Polish immigrant, divorced her, became a roofer, moved to Florida, and found a second Polish wife.

The last time I talked to Pavel, he had joined an Evangelical church and told me I'd end up doing the same someday once I found God.

As for Vladimir (Vova), I never saw him again. About a year later, after arriving in what had re-become St. Petersburg, I headed over to the communal apartment where he and his "wives" lived. I ascended the stairwell and knocked on the door. A man pried it open just enough for me to see inside. He didn't have to ask who I was looking for.

"They're all gone," he said with a sigh of relief, shutting the door quickly. I made some phone calls, trying to find Lena or Vova through a network of acquaintances, their numbers scribbled on a slip of paper. No one knew where they had gone. As for Ellie, I had no idea where to look for her.

I rang Vova's parents' telephone number. His sister answered the phone. She recognized my voice and accent. But there was silence on the other end when I asked for Vova. I asked again if he was there.

"No," came the belated reply.

"Do you know when he'll be back?" I asked.

"No," was the response after an even longer, more awkward pause.

"OK, do you know where I can get ahold of him?"

"No," said the female voice. Then she hung up the phone.

I wondered where to look, or if to, and whether a prison—or a graveyard—might be the best place to start.

SICKLE AND HAMMER DOWN:
AN EMPIRE'S LAST HOURS

The date was Wednesday, December 25, 1991. It was Christmas Day in much of the world, but in Orthodox Russia, just another day. Except it would turn out to be the USSR's last. I had come to Moscow two months earlier with thoughts of pursuing foreign correspondence. I grabbed a cab and headed out in search of some groceries.

"Under Brezhnev there was even cocoa in the stores, God damn it!" The taxi driver slapped his hand on the wheel of his Volga four-door. "Even fucking cocoa!" He laughed uncontrollably through his gold teeth, as if the very idea of cocoa sitting on a store shelf evoked wonder. "Look what they've done. Gorbachev and his cronies have destroyed a great country. Everyone feared us. Now I don't think even Upper Volta is afraid of Russia."

Gorby had still hung on as one by one every last one of the fifteen so-called titular republics that made up the USSR declared independence and sovereignty from the center outward: Armenia, Azerbaijan . . . Kazakhstan . . . Kyrgyzstan . . . and when Russia declared itself free and independent of the "Soyuz" (Union), Mikhail Gorbachev had effectively become a president without a country.

But when his nemesis, Boris Yeltsin, now president of the reborn Russian Federation, led the effort to cobble together a post-Soviet entity called the "Commonwealth of Independent States," known by its clumsy-sounding acronym CIS (SNG in Russian), it was all over. Many Russians still had no firm idea as to whether the USSR (SSSR in Russian) still formally existed. The hammer-and-sickle flag was still flying, after all.

"Can you tell what this SNG thing means?" asked the gold-toothed taxi driver as I got out of his car. "SSSR (USSR) sounded a hell of a lot better." He slammed the door behind me.

While I scurried around town looking for supplies, Mikhail Gorbachev was spending his last day in power behind the massive red walls of the Kremlin. He'd been under a virtual news blackout about his fate, but not of the nefarious kind. None of the Soviet television networks was even documenting the last days of the empire, because none of them seemed to care. By contrast, some foreign networks spent days in the corridors of fading power, recording everything now that the once-feared foreigners had easy access to the nerve center of the erstwhile Evil Empire. The irony was not lost on Gorbachev's closest aides.

"It's shameful for us that only Western TV journalists hovered around him," wrote Anatoly Chernayev in his account of Gorbachev's final days in power.

While I was at the market "Christmas shopping" for bread and cheap sausage that morning, Gorbachev asked to have a telephone call arranged with US president George Herbert Walker Bush, during which Gorbachev informed Bush that he would be making a special televised address at seven p.m. Moscow time. He also told Bush that he had signed an order transferring control over the Soviet Union's "nuclear briefcase"— the means to launch Soviet nuclear missiles—to the Russian Federation and its president, Boris Yeltsin. "As soon as I make my announcement, the order will come into effect," he told Bush. "So you can peacefully celebrate Christmas and sleep without worry tonight," Gorbachev added.

Bush is said to have waxed emotional about the close personal ties they had developed over the years; it is not known if Bush offered Gorby asylum.

Meanwhile, I had gone back to an apartment I shared with a friend, Sergei Lazaruk, who at the time was deputy dean of the prestigious Soviet State Institute of Cinematography (VGIK) and trying to eke out a living on the equivalent of a hundred dollars a month. We had met earlier that year, when I'd led a group of American film students to the USSR as their interpreter.

A sundry group of other Russian friends had also come over to watch the TV broadcast with us, including Mikhail Zhivilo, then a small-time currency speculator who used to change fifty bucks a time for me at the black market rate. Zhivilo, well dressed and soft spoken, had just started work at Moscow's first commodities exchange. He talked about the unique economic opportunities amid the chaos and how the period would not be repeated in terms of its potential for making big profits. His optimism seemed absurd given the dire state of the Soviet (Russian) economy. He suggested I join him and his business partners in the precious metals business. I declined, and he openly laughed at my desire to pursue foreign correspondence. His laughter was well vindicated. Within years, Zhivilo was running one of Russia's biggest aluminum plants. He made tens of millions before falling out with a regional kingpin governor and going into exile with his fortune. (Meanwhile, I am still working a day job, whereas I doubt Zhivilo feels much compunction to—beyond philanthropy.)

Sergei was the only one who seemed interested in watching Gorby and the passing of the empire, to be announced live on TV. Then the clock struck seven p.m., and Gorbachev's familiar image filled the screen. He began to speak.

Gorby expressed deep regret that it had proven impossible to save the Soviet Union. He opposed its dissolution. Upon assuming the mantle of power in 1985, he had had no alternative but to try to radically reform the system. "It was clear not all was well with our country. . . . I understood that to begin reforms of such a scale in a society like ours was extremely difficult and even dangerous. But even today, I'm convinced of the historic correctness of the democratic reforms that were begun in the spring of 1985."

Gorbachev spoke for all of ten minutes—a historically short address. He concluded with the words "I wish you all the best." Then he was off the air, and the Soviet Empire, which had endured for sixty-eight years, eleven months, and twenty-five days, was no more—and few seemed to immediately understand the significance of it all. Later, I learned a few more details about the aftermath: Immediately after his last address, Gorbachev turned to his final task: turning over the Soviet nuclear brief-case. Yet even this moment was tinged with absurdity. Boris Yeltsin, known for his tirades and unpredictability, had for unclear reasons taken offense at Gorbachev's resignation speech. According to Gorbachev, Yeltsin refused to show up in the Kremlin to take over control of the "nu-clear button," as it is called in Russian. Gorbachev writes of the incident with bitterness. Yeltsin offered to meet "on neutral ground." In the end, Gorbachev handed over the means to destroy the world many times over to Marshal Yevgeny Shaposhnikov and several senior military officers.

Gorbachev went into a room with several aides who had stayed to the end.

They poured themselves a round of whiskey, bitter solace for the USSR and its last leader's having already become an afterthought. Gor-bachev recalls:

> There were no other procedures for seeing off the president of the USSR, as is the accepted norm in civilized countries. Although many years of close, comradely relations connected me with most of them, not one of the presidents of the sovereign states—the former Soviet republics of the USSR—considered it necessary to come to Moscow in those [final] days, or even to call me.

Within forty-five minutes of his resignation speech, sentries lowered the proud red hammer and sickle from the Kremlin and replaced it with the Russian red, white, and blue tricolor.

My friend Sergei Lazaruk, in despair, suggested we go into the cen-ter of Moscow for some drinks. In the streets around Red Square, life went on as usual, oblivious to the empire's passing. People were strolling around, what few cafés that were open were packed, and one would not have known that 300 million people had just become citizens of different countries.

But the quiet bordering on indifference about the demise of the

"Common House" that had been the USSR masked a churning fury beneath the surface. The genie of independence was out of the bottle, and the roller-coaster ride of "parading sovereignties" and extreme nationalism had just begun.

One of the first places to blow was at first glance one of the least likely—the wine- and song-filled and (now former-Soviet) Republic of Georgia, which just happened to be Stalin's homeland.

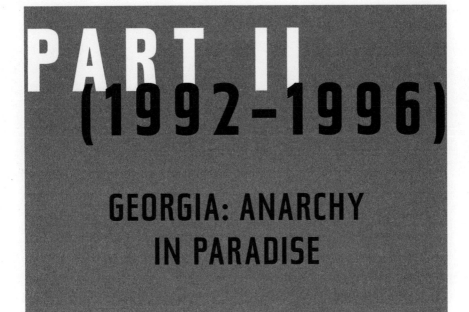

PART II
(1992–1996)

GEORGIA: ANARCHY
IN PARADISE

Last Georgian volunteer units head to front lines, days before Sukhumi is taken over by Abkhaz, September 1993.

My boss from Reuters TV says: "Pack your bags and get to Georgia." It is August 1992, and I've been working in Moscow in the eight months since the USSR's disintegration. There's another war on there, this time in Abkhazia [Georgia]. I'd been to Georgia twice, most recently earlier that year after a two-week civil war reduced the heart of the capital to a smoking ruin. I'd only covered one war, a few months earlier (and even then for only a few days) in the former Soviet republic of Moldova. For some reason this made me a kind of war specialist to my boss, or at least foolhardy enough to embark on this latest Georgian "adventure."

The two-hour flight from Moscow south to the Caucasus Mountains reflects the now-dead empire's geographical complexity. Flat fields of wheat punctuated by birch forests give way to bursting rivers and rolling hills. Just an hour or so out of Moscow, our plane starts to pass over lands conquered by the Cossacks in the eighteenth century, the traditional homelands of dozens of indigenous peoples—Ossetians, Ingush, Kabardins, and Chechens, to name a few. . . . Then rise the Caucasus Mountains, snowcapped, knife-sharp granite fingers sticking up out of the blue. Georgia comes into view.

Georgia seemed an unlikely backdrop for failed-state status. The Soviet Union's richest corner—Black Sea beaches, snow-covered mountain peaks, subtropical sunshine nurturing mandarin and tea groves and vineyards—it had a reputation for producing painters, ballerinas, and poets, bacchanalia and boundless hospitality. "Get rid of the Russians and we'll live off our wine and cognac!" was a typical common refrain.

Yet in another way it was indeed a very likely place for trouble. It was a mix of the majority Georgians, "autonomous" republics, and corners dominated by ethnic minorities. And, given its bountiful attributes, Georgia was naturally coveted—home to resorts owned by the Soviet military, political, and cultural elite. What's more, Georgia had been part of the Russian Empire far longer than the effective birth of the Soviet Empire in 1917. Georgia had entered Russia as a protectorate in the late 1700s, as its rulers of the time saw it as a chance to avert another threat from Persians, Turks, or Muslim raiders from the North Caucasus—it even shared Orthodox Christianity with the Russians. Georgia and Abkhazia, the most valued jewels in the empire's battered crown.

The Abkhaz were, in fact, by the time of the empire's breakup, just 17 percent or so of the population of that region—fewer than 100,000 souls. They blamed a deliberate policy of assimilation led by Stalin and his henchman Lavrenty Beria on their decline. Beria was also a Georgian— or, to be more precise, a Megrelian—a Georgian subethnos. The Georgians became 45 percent, the rest Abkhaz, Russians, Armenians, and a smattering of others. Tensions smoldered for years, the Abkhaz local parliament declared independence, and through a series of deadly miscues, the war was on.

And so it was with beautiful Sakartvelo—"the land of the Georgians"—in their own, very non-Russian language. Independence had arrived, and I was suddenly sent there to record the pathology of upheaval that would ensue.

NOBODY STARTED THIS WAR

N obody started this war," stammered the woman manning the one phone in the Parliamentary Press Department of the Republic of Georgia. It was disingenuous, of course; somebody started it. Maybe she was just in denial. But she's partially correct—the war's commencement is anarchic, absurd, seemingly starting on a whim.

A paramilitary gang, the "National Guard," gets permission to enter a few miles into autonomous Abkhazia and guard passenger trains, which are being raided and robbed at will. Georgia has agreed with the local Abkhaz authorities on guarding the trains. How will the National Guard accomplish this act of ensuring safety? With tanks, among other toys. *Tanks to guard passenger trains?* Tanks were not part of the deal. It is absurd, of course, the sight of the tanks evoking deep fears in Abkhazia, helping ignite the war. Not to mention the fact that they are worthless for guarding passenger trains.

Tengiz Kitovani is the potbellied leader of the National Guard. His mission supposedly has nothing to do with Abkhaz separatism; it's to prevent a wave of recent kidnappings. No one told Kitovani to crack down on Abkhazia, they say. No one gave the National Guard permission to enter any which towns, just guard the railway. But someone took some potshots at Kitovani's guys, and they fired back. Looting and excesses began. Alcohol and testosterone were also involved. Need I add that Tengiz Kitovani is a large-canvas painter by trade? Did I mention that some Georgians accuse him of being a KGB agent sent in by the Russians to do a fifth-column job?

Kitovani's men ditch their railroad-guarding mission and angrily march into the regional capital, Sukhumi. The predictable wave of looting and revenge against some ethnic Abkhaz, and other local non-Georgians, ensues. The Abkhaz flee north for the coastal town of Gudauta, where they set up their own administration.

It's a mere few days after the war's start. I wander the halls of the parliament and strike up a conversation with Eduard Shevardnadze, the effective "head of state" of the new Georgia. (At the time, he is officially known as chairman of the State Council; later, he'd opt for the title of president. At this stage in Georgia's statehood, "Shevy" has but one bodyguard, and security is almost nonexistent.) To many in the West, he's the Man Who Ended the Cold War as Mikhail Gorbachev's Soviet foreign minister. He's on his way to a raucous parliamentary session. Shevardnadze smiles and rattles off a few platitudes to me about how there is still "hope." In other words, it's not too late to stop the conflict in Abkhazia.

Shevardnadze has problems: The "head of state" is clearly not calling the shots. He is not even formally commander in chief of the National Guard. The dim-witted loudmouth Kitovani is.

Kitovani is one of the warlords who brought Shevardnadze back to Georgia as a fig leaf for their questionable legitimacy. Because they have the men and the guns, they are in control, at least for now. The Abkhaz don't buy it: They are convinced Shevardnadze's behind the war. Shevardnadze tries to reach Kitovani by phone or military radio. The rabble-rousing artisan Kitovani, once inside Abkhazia, even refuses several times to take phone calls from the "head of state" as he helps lead Georgia into its latest disaster.

I wander down the street from the parliament.

It's a molten August sky, as if dripping hot lead. Armed men are milling around in a downtown park, near Tbilisi's Central House of Chess. The air is a simmering pot boiled over. These fighters belong to yet another parliamentary group, the Mkhedrioni ("Knights"), and the Chief Knight is about to speak. His name is Jaba Ioseliani, and he is a smiling man with a dramatic aura. In the sixty-seventh year of his life (born 1926), Jaba (Georgian men, even presidents, are referred to by their first names, preceded by "Batono," a term of respect roughly meaning "Sir") is well preserved, dapperly dressed (he prefers bow ties), and armed with a deceptively warm smile. By age sixty-six, most paramilitary leaders have well-established military careers. Jaba's, by contrast, is about two years old. He helped topple the erratic elected president, Zviad Gamsakhurdia, over the winter. Now he, together with the big-canvas painter Kitovani, is the other main protagonist in Georgia's newest war, against the Abkhaz. Life imitates art. Jaba's current "official" job description? Dramatist, playwright.

An earlier job of Jaba's came as a student in Leningrad. In this case, a woman's finger was allegedly chopped off in order to make it easier to steal a ring she wore. Toss in a second jail stint for manslaughter, and all in all Jaba earned more than fifteen years in a Soviet (Russian) prison before reclaiming his status as a dramaturge in Georgia, just when the place was falling apart. And now as a warlord.

Hundreds of armed men have shown up to hear the Great Man, who is pontificating from a stage inside the House of Chess. The gathered are an eclectic lot, and they and the Great Man seem props in a grand show. Uniforms? The favored dress code is a T-shirt and jeans, preferably baggy ones. Dark sunglasses, worn night and day, sun or clouds, also seem obligatory. Oh, and make sure you bring your own Kalashnikov, or share one with a friend.

Jaba's speech is a colorful rant about pride and honor, or at least his interpretation of such values. Loud chatting among the crowd of fighters drowns him out. Many are sprawled out between theater chairs. The rabble is nonstop, extemporaneous; Georgians have a habit of talking all at the same time, and this is no exception, especially since many of the "Knights" are inebriated.

The Knights are accountable only to themselves and, occasionally,

Jaba, who is accountable to no one. They make sure everyone understands that. The license plates on their automobiles are uniquely personalized: Often they have none.

Jaba jumps into a waiting car, followed by me and the makeshift army of men in cars with no license plates. The several hundred fighters head for the airport.

The Knights have no planes, and the government has no real air force, even troop transports. Odd aircraft on the tarmac (usually Tupolev-154s, the standard Soviet passenger planes) are commandeered on the spot and converted for use in minutes.

The lucky get seats, if they haven't been torn out. No seat, no problem. Stand in the aisles, in the cockpit, in the toilet. Some men pile into the cargo hold along with a new supply of artillery shells. Everyone poses for pictures, partaking in this moment of history.

"Gamarjos Sakartvelos!" "Long Live Georgia!"

The empire is dead and the pent-up emotions of hundreds of years under foreign tutelage boil over in a paroxysm of nationalist fervor. The result is a ruinous, pointless, internecine bloodletting pitting Georgians against Ossetians and now Georgians against Abkhazians and finally Georgians against Georgians, during which most of the original objectives (such as independence) get lost in the mayhem.

The Knights have vague notions about their upcoming mission in Abkhazia. "We are going to fight for the Motherland" is a typical refrain. Blank stares greet me when I ask what that means in practice.

Well, it's only been going on for a week. So, is it really a war? Well, people have been killed, so let us call it a "conflict," but not a "war" yet. We can reserve that designation for another year, by which time there will be ten thousand dead and hundreds of thousands homeless.

I'M READY TO make my way to the "front," if there is one. Groups of Georgian fighters are still clamoring to get there too. Miraculously, some commercial flights are still flying! I buy a twelve-dollar ticket on a twenty-six-seat Yakovlev-40 plane. I seem to be the only paying passenger, however. The rest are either Batono Jaba the dramatist's "Knights," or Kitovani's National Guardsmen. Why is it that paramilitary gurus around these parts all seem to be led by artists of one ilk or another?

It is hot on the asphalt. Burning hot. Shoes sink in the half-melted tar. The flight was supposed to leave at three p.m., but now it is four and then five, then six. "We're waiting for a VIP," blurts out an airport official. Who? No one will say. We take refuge from the heat by sitting on our bags underneath the wings of the little plane. Three fighters are next to me, along with a lamb on a tether. They do their best to show me the legendary Georgian hospitality, pouring shot after shot of *chacha,* or hard-core Georgian moonshine made from grapes, into a common glass and down shot after shot. Sweaty with gregariousness, they act like they're going to a party. Or a funeral pyre for the empire. They drink to my health, even as they slowly ruin theirs, and insist I join them in the festivities. But I'm in no mood for this and turn down their entreaties until someone reminds me that snubbing a toast is an offense to Georgian honor, an issue that is treated with infinitely more gravity than the newly ignited war.

Finally, the pilot appears. After some two dozen men with their sundry weapons board, I climb up the stairs followed by my three fighter friends and the lamb. It bleats and baahs the entire way to Abkhazia. So does one of the liquored-up fighters, chattering away in Georgian in my ear the whole flight, which I don't understand a lick of yet. That fact does not trouble him.

It's dark by the time we land in Sukhumi, and I can't see a thing from the air. My fighter friends disappear with their bleating future dinner into the chaos on the tarmac. As the reinforcements have arrived, other armed men fight for seats for the flight back to Tbilisi. Across the runway, a much larger passenger jet is getting ready to fly a scheduled route to Moscow. Most of the would-be passengers are Georgian men, dragging enormous bags filled with produce to sell in Russia. They make their way toward the plane but are stopped by furious fighters who charge the merchants with desertion of the Motherland. "Stay and fight!" they scream at the perceived turncoats, firing their weapons in the air. The war that nobody started does not seem to be going well.

I make my way through the throng to the road outside the terminal and try to find a lift into the city, some twelve miles away. There are no cars on the road. Another fighter approaches and introduces himself as "Commander Dato," the Georgian short form of the name David. He is tall and his head droops toward me, like an overripened sunflower. With him is a local woman, Irina. "I'm a Jew," she says, out of the blue. For the next two hours, Dato talks up a storm. He's already called HQ, he says. Every so often he promises a car is on the way. "Ten minutes," he says for the thirteenth time.

Later, instead of a fourteenth broken promise, he admits, "No more cars tonight," and points in the direction of a forlorn barrackslike shack. I stumble in the dark and enter. The floor is a mixture of concrete and dirt. A bunch of grunts snore away on cots. I find a free one and pretend to sleep. At dawn, I leave the slumbering paramilitaries and wander onto the long airport access road, which leads to the main highway.

There are still no cars in sight, but the morning sun reveals a lush cover of palm trees, mandarin groves, and tea plantations along the main road. Cows wander through tea bushes. The Black Sea coast arcs on the left. On the right—the snowcapped peaks of the Caucasus. I'd heard of Abkhazia's beauty but wasn't prepared for the Malibu-at-war I'd entered.

A car stops along the road, another rattling, ubiquitous old Soviet Lada. The man behind the wheel is Aleksandr Berulava. He's wiry, edgy, with ruddy cheeks. Although he claims to be a local journalist, he's wearing military fatigues and is now doing PR for the Georgian war effort.

"They had all the best houses, all of the best jobs," Berulava complains, insisting the Abkhaz and the Russians started the war through a carefully calculated set of "provocations." He pulls up to the Georgian HQ, hastily set up in a palatial coastal mansion in a lush botanical garden that once served as summer digs for Uncle Joe Stalin. Peacocks strut about the yard, barking. Placards identify rare plants and flowers, visual and olfactory sedatives for Stalin and other strongmen who've inhabited this piece of paradise.

We ascend the steps, and I am led in and introduced to Giorgi Khaindrava, the city's "military commandant." Just like Jaba the dramatist and the painter Kitovani, Georgi is yet another artistic figure—in this case, an actor by profession. The war is feeling more and more like a big stage production.

"Welcome, welcome to Sukhumi, my friend!" crows Commandant Khaindrava. He is boisterous, hosting—as if the mythology of Georgia's endless wine- and feast-fueled bacchanalia is obligatory even in these difficult circumstances.

I mention to Khaindrava that the "Knights" and "Guards" have not ingratiated themselves with the local Abkhaz and non-Georgian population. They've accused them of looting, booze-fueled vandalism, and random violence.

He nods his head slowly. This is a problem among his men, he admits.

When the military commandant tells you he's got a problem with random violence and uncontrolled marauding, you know there's more trouble brewing. I ask about getting to the "front." The problem is, there isn't much of one. Most of the Abkhaz have retreated to the north of the region and are busy setting up an "army"—with the covert help of the Russians and some allies from ethnic brethren in Russia.

In the heady first days of the war, the Georgians demonstratively marched all the way up the coastal highway to the Russian border, planting Georgian flags, kissing the local women, and drinking with local men.

But marking territory is not the same as holding on to it.

Eighteen years later, in 2010, Giorgi Karkarashvili, a young Georgian top commander in the Abkhaz war who later became Georgia's defense minister at the ripe age of twenty-six, makes a startling admission:

"We entered Abkhazia in a very disorganized way. We didn't even have a specific goal, and we started looting villages along the way," Karkarashvili says. "As a result, in the span of a month, we managed to make enemies out of the entire local population."

With such sage military planning (more driven by testosterone than strategy), the end result of the War That Nobody Started would be predictable.

I ARRIVE BACK at my apartment in Tbilisi from Abkhazia after midnight, covered in subtropical sweat and grime. Images of rare luxury swirl in my head. In this case, of hot water. One of the few perks central planning did offer was nonstop, almost-scalding tap water on demand. In urban USSR centers, one could take virtually endless free steam showers, the water pumped from giant central heating stations. Any American who grew up in a large family knows this is not something to be taken for granted.

I went to the shower and turned it on, but the water was an icy rain. I waited, but the stream remained glacial. The central hot water system never was switched back on again in Georgia; heating stations could no longer afford fuel—the end of another era.

I get a late-night phone call from a colleague. "Head of State" Eduard Shevardnadze was flying to New York the next morning to speak at the United Nations. I assumed it was already too late to sign up. "Come to the airport and just get on," said the reporter, Zhorra Vardzelashvili.

"What do you mean 'just get on,' " I countered. "We're talking about the president's plane. And he's leaving in a few hours."

"Just show up," he said.

Rules of deference and feigned respect common to the rest of the governed world had yet to catch on. The Georgian officials were often embarrassingly deferential to foreigners. The guards at parliament barely bothered to emerge from a slouch when I passed through. There were metal detectors for show—usually switched off.

I got to the airport minutes before takeoff. Shevardnadze stands, waiting. The Man Who Ended the Cold War seemed a bit out of place in the VIP lounge, with its stained brown carpeting and sofas with cigarette holes, where cows often wandered near the molehill-bumpy runway.

"Go ask him if you can come along," Zhorra told me.

"He's the head of state. I can't just ask him like that," I said.

Zhorra looked exasperated with my formality. He knew what he was doing—himself a former aide to Shevardnadze during Communist times. Zhorra sauntered up, then whispered to Shevardnadze, who quickly flashed his Cheshire-cat smile—sometimes described as "warm" by westerners, but as "Machiavellian" by some Georgians (not to mention the Abkhaz). "Come along," Shevardnadze lip-synced.

Shevy's plane was in effect making its maiden voyage as the most modern aircraft in the Georgian fleet. It had just been retrofitted with extended fuel tanks and other updates.

After takeoff, Shevardnadze's personal stewardess took command of the in-flight program. She was a twenty-five-year-old pop singer by the name of Anna Jacki. Anna had curly red hair and a petite body, and was well known for what by Georgian standards were her racy music videos. Her clothing was so tight, it appeared to be sprayed on.

Anna helped hand out the meals, which consisted of hand-sliced blobs of fatty beef on blanched, tasteless bread. The meat also turned out to be rancid. As a consequence, I spent two days in New York looking into a toilet bowl.

We stopped for fuel in the Icelandic capital, Reykjavík. The city was wrapped in one of its legendary fog attacks. The runway appeared out of nowhere as the pilot tried to land. Unsurprisingly, we overshot it. The plane groaned as he violently jerked it back up and banked hard to the left, over the icy Atlantic below.

We landed safely on the second attempt. By this time, however, the plane full of normally boisterous Georgians was shaken into silence.

The Icelanders wheeled out their prime minister to meet with the Man Who Ended the Cold War, Shevardnadze, now more a curiosity piece than statesman to the West, as if his plane were a UFO and those aboard it green men with antennae. The Icelanders hurried him and several of his ministers off to a meeting room, giving the diplomatic nonevent (fuel stopover) an air of mysterious intrigue.

The real fruits born of the first and possibly last Icelandic-Georgian summit remain a mystery to this day. Back on the Presidential Plane, nervous faces greeted us. A crew member agitatedly discussed something in the front.

Anna the pop-star-presidential-stewardess later revealed the reason for the commotion: The windshield of the plane had cracked in a spiderweb pattern. Aviation rules mandated that it be unconditionally grounded. The crack was a decompression risk, and we were about to head over the frigid Atlantic again.

The irony that our intended path was similar to that of the *Titanic*—almost exactly eighty years earlier—was not lost on us.

Shevardnadze had other ideas.

"Fly on," he calmly told the pilots, after learning a replacement would have to be brought from Moscow, at least a two-day delay, including repair time, which would have meant missing the UN session.

There was only a small, low-level State Department retinue waiting on the tarmac when we landed at JFK. The Cold War was over. Shevardnadze's once-tall standing carried a lot less coin. As we taxied in, broken windshield intact, a tiny retinue of unknown US State Department officials waited below to greet him, a sea change from the red-carpet treatment he was used to from world leaders as the Soviet foreign minister. Shevardnadze, who rarely took insult to heart, grunted something in disgust to an aide. Here was a global giant who had been confused with the leader of a Third World country. Which in fact he now was.

Shevardnadze got a better reception at the United Nations, where he made an impassioned speech about the dangers of what he claimed was "aggressive separatism" in Abkhazia. However, some of the Georgian journalists and government officials on the trip never saw it—they skipped the protocol bit and busied themselves scouring the bowels of the Bronx for cut-rate TVs and stereos.

Once we took off for Georgia a few days later, the Man Who Ended the Cold War made his customary foray into the back of the aircraft to greet those aboard. He did a quick double take, however. The rear half of the plane was jammed with boxes reading SONY, JVC, and PIONEER. They'd converted the Presidential Plane into a flying warehouse of cheap electronics.

As the shop tour continued, the war in Abkhazia was escalating. Cease-fires had been signed and broken, the fighting escalating, the Georgians retreating. By late October, the Georgians controlled only the capital, Sukhumi, and a few lesser towns.

Later that month, possibly as a burst of revenge or effort to wipe out the historical record of the Abkhaz's presence in the region, a group of Georgian fighters torched the building housing the Abkhaz cultural archives in Sukhumi, effectively destroying history. Saved were only a few thousand out of some 170,000 unique documents and artifacts. This greatly embittered the Abkhaz in a way that has never been forgotten.

The war was now Shevardnadze's, even though he appears to have been opposed to launching it. He had gone from Berlin Wall smasher to returning to power in his smallish, chaotic, but now independent Georgia. Shevardnadze's detractors in Moscow hated him for "destroying" the USSR—along with Gorbachev—by "giving away" East Germany. Now the man who helped bring down the big empire was left trying to hold together the remnants of another fragmenting land, his native Georgia.

EXODUS

Autumn gave way to a winter and spring of pitched battles, the Georgians barely hanging on to Sukhumi. The "War That Nobody Started" was clearly not going according to plan. Not that there had ever been a "plan."

As sultry summer set in, fighting periodically severed the only road link to the capital, cutting it off from the outside world. The Georgians launched bloody counteroffensives, reopening the meandering coastal highway for a few more days. Soon after, it would be sliced again, reopened, and recut. The strangulation of a dying man, then easing up ever so slightly just as he loses consciousness, allowing mocking reprieves of oxygenated euphoria as the inevitable approaches.

I, a few other reporters, and the odd aid worker stayed near the front lines, at a sprawling old facility built for Red Army bigwigs. Its official name was typically Soviet: the Resort Sanatorium of the Moscow Military District. Palatial digs by Soviet standards, the sanatorium sits amid twenty sensual acres of palms, orchids, and oleanders: a botanist's subtropical dream. It was the only place left to stay. Georgian units had commandeered the rest of the hotels. The Abkhaz had shelled others into disrepair.

The sanatorium oozed with the air of empire, a coveted Kremlin colonial outpost. Russian generals had vacationed here for decades. You could feel their ghosts frolicking on the spacious balconies. The foamy waves of the Black Sea lapped onto the beaches below them.

Most of the "resort" workers abdicated as the war intensified—leaving behind a crew of local caretakers. The gaggle of clerks, cooks, and cleaners had long been at the condescending beck and call of vacationing generals. Now, like a group of mutinous deckhands who'd thrown their sadistic captain overboard, they reveled in ironic revenge. There were almost no guests, no running water, and little food. Notoriously inaccurate missiles fired by the Abkhaz regularly scored direct hits on the sanatorium grounds, blasting out windows. The now-ruling worker class was oblivious to these inconveniences. The estate was theirs, and they relished it.

One of the newly crowned was Marina, a chambermaid. A gregarious, wispy fifty-something, Marina was permanently clad in homemade black ruffled skirts that reached her ankles, even in the most oppressive of sea humidity. She derived great joy from her newfound powers. Marina took special delight in one particular act: conferring the keys to rooms once reserved for the top Soviet military elite unto hitherto unauthorized ruffians like me.

Leading me to my room, Marina would dangle the keys suggestively from their carved wooden tags and then carefully glide them into the locks. With the weight of her small body behind her, she'd dramatically push open the doors to reveal my double-roomed chamber with twelve-foot ceilings. There were large beds with ruffled spreads, kitsch red-velvet love seats, and amenities like the crystal water decanters that doubled as receptacles for my morning birdbaths. The decanters were a godsend, for when I turned on the wheeled taps in the bathroom, usually nothing came out. At best, foul-smelling brown water trickled down.

"General Ivanov once holidayed here for two weeks," Marina cackled. "I'll tell you something else: Comrade Belinsky's wife used to love to sleep in this bed, and not always alone." She giggled, placing the keys in my hands as if they were diamonds.

Every evening as the sun was setting over the sea, at precisely eight o'clock, the caretakers switched on a rumbling old diesel generator. The sanatorium became practically the only island of light in the darkened capital. The few of us who called the sanatorium home gathered nightly on the veranda. We drank from jugs of crude homemade wine and smoked the chokingly acrid local Abkhazian-produced cigarettes, Astra. With little else to do, we watched and listened to evenings of exploding artillery shells.

We could often see blasts from a pier a few hundred meters away. The Abkhaz shelled it nightly. In the lush hills surrounding the city, firefights erupted in quick bursts. We traded vacuous interpretations about what was going on, trying to make sense of it all. It was a way to pass time, aided by bravado about the ongoing battles.

Neither the Abkhaz nor the government shed much illumination on the situation. They bragged of astounding but nonexistent battlefield triumphs. They underestimated their losses with equal shamelessness. Yes, one could visit the front, but that offered few real clues about what was going on. This was a war being fought mostly with random barrages. Both sides favored rockets whose nickname *grad* means "hail," as in a hailstorm. They were just as inaccurate as their name. During attacks, they rained on the besieged capital from truck-mounted batteries that could fire off a couple of dozen of the treacherous things at a time. *Grads* were conceived by Soviet munitions designers to frighten incoming infantry, not for precision. The effect was, predictably, devastating. The attacks rarely hit anything strategic. Sometimes they simply decapitated innocent pedestrians brave enough to venture out for food or supplies. The Georgians would answer by firing the same inaccurate *grads* at the Abkhaz positions.

From our nighttime perch on the veranda, we had a perfect view of the entire bay. It would have been possible to watch the movements of naval ships or patrol boats. Except that neither side had a real navy.

Life went on, amid the bombardments. From my post along the veranda, I occasionally heard cries of passion wafting from rooms of the sanatorium. I wondered if it could be Marina. I wondered if she was gleefully taking revenge on the wives of those haughty military generals. They had sometimes vacationed at the sanatorium alone, away from their military husbands. Perhaps Marina was making the most of those oversized beds, before the war took that away from her.

More cease-fires came and went, and as missiles continued to rain down on the city, a silence descended. The wide avenues, lined by incongruously pastel buildings and botanical gardens, emptied by the day. Pedestrians deserted the promenade along the seafront, where ships full of tourists had docked just a summer before. The exodus began with the start of the war. Now it accelerated. It was a gradual march out of the capital, done stealthily, like a family facing eviction. Just as no one wants the neighbors to see the truck backing up at the door, the men who could have fought at the front did not want to be seen abandoning their city. They seemed to look away on their way out, avoiding eye contact.

THE STREETS STREAMED with women dragging bags, bright woven bags with stripes, full of family albums, heirlooms, and clothes. Bags became a main topic of discussion. Who was selling them, where to buy them, when more might arrive at the bazaar? Which kinds were strongest and which would rip, which were the easiest to sling over one's shoulder, which ones were waterproof? Once the bags were filled, families would haul them to a curbside and wait for a passing bus to come, at least during times when the only road out was not cut by battles. The lucky drove out with their cars stacked high with belongings. But the preferred method of escape was through the airport.

Of course, by now, scheduled passenger planes were no longer flying. People wanted out, not in. Getting onto one of the departing planes was a matter of persistence, luck, and social position. I had an unfair advantage. At the press center, a man handled getting journalists out of the capital.

Aleksandr Khaindrava was the uncle of Sukhumi's military commandant—the actor Giorgi Khaindrava, whom I'd met on my first trip. A septuagenarian, Alexander projected the avuncular aura of a southern college professor. He occupied a room in Stalin's summer retreat. As a young man, he'd grown up in China, in the city of Kharbin, among a community of Soviet exiles who fled amid the Bolshevik Revolution. His King's English empowered him to deal with the press. Few other people around spoke English at all, and he delighted in me as a captive audience.

ALEKSANDR KHAINDRAVA WAS a man shipwrecked by the shifting fortunes of empires and exile. This made a lonely soul of him. And so, instead of expediting my way out of the city, he impeded it. He pretended not to know when the next plane full of Georgian paramilitaries would land, making space for escapees. On an old plastic rotary phone, his long crinkled fingers dialed the numbers for the airport with excruciating slowness. He knew himself that the city's telephone lines were so bad that barely one call in a hundred might get through.

When Aleksandr did get through to the airport, he'd often say, beaming, "I'm so sorry, the plane just left." For him it was a reprieve that meant another hour of conversation over tea, sixty minutes less loneliness in a country that was his, yet not altogether his, in a war that was neither his nor anyone's in particular.

The airport, once I did reach it in spite of Aleksandr's gentleman's loneliness-laden chivalry, was a war zone of a different kind.

When one of the planes would land, near-riots ensued. Screaming women fought with the paramilitaries, themselves trying to escape. The fighters waved Kalashnikovs and barged their way into the planes. The power of their weapons determined who would get on. The battles were nonsensical. The planes landed and took off until everyone who wanted out was out. Then the fighting would die down again. Ethics held little sway. It was often women and children last.

There was, however, one cardinal rule.

The dead were given priority.

In Georgia, the dead are more alive than the living. The culture enshrines a cult of funerals and wakes. Georgians—as well as Abkhaz and many in the Caucasus—feast around the graves of their departed every year on their birthdays. They leave succulent food, jugs of wine, and even cigarettes for the dead.

The dead.

They were stacked in simple zinc coffins and loaded onto the planes. Not military aircraft—just more requisitioned former Aeroflot passenger jets.

A fighter with a clenched face guided me up the ladder and past the screaming women and shouting paramilitaries. The Georgian custom of chivalrous hospitality can reduce one to a state of embarrassment. This was, after all, a flying hearse, and I was jumping the line. Below the plane echoed the shrieks of women and yells of men, and the larger sense of noisy Georgian chaos of the time. But inside, those shimmering, clean, perfect zinc rectangles of coffins stacked high conferred a feeling of pedantic order.

The fighter took me into the cockpit. The Pilot was a thickset man with a pencil mustache. He welcomed me in the same cheerful, oblivious Georgian spirit, as if I had walked into a wedding party, not a plane of rotting bodies.

From the cockpit, the Pilot watched nervously out the window as more people jammed aboard the plane. I tried to open the door to the cockpit to take a photo of the cabin, but it was so overloaded with coffins, refugees, and fighters that I had trouble pushing it open. The air was stifling, one hundred degrees of sweltering humidity.

His face turned from apprehension to anger. He looked at a weight indicator dial nervously. "We're overloaded by thirty percent. We've been flying regularly twenty percent overweight," he told me. "But thirty is pushing it. You see the condition this plane is in. The tires are bald. The fuel is of rotten quality; I think they've been watering it down."

The Pilot put on his headset and barked at the dispatcher. "We're not taking off. Do you want us all to die or something? We're overweight. Unload some of them or I'm not flying anywhere."

No one budged.

I could hear commotion coming from outside the cockpit. It swung open, and a fighter glared at the Pilot, gripping his AK. "Start those damn engines or we'll bring another pilot and leave you here."

The Pilot swore and began going through the preflight checklist. Sweat accumulated on his forehead. The engines roared to life. We taxied to the runway and then went all the way back to the end of it—to give us as much length as possible to take off. The plane groaned and picked up speed. We hurled toward the end of the runway. We lifted off with only a few feet to spare.

FROM THE WINDSHIELD, I watched the crowd of waiting women would-be escapees with their woven bags. They and the fighters left around them slowly faded from view. We passed over those bright mandarin groves full of wandering cows, derelict tea plantations, and the bougainvillea-lined main road along the beach. That misleadingly serene beach, devoid of holidaymakers, devoid of women in bikinis, devoid of children with sand pails and old men gathering shells. From the cabin the sound died. The shuddering craft was filled with the scent of sweat and death.

The Pilot wiped his brow. He aimed the plane in the direction of Tbilisi. He said we'd fly lower than normal to save fuel. I nodded as he told me the story I'd already heard hundreds of times. Georgians, he said, had not expected freedom to be so tough, or so brutal.

THE PILOT PUT the plane at cruising altitude and then performed his obligatory duties as a good Georgian host. "Now it's your turn," he said.

He sat me down in his pilot's seat. I took my place at the controls. Tupolev-134s, now mostly obsolete, are low on automation—therefore many veteran pilots actually relish flying them, rather than running what is essentially a mainframe with wings. This one had an old-style transparent nose cone. I could see everything around, like in a glass-bottom boat.

The plane pitched slightly as I moved the controls. Crazy thoughts filled my head. If I turned too sharply, those neatly stacked zinc coffins would tip over and the corpses would spill out. If I aimed the nose down, we would descend into the aquamarine waves of the Black Sea. Then the Pilot retook the controls as we reached the midpoint over the water.

Tbilisi came into view and we began our descent. As we approached, he turned to me.

"Friend, do you know what happens when you try and land a plane that is this overweight?" the Pilot asked me.

I did not, I said.

"When a plane is this heavy, it's very dangerous to put down. We could swerve off the runway. We could run out of runway. Or one of the tires could burst, and with all the extra weight, we might spin out of control and flip over." He seemed relieved to verbalize all the apocalyptic possibilities.

I didn't ask any more questions.

The wheels hit with a thud, and the plane bounced back up. The women jammed in the toilet and amid the coffins shrieked. The Pilot gritted his teeth. We shuddered to a halt at the very end of the runway. A crowd of civilians and fighters surged along the sun-drenched route toward us, looking for relatives, dead and alive.

OVER THE NEXT few weeks, the Georgians were forced to consent to a peace plan to end the war in Abkhazia. As a condition, they agreed to pull out their military hardware: tanks, artillery pieces, and armored personnel carriers (APCs). But the truce would not last. Too much blood had been shed. Both sides accused the other of cease-fire violations. The Abkhaz, backed by the Russians, smelled victory. In late September, the Abkhaz again cut the main road.

The provincial capital of Sukhumi was surrounded. The Georgians had little left to fight with. Again, Shevardnadze flew to the city to rally his troops.

The next day, I followed his path in another converted passenger jet. It was, as usual, stuffed to the hilt with ammo.

The pilot of this plane also told me to ride in front with him. "If we take fire on our approach, the cockpit is the safest place to be," he explained, not so reassuringly.

Sure enough, as we approached the city, we saw a gunboat in the harbor. It was one of the small vessels the Abkhaz had rigged up with crude antiaircraft missiles. The pilot pointed at the boat below, like a warped tour guide. He banked hard left as an evasive maneuver. Again, we landed hard. It was a relief, as if being delivered to a doomed city can be called that.

OURS WOULD BE one of the last Georgian planes to ever land in the city. I headed back to the sanatorium with a group of Georgian fighters. More Russian officers had arrived. They were there as monitors for the now-doomed peace deal. In reality, Russia had sided with the Abkhaz—for the Abkhaz, alliance with the Russians was pragmatism. The Russians helped arm and train them; this was openly admitted to me later by top-level Russian military officers in Abkhazia. For the Russians, a part of the reasoning was cultural—the Abkhaz being perceived by the Russians as more "Russified"—but mostly it was strategic (Abkhazia had excellent military facilities, resorts for the Soviet military brass, and seaports); add to that the Kremlin's hatred toward Shevardnadze for his role in "destroying" the Soviet Union as Mikhail Gorbachev's foreign minister. Some of them were out to return the favor by helping to, as they saw it, destroy Shevardnadze and shatter Georgia into its own fragmented state.

The world had responded to the crisis by sending a tiny team of eight United Nations "observers" and their Danish commander, Brigadier General Hvidegaard, all of whom had also taken up residence at the sanatorium. They were powerless to do anything.

Condemned cities are repositories of the poor, the foolhardy, and the naive. They are also sanctuary to the eccentric and the twisted.

I NOW FOUND myself sharing a room with Ed Parker, a sinewy, excited Brit. His jerky body movements and taped-up wire-rimmed glasses infused him with the aura of an unhinged chemistry buff. Parker had arrived in the capital as a fixer for a British TV crew, ITV. The telecrew stayed one day and then hurriedly flew off on one of the last planes out.

But Parker stayed behind. He told the TV crew to "go to hell," even though he had no outlet to report to and no means of filing news. He stayed out of ghoulish interest, a war tourist.

Ed told me he had fought as a mercenary on the Croatian side during the war in Bosnia.

"Did you kill anyone?" I asked.

"Hell, everyone asks me that question. OK, man, yeah, I killed some guys. There were a bunch of Serbs in a truck. We saw them over a ridge and blasted them with a bazooka. Don't ask me that fucking question again."

Ed relished his apocalyptic situation. "When I got here, I was determined to be the last one out," he told me proudly.

THEN THERE WAS the Preacher Man.

I found him wandering amid the palm tree—lined grounds of the sanatorium with an accordion slung around his neck. A proselytizer from the southern United States, he spent his time wandering around various post-Soviet war zones, trying to save the souls of those about to enter the other realm. He had a serene twinkle in his eye, probably because he sensed he had plenty of work ahead.

The Preacher Man had just done something even the most adrenaline-crazed war junkies hadn't: He'd walked across the front lines as Georgian and Abkhaz shells crashed down around him.

I told him it was a damn fool thing to do. Suicidal.

The Preacher Man just shrugged. "You never know when you're going to meet your maker!" he said with a big grin. Then he raised his elbow and mashed his fist into the side of the accordion. His folksy voice and the accordion's toyish vibes seemed to echo in unison along with the swaying tops of the palm trees.

All-consuming fire
You're my heart's desire and I love You, dearly, dearly Lord
Glory to the Lamb,
I exalt the great I am . . .

The Preacher Man continued with his Armageddon talk. He'd spent several days with the Abkhaz on the other side of the front. They told him the final assault on the city would come soon. The end would come in a few days. Of that he assured me.

Later, the Preacher Man's information would prove to be more accurate than that of any pontificating journalist or the UN "observers" (who were observing almost nothing, having just arrived a few days and weeks earlier and being confined to their quarters by the bombardments).

The Georgian defense of the city was quixotic. They had virtually no heavy armor left, save about a dozen rusting T-55 tanks of 1960s vintage. The covers to most of their artillery pieces were locked as part of the collapsed cease-fire, and they said the "mediating" Russians refused to provide the keys to unlock them. They were down to a few howitzers.

Two Georgian volunteers with soot-black hands did man one old artillery gun. They set it up on a jetty, just behind us and the sanatorium. We were now in the direct path of direct artillery barrages from Abkhaz positions. Dozens of boxes of ammunition were stacked up around the aging gun on our side. The Georgians took turns firing toward the front. The Abkhaz and their allies blasted back. But since they were using equally inaccurate firepower, many of the shells just exploded on the grounds of the sanatorium, blasting out our windows and scaring the few remaining residents to death.

Moreover, the Georgians were not bothering to change the location of the gun every few hours, as military logic demands. They blasted away, violating the cardinal rule governing artillery. Many of the Georgians had almost no weapons training. I saw one confused fighter struggling to jam his Soviet-made AK with ammo made for Romanian or other ex–East Bloc AKs, which can cause the guns to jam and explode. I didn't hang around to see the outcome.

General Hvidegaard, the UN man, sat on his balcony, smoked a cigarette, and philosophized over the shrill whistling of the gun. He said there had been negotiations to save the peace deal. But in the typical bravado of so many wars, the sticking point was the ownership of a dozen or so AKs. The guns had belonged to the Georgian-Abkhaz-Russian commission monitoring the cease-fire. The Abkhaz and the Georgians were bickering over their ownership.

"The sides insist this is a matter of honor. Unfortunately, this is the level we are dealing with," Hvidegaard told me.

On the jetty behind the sanatorium, the lone howitzer kept blasting away. "That gun's been firing every forty-five seconds for the last three days," the general said nonchalantly. "It can't continue forever. Either they will run out of ammunition, or . . ."

We spent the days of the siege running between the "resort" and the provincial capital's main government building, a hulking nine-story edifice ringed with palm trees.

On the third day of the siege, Shevardnadze convened a press conference. He appealed to his countrymen to come to the aid of the city, saying Georgia was at war with Russia. The entreaty was broadcast over Georgian TV.

In response, several hundred tried to come to the front. They flew out from Tbilisi in another TU-154 passenger jet loaded with ammunition and fighters.

But as the jet attempted to land, the Abkhaz shot it down with a heat-seeking missile. The crippled craft broke into several pieces on impact. More than a hundred people died, including a journalist from the *Wall Street Journal*, Alexandra Tuttle. I had met her only once, coincidentally at the very airport where she would meet her death. It had been a few weeks earlier in the summer, ironically when I was arriving in Sukhumi and she was leaving to go back to Tbilisi.

Also aboard the plane was Aleksandr Ivanishvili, the thirty-three-year-old brother of my friend and colleague Nino Ivanishvili. A violinist and physicist who had never held a gun in his hands and regarded the war in Abkhazia a mistake, Aleksandr and seven of his friends—one an artist, another a doctor—headed for the front only after hearing Shevardnadze's desperate radio exhortations that Georgia was at war with Russia.

Aleksandr's body was never found amid the wreckage of the burning jet, but unknown charlatans hounded his sister Nino for more than a year after the war ended, saying Aleksandr was alive and extracting money from her for supposedly arranging for his release. After the con men had their cash, their promises gradually ceased, and Aleksandr was of course never heard from again.

The Georgians coming back from the front were getting pulverized. Thomas Goltz, the war reporter, and I watched one carload pull up to a hospital. One of the soldiers was dead—coated in blood. Part of his head had been blown off. His three comrades were sobbing and slapping him in the face, as if trying to wake him.

A few minutes later, the Abkhaz rained shells onto the capital again, and smoke rose in velvet plumes into the sunny September air. They managed a direct hit on the TV tower, which had beamed Shevardnadze's exhortations from atop a hill. A few hours later, I saw huge flames coming from the shore near the sanatorium. The howitzer battery had been hit. I thought about what had become of the two soot-faced men who had been manning it.

Finally, the phone lines with the outside world were cut. I felt a sense of despair mingled with relief. There were no satellite phones, no way left to report. We were alone with the fate of the city.

Freed from the demands of conversing with my editors, the next day Goltz and I decided to take a bar of soap into the Black Sea and bathe our filthy bodies. It was an otherwise perfect late-summer day, and I thought about the incongruity of a serene swim along the shore of a condemned city under constant bombardment.

Suddenly, two Georgian air force Sukhoi-25 fighter bombers appeared on the horizon. They streaked low and passed almost exactly ninety degrees above our heads. We dunked ourselves underwater, as if that would be any defense use had their bomb doors swung open and dropped one.

As we reemerged for air, I saw the two planes race toward the Abkhaz positions. There was an earth-shattering blast. Then just one plane returned our way and headed back across the sea. I knew that the entire Georgian air force had consisted of four aging Sukhoi-25 fighter bombers. Now there were three.

After our bath was cut short, I returned to the sanatorium and called the military press center. Although the phone links with the rest of the world had been cut, the phone lines within the city were still intermittently working. With the lack of people left behind to use them, they were working better than ever. It was one of those strange, snickering ironies that one finds amid total chaos: Bits of life still function normally, out of inertia.

A Georgian press officer whose voice I recognized picked up the receiver. I asked about the planes that had just streaked over the city with their unmistakable scream. "Whaaaat planes?" he slurred. He was stone drunk.

The wake for the city had begun.

WITHIN TWO MORE days, the Abkhaz closed to within a few hundred meters of the main government building, the mini-Reichstag of this empire war. Inside, the food had run out. Shevardnadze convened a final press conference, but it was mostly a rant about the Russians and how they had deceived him. With no one to translate his comments into English, one of Shevardnadze's assistants asked me to interpret for the few remaining journalists.

Ed Parker, in attendance out of a sense of history, even though he had no outlet to report to, leaned over. He told me about how he'd been to the airport and seen "a hundred bodies" of those killed when the last plane full of reinforcements had been shot down. "Mate, I've seen more bodies in one day here than in two years in Bosnia." His eyes were full of sick excitement.

On the seventh floor of the local "Supreme Soviet" building, the members of the provisional Georgian government gathered. Those who wanted to flee had already availed themselves of the opportunity. Those staying behind had reconciled themselves to either capture or death. Georgians have a tradition known as *datireba,* a form of mournful singing performed at funerals. Relatives and loved ones literally cry to the deceased as a type of protest, scolding them for having left them to flail about in the temporal world. They also have a tradition of bacchanalian toasting and drinking, a tradition designed not only to celebrate life's more felicitous moments, but also to paper over the saddest of them. The mood among the government officials was a mixture of all of this.

One of the officials, a barrel-chested man, was also a well-known jazz musician. He invited me in, pounded on his desk, shouted and laughed boisterously, poured a glass of cognac, and belted out a loud song.

And then there was Aleksandr Berulava, now "vice commandant" of the city. He had given me a ride that first day in Sukhumi a year earlier. He was reviled by the Abkhaz, who accused him of tolerating abuses at the start of the "War Nobody Started." Berulava resented journalists for not taking the Georgian side—as he saw it—in the war. He had been morose for days as the fate of the city hung in the balance.

Now, with the end near and only the details of his fate to be decided, he seemed relieved. In fact, he was beaming. He sensed closure. His choice to stay had been made. I tried to understand his fatalism.

Outside, the shelling was getting heavy again, and the sun was setting. I got ready to dash the half mile back to the sanatorium. As I left the building for the last time, Berulava ran after me onto the grounds with something in his hands. For a moment, I thought perhaps he wanted to harangue me. Instead, he clutched a book. It was a collection of essays by Shevardnadze, called *My Choice for Democracy and Freedom*, signed and dedicated personally to Berulava just two days before:

Dearest Aleksandr,
for your support during the darkest days in Sukhumi.
Yours truly.
Eduard Shevardnadze.

He pushed it into my hands. "Here. I want you to have this. If I get out alive, you'll return it to me. If I don't, please keep it. . . ."

It was the last time I would see Aleksandr Berulava. I still have his book.

Back at the sanatorium , the shells pummeled us all night and all of the next day. By now there was no food. Even the battle-hardened Ed Parker was becoming more unhinged, as if that was possible. He, Thomas Goltz, and a marooned relief worker from the French aid group Médecins Sans Frontières argued over the ownership of a piece of processed cheese. Parker threatened to disembowel the aid worker. We restrained him, arguing that a Tolstoyan duel over a piece of processed cheese was not worth the trouble.

Parker and I walked through the grounds of the sanatorium. A big jeep belonging to the aid worker was parked nearby. The door was emblazoned with a huge emblem reading MÉDECINS SANS FRONTIÈRES. Parker's eyes lit up. "Mate, I've got a great idea. Let's steal that jeep, cut off the top, and rip out the seats. We'll give it to a bunch of drugged-up Georgian fighters and have them bolt an antiaircraft gun to the floor. Then we'll take pictures of them firing the thing into the air with the emblem MÉDECINS SANS FRONTIÈRES on the side. We'll publish the photos all over the world. When the Abkhaz get here, they'll hang that aid worker from a lamppost."

That night, there was nothing to do but listen to the particularly fierce pounding of artillery. One shell landed in the doorway to our building, shattered the windows, and disfigured a tile mosaic in the yard featuring the face of Soviet Union founder Vladimir Lenin. It was a dramatic night, but I had no way to report any of it. It seemed like time had stopped, existence suspended.

IT WAS TIME to get out of the city.

Rumors flew.

There would be a plane out.

Or a boat. The information spread like wildfire. We waited for a lull in the fighting. When it came, our Ukrainian cameraman from Reuters, Sergiy Karazy, and another cameraman and photographer, the Azerbaijani Farkhad Kerimov, and I set out on foot for the airport, fifteen miles away. (Two years later, Farkhad was executed by a group of Chechen rebels who mistook him for a spy.) On the misleadingly peaceful-looking road, there was not a single vehicle. We encountered a few pedestrians hauling sacks, a trickle of humanity headed out of the city. Near a train depot, an artillery shell landed about thirty yards from us. We hit the ground.

When we approached the airport, I saw a TU-134 passenger plane approaching. Slowly it circled and then landed. A mass of fighters and a few civilians rushed it, believing they'd found their ticket out. Faces turned somber when they realized that the craft was going nowhere; as it pulled to the terminal, jet fuel leaked like rain from the wings. From a jerry-rigged gunboat in the harbor, the Abkhaz had peppered the fuel tanks with bullets, puncturing them. Soldiers rushed to and fro with buckets, trying to collect the valuable liquid before it spilled onto the ground.

We wandered away from the bucket brigade and the airport. To where, we had no real idea. It was pointless to continue down the coastal road. The Abkhaz had cut it ten days before. There was no way out.

We walked into a village across from the airport road. Most of the houses were deserted. But in front of one, an old woman in a long black dress and head scarf was standing in the yard. A widow. Widows in rural Georgia usually dress in black, no matter how many years have passed after the death of their husbands. They are never invisible.

Strangely, the woman was smiling.

She invited us in. Her name was Eteri. There was a persimmon tree in the yard, and she went outside and plucked several of the bright orange globes and tucked them into her apron. The inside of the wooden farmhouse was a typical Georgian shrine to her dead husband. It exuded timeless warmth. There was only a repressed sense of worry on her face. She cooked up a meal of chicken and soup, the *supra,* or Georgian feast, trumping the bleakness of the situation. She fetched some home moonshine, made from tangerines. We drank it copiously, in between her toasts to Georgia, to God, and to her dead husband, who had passed away years previously.

I asked her if she planned to try to leave. "Of course not," she said, nonchalantly. "The reinforcements will be here soon." We tried to con-

vince her to reconsider. She smiled and refused. I did not have the heart
to tell her it was all over. Eteri put a kerosene lamp in a window and
poured more of her moonshine. I slept deeply, with the bittersweet taste
of fermented tangerines on my lips.

In the morning, I peered out a window. The shore was visible. Large
naval ships were emerging on the horizon. The Russian and Ukrainian
navies had sent boats in to evacuate those who wanted to leave, and that
meant just about everybody. I gathered my things and turned to say
good-bye to Eteri. "Are you sure you don't want to go with us?" I asked.

There was no answer, just a slight smile.

"I'll be here," she said. I did not know if this was naiveté or a bow to
fate. After the war was over, I returned to the area and got close enough
to see her house in the distance. The windows and door were flung open,
and a breeze was blowing curtains back and forth. Predictably, the house
had been looted. Eteri was gone.

A mass of locals moved toward the ships. Many were sobbing. They
were coming to terms with the fact that they would never see their homes
again. The Georgians were leaving, knowing the Abkhaz would make
sure they did—or worse—if they arrived before they fled. They would
not be allowed to return—collective punishment for the war.

The ships could not move close enough toward the shore; the water
was too shallow. Women swam in their flowing dresses toward the waiting boats.

And then there were the dogs.

They moved in several packs around the area where the ships had
pulled up. Labs, huskies, and German shepherds. Mutts and purebreds.
Their owners had abandoned them. They yelped, they barked, they ran
about excitedly.

We waded out to sea with the refugees. We were hoisted on board a
boat full of them. We started to pull away. One of the dogs jumped into
the water and paddled his way toward the boat. A woman screamed.
The captain stopped the craft. We waited, and the dog was hoisted to
safety.

Then we pulled away from the shore. Across the city of botanical gardens, palms, and pastel-colored buildings, a great many fires now burned out of control. The yelping of the dogs faded to a collective whimper as we moved toward the horizon.

They—and we—were the lucky ones. Hundreds of people walked days through icy high-mountain passes, starving. Road bandits—of their own ethnicity—often stole their belongings as they tried to walk to safety. Dozens froze to death along the way.

WHEN WE REACHED the shore on the other side at Poti, we piled onto a bus. We headed toward Tbilisi. In the seat in front of me sat an older man. A rotund man, balding, the type of man you expect to see singing loud Georgian songs and toasting with wine around one of their legendary feasting tables. The man was sobbing uncontrollably. The sound rippled through the bus like a throbbing knife. He kept repeating the same word, *"shvilo! shvilo!"* meaning "son" or "children" in Georgian. It can also be used as a simple exclamation. In this case, it sounded more like a moan. The man glanced at me, quieted, and then burnished an apple with his coat. He turned and handed it to me.

"Here," he said. "You remind me of my son." The son had heeded Shevardnadze's call to come to the defense of the city, and he was killed in the war's final days.

ON THE TENTH day of the siege, the capital of Abkhazia fell to the Abkhaz, or was "liberated," in the terminology they used. Shevardnadze escaped. The Georgians had patched up the wings of the plane I had seen, the plane whose fuel tanks had been shot full of holes. I wondered if the son of the man who had given me the apple had been on the same plane with the president, his body in one of those gleaming zinc coffins.

A FEW DAYS after the fall of the city, cameraman Sergiy Karazy and I grabbed a plane from Tbilisi to the Russian city of Sochi. We made our way down the Black Sea coast. We crossed the Psou River back into Abkhazia.

A Russian border guard whom I recognized greeted me. Trucks full of looted goods were pulling up to the border between Russia and Abkhazia. Some of the more absurd aspects of the war had unnerved the man.

"A couple of days ago a Polish guy tried to cross the border, saying he wanted to fight for 'little Abkhazia.' I asked him, 'Can you tell the difference between a Georgian and an Abkhaz?' He told me no. They let him through anyway."

On the horizon, hundreds of trucks filled the roads. They were stacked high with war loot—carpets, furniture, appliances, somebody else's bric-a-brac.

When we got to the capital, looting was in full swing. I walked up to a house where Abkhaz partisans were loading furniture into a truck. They were bickering about what to do with the spoils. I recognized one of the men immediately. He looked more erudite than the rest of the group, mostly rank-and-file fighters on a victory high. He identified himself as a member of the Abkhaz parliament. He acknowledged me, embarrassed. The fighters continued loading their war trophies into the truck unabated.

"What you see here is sad, but it is true," he told me. "This is the way of war." (And it was. There were elements of this on every side in all the post-Soviet wars I witnessed: Few passed up the chance of looting or "taking trophies" when given the opportunity.)

Behind a building near the sanatorium where we'd stayed, I saw two bodies, one of an old woman and another of a middle-aged man. They had been shot. Kerchiefs covered their faces.

A monkey stood on a bridge nearby, looking rather confused and evidently pondering his next destination. Monkeys are not native to Abkhazia. He was from a scientific research center full of hundreds of primates nearby. They had been used in medical experiments, and a few had actually been sent into space in the Soviet space program. Georgian troops stole many of them and turned them into pets. They elevated some to war mascot status, riding about in their tanks with the monkeys atop—like slapstick commanders. Now primate conscription had ended, and the monkeys were relishing their newfound freedom.

LATER, I SAW an Abkhaz journalist whom I recognized. He greeted me warmly. Behind us, the "Supreme Soviet" was charred. Some of those inside had resisted, and the Abkhaz and their allies had set it ablaze after dragging out those last Georgians who had stayed behind.

I asked about Aleksandr Berulava, the man who had given me Shevardnadze's book to keep for him.

"Berulava?" the journalist asked wryly. "Berulava was executed."

His death was likely a gruesome one. Both sides, especially during the waning days of the war, had, among other things, taken to chopping off ears from dead adversaries or plucking out eyes (often before they were killed).

I SAW THE Preacher Man again. He smiled broadly. In his broken Russian, he shouted, *"Slava Bogu!"* several times. Literally, the term translates as "Glory to God." But it is used as an interjection, rather than literally, something along the lines of "Thank God for that" or "luckily."

The Preacher Man was oblivious to having misused his limited Russian syntax, however. Instead, he kept repeating the phrase. *"Slava Bogu! Slava Bogu!"* It lilted like a feather in the sultry, smoke-scented air.

The Abkhaz journalist turned to me and whispered, "What the hell does he mean by that, *"Slava Bogu!"*?

"He just means it," I answered. "He just means it."

We moved south out of the city on foot, in the direction of the airport. All along the horizon, houses were burning and being looted.

Though several days had passed, there were still packs of dogs running aimlessly along the road, searching for their abdicated owners. I swear I recognized some of them.

The War That Nobody Started had ended.

At least for now.

BURIED FIVE TIMES: INSURGENTS IN FLAT BLACK NYLONS

Eduard Shevardnadze (The Man Who Ended the Cold War) fled Abkhazia not in a boat or on a freezing mountain pass. He flew out in that same last, ravaged, jet-fuel-dripping plane we saw at the Sukhumi airport, its wings full of bullet holes. Workers had patched them with metal strips and scavenged up just enough fuel for a quick escape back into government-controlled territory.

Or what was left of it.

This latest insurrection was under way even before the War That Nobody Started ended. Georgia was entering its fourth war in less than two years of independence. From the empire's crown jewel to failed state.

The protagonist was none other than Zviad Gamsakhurdia, elected president in 1990, but quickly having evoked the ire of many within months, including the artists-turned-warlords Kitovani and Ioseliani.

Proclaiming Gamsakhurdia an autocrat and demagogue, they felt the best way to unseat him was to lug large-caliber artillery pieces into the upper floors of the nearby Intourist hotel and fire them directly at the parliament from less than a hundred yards away.

It was an excessive use of firepower, to say the least—like going after ants with a sledgehammer—done more for the warlords' warped sense of "Georgia as Vaudeville" effect (there were TV crews to show off for, after all) than for anything faintly resembling military logic. After a couple of weeks of blasting away, a once-elegant city center was reduced to a series of smoking holes and gutted neoclassical facades. They could indeed boast, at least, of forcing Gamsakhurdia to flee—to Chechnya, where he found a fellow traveler in the rebel, rabidly anti-Kremlin leader there, Dzhokhar Dudayev.

That did not mean Gamsakhurdia had lost all backing, especially in the countryside or outside Tbilisi. To call them "supporters" would be an understatement. These were devotees, worshippers of a kind, and Gamsakhurdia was a near-deity for many of them.

The evocation of this allure seems simple enough on the surface: Zviad was the son of Georgia's most famous twentieth-century writer, Konstantin Gamsakhurdia. While the Western reader may have never heard of such epics as *The Smile of Dionysus,* these works have deep resonance in the literature-obsessed Georgian soul. Konstantin's bitter criticism of the Bolshevik takeover of Georgia and his exile to an island in the Arctic Ocean, where he came close to suicide before distracting his mind by translating Dante, reinforced his credentials.

Zviad was a linguist and ethnographer with an explosive temper and a penchant for rants against ethnic minorities like the Abkhaz. He once said that the Abkhaz should "leave Georgia and go back where they came from," embracing a radical claim that the Abkhaz were originally mountain dwellers from outside Georgia who had gradually migrated to the Georgian Black Sea coast. "The Abkhaz nation doesn't exist," he yelled through a megaphone in front of the Georgian parliament during one rally in 1990. Today in Georgia such statements sound absurd. But in the supercharged ethnic frenzy of the Soviet collapse, they found resonance.

Aside from his nationalist creds—important at that time—Zviad's ascension was bolstered by his taking over the mantle of Georgia's leading anti-Soviet dissident. He was tossed, KGB-style, into a mental hospital for a spell, further boosting his own standing. Deeper reasons prevailed for the mystic adoration he inspired among his devotees. The surrealism surrounding his death helps illustrate some of them.

But Zviad in the autumn of 1993 was far from dead.

• • •

SHEVARDNADZE'S LOSS OF Abkhazia gave him a chance to reclaim power. Wild throngs greeted Gamsakhurdia upon his return from exile to western Georgia, his power base. He proclaimed himself president again and, with a few hundred ragged troops, advanced toward the capital, most of the remnants of the government's "army" having scattered or getting ready to.

Alas, he had barely unpacked his bags when Shevardnadze pulled a desperate move. The same man who accused the Russians of engineering his defeat in Abkhazia now invited those same Russian troops to intervene to save his own regime, even greeting them as they docked on the Black Sea coast. In exchange, the Man Who Won the Cold War signed Georgia up to the Russia-led Commonwealth of Independent States, Moscow's pitiful effort to cobble some loose USSR fragments back together.

With the Russians pouring in and his insurgent forces vastly outnumbered, Zviad retreated for a last stand in the western Georgian town of Zugdidi. We prepared to scramble off to find him before the inevitable occurred: his capture, escape, or death.

I lay awake the night before, thinking about the imprudence of trying to gain entrance to yet another besieged city. Wind and rain drummed against Tbilisi's endless maze of galvanized zinc roofs, an electric heater inert at the foot of my bed. The device itself was a thin piece of wire wrapped around a ceramic cylinder; a death trap in a midnight stumble. Happily, a power outage had rendered the thing temporarily impotent, and me freezing.

Tbilisi had taken on the kind of atmosphere that often follows humiliating defeats: resigned apathy, mixed with an increasing sense of nihilism.

Violent young men lurked in the shadows, and you knew it.

In the morning I forced myself out of bed and headed toward our office on Rustaveli Avenue on the fifth floor of a building with a semipermanently broken elevator. There I met up with my cameraman, Sergiy, to figure out how to get to Zugdidi for Zviad's last stand. There was such a plethora of great bad options. The main road was cut by skirmishes, and the rest of the roads were usually little more than neglected dirt tracks.

As we prepared to head out, a group of scruffy paramilitary-looking types (by now simply meaning men with guns) banged on the office door, mistaking it for someone else's. They were headed for the "front" to do battle with the "Zviadists," they explained.

One of the men eyed a cheap, poorly produced, and (as it turned out) inaccurate road map of Georgia that I'd taped up on the wall behind my desk.

"Where is Samtredia?" he demanded.

"Here," I said, pointing to the town in western Georgia of that name. It was along the main highway, supposedly the epicenter of the new war.

"*Gmadlobt,*" said the man, thanking me in Georgian, and turned to go.

"Just a second," I said, ripping the fifty-cent piece of cartography off the wall and thrusting it at him. "Take it!"

If these "government forces" had no idea where Samtredia was, they were in far worse shape than we were but at least might recognize us before they shot, thanks to my map gift.

The boys left on their mission, and Sergiy and I soon followed them westward toward the Black Sea and the "front lines" (a loose designation at best) in our beat-up Russian Niva four-wheel drive. The road was full of potholes, meaning, by the standards of the time, in fairly good shape.

WE STOPPED FOR a meal in the lone functioning canteen in Georgia's second city, Kutaisi, the legendary capital of the ancient kingdom of Colchis. The eleventh-century Bagrati Cathedral, still in ruins 301 years after Ottoman conquerors blew it up in 1692 (talk about a slow repair job), brooded over the city from atop a cliff. Jason and the Argonauts, in their epic quest for the Golden Fleece, had Kutaisi as their final destination—King Aeëtes' seat of power.

The canteen had no seats, so we stood while eating beef stew and large pieces of Georgian *tonis puri*, bread baked on the sides of an ancient kiln, washing it down with a quirky, unique-to-Georgia, antifreeze-colored, tarragon-flavored soft drink. At 6,400,000 and something, the bill sounded steep for some slop and bread. But the currency at the time was the infamous interim Georgian "coupon," looking like xeroxed Monopoly money and then trading on world currency markets at something like 2 million to the dollar. I'd never given a million anything as a tip. I did so, and my mood improved.

We continued west along the main road under a light rain. There was no point in continuing on the main highway through Samtredia. It had been "conquered" and "retaken" by first the "Zviadists" and then the "government" on almost a daily basis. One day, a few "government" troops would roll forward with a tank or two, stand around, and pull back when a few dozen Zviadists—those who hadn't fled Shevardnadze's Russian enemies-turned-allies—would roll in. The next day, the reverse would happen.

Rather than endure such theatrics, we chose a route marked yellow on our map, designating a secondary road, supposedly in reasonably good condition, that would bring us across the lines. Instead we found a wide, formerly asphalted rut leading through a forest.

Places of war need not be tormentingly depressing, although many, if not most, are. Yet in much of western Georgia, it was hard to believe any conflict was going on at all.

Streams of gentle autumn light poked through the lush subtropical foliage.

Palms whispered in the breeze.

In tiny villages, women in straw hats sold sunflower seeds wrapped in pages ripped out of discarded editions of Gogol.

Cows meandered amid tea plantations.

As we admired the landscape, three more scraggly, Kalashnikov-toting men (God knows fighting for whom) flagged down our car.

They were proud Zviadists, they explained, but on the run in the face of the Russian intervention.

"That fucking Shevardnadze," one said. "He lets the Russians take Sukhumi, and then he brings them in to do his dirty work. He is nothing but an occupier and a KGB agent."

"Turn down that road," one said, pointing to another muddy track with bits of asphalt remaining here and there.

We didn't argue.

Within five minutes we hit a water-covered rut with such force that the speedometer console fell out onto my lap. I argued with the gunmen about where the hell they were taking us. Another five minutes later, the trio hopped out at an intersection, expressing no remorse for the assorted gauges now adorning my lap. I ripped out the wires and tossed them in the back of the car. Our relief in reaching Zugdidi, Gamsakhurdia's last-stand fortress, was short lived.

No one was really in control of the Zviadist "capital." A panicky gathering milled around the local administration building, speculating about the Russians being on the way or trading rumors. We deferentially checked in to see if we needed some sort of "accreditation" from the "authorities." Instead we found only a room full of "officials" chattering away. One wrote down our names. Accreditations? "No, we don't have any of those," he said.

We asked for a meeting with "President Gamsakhurdia." Loud assurances were given that he was on his way. When? Soon! Where? "Right here." "Over there." "At the stadium." "In the central square."

Gamsakhurdia was trapped. Confusion reigned. Some of his fighters were driving up and down the main street in a stolen Red Cross four-wheel drive, aimlessly, an act of final defiance. The sight of the vehicle, jammed with paramilitaries, Kalashnikovs pointed out the windows, fit the mood perfectly because the more delirious Zviadists were convinced the International Red Cross was an intelligence front.

We crossed the street to a building where we were told we could find a man by the name of Jambul, Zviad's self-described "chief of security."

We found him, but the man was so drunk that he was swaggering as he stood. "The president is not available," Jambul said gravely.

Suddenly shooting began outside the building. We were convinced the government had decided to storm the city. We hit the floor. But the crackle of Kalashnikovs ceased abruptly after a minute. We emerged from the building. A warlord by the name of Vakhtang "Loti" (meaning "The Drunk" in Georgian) Kobalia had arrived; the volley of gunfire was a celebratory greeting.

Kobalia's nickname was said to be fitting. The root of his surname was equally ironic. *Kobali* means "bread" in Megrelian, the local Georgian dialect used in the area, and Kobalia had indeed been a bread truck driver in Soviet times before launching his paramilitary career.

Vakhtang "The Drunk" had fought on Zviad's side during the first civil war, running the Megrelia area as a kind of fiefdom and a safe-haven for supporters of the ousted Gamsakhurdia government before making some sort of peace with Shevardnadze. But Kobalia's detractors said Kobalia's forces fought halfheartedly in order to ensure Shevardnadze's defeat in the final days of the war in Abkhazia, ultimately switching back to Gamsakhurdia's side, just in time for his last stand.

I AGAIN ASKED Jambul about Gamsakhurdia's whereabouts. "That's a state secret," he said, as if Gamsakhurdia actually controlled a county, let alone a country. There was no chance of an interview, he said. "It's getting dark. I'd advise you to get out of here, for your own safety."

Drunken security chiefs not being known for caution, we promptly obliged and headed down a back road again toward Tbilisi, becoming completely lost in a worsening downpour. Two men stood near an intersection, both of them brandishing Kalashnikovs. Sergiy decided to ask them for directions.

Not a good idea, it turned out.

The two were agitated and demanded to see our documents. We assumed they were Zviadists, so we tried to get in their good graces by emphasizing that we had just come from Zugdidi, where we had met with members of his "government."

"We're Zviadists, all right," growled one of the pair. "But we could drink his blood tomorrow if we want."

Loyalties were breaking down, and the conversation soon grew from uncomfortable to threatening. I was ordered by the gunman on my side of the car to empty my wallet. It contained $140, but I was not particularly upset, because it could have been much worse: I had $5,000 stashed in a duffel bag in the back of the jeep, having made a cash run to Reuters in Moscow a few days earlier and forgotten I'd stashed away the money. Happily, the thugs weren't very thorough with their shakedown.

Then came the subject of our TV camera, which Sergiy was holding in his lap. It was a Sony professional unit, and worth ten thousand dollars. The gunman on the passenger side grabbed the lens and began pulling the camera away. Sergiy tugged back, an act of audacity that startled the gunmen.

"Look," the one on the left explained. "We could kill you right here and toss you in a ditch to die," he raged. "Give us the fucking camera." The tug of war resumed.

Sagely, Sergiy appealed to the men's sense of masculine honor, a holdover from better times before their homeland and Georgian way of life were ravaged by poverty and upheaval.

"Please understand," reasoned Sergiy. "If you take this camera, which is of no use to you, you will deprive me of my livelihood. I have hungry mouths to feed at home. I won't even be able to buy bread for my children."

Suddenly, along this muddy, rainy road in the middle of a forest where the thieves had no reason not to strip us of everything we owned, time stood still.

The gunmen went silent.

Sergiy had uttered the magical words: *children, bread*.

These were brutal days: creeds, rules, and laws eroding quickly.

Yet the storied sense of Georgian respect for guests, and the country's cult of the sacredness of the child, still held sway.

The gunman released his grip on the lens, his hands slipping away, as if greased, leaving Sergiy with the camera, and the man with the gun, and the power to exterminate us, slowly closed the car door himself.

WE RETURNED WITHOUT our interview. In fact, Gamsakhurdia never gave another one, melting instead into the hills and gorges to ponder the last days of his life.

Within a few weeks, on New Year's Eve of 1994, the end came. A single shot from a pistol penetrated the side of Zviad Gamsakhurdia's head. The venue was a farmhouse amid a nondescript village in western Georgia, far from presidential glory in Tbilisi. The government claimed it was a suicide. His devoted followers shouted murder. Gamsakhurdia was dead, but a decade-and-a-half epic had been born—the story of his wandering corpse, and the unclear circumstances of his demise.

AT FIRST GAMSAKHURDIA'S resting place next to a farmhouse is kept secret, a select few performing the burial. Then he is dug up a second time and moved again, just in case a mole had leaked the location. Zviad's supporters, however, see the lack of a body as proof that he is alive. He is not dead, they insist; all such reports are merely propaganda.

Then, in late February, a Chechen plane lands in western Georgia on a special mission. Gamsakhurdia's volatile widow, Manana, refused to let his corpse rest in the "junta-dominated" Georgia of Shevardnadze, as Zviad's supporters called Shevardnadze's government. A Georgian delegation meets the Chechens, and together they fly by helicopter to the obscure village where Zviad is buried. There, men with simple shovels dig clinically, deliberately. Their expressions bear neither gravity nor sorrow. The process is not a long one. A simple handmade wooden coffin emerges, the type that a typical villager might be entombed in. The men hastily carry it off to the waiting helicopter. Stalks of straw from the farmhouses fly about as the whirl of the blades carries the coffin into the sky.

A BITING COLD envelops those of us assembled along the tarmac as we wait for the flying hearse to land.

But once the wooden coffin is unloaded, the Chechens who came to fetch Gamsakhurdia's remains look startled. They evidently assume the dead president had been buried Muslim-style without a casket. The Chechens have brought along their own zinc coffin in which to transport him to Grozny. An eerie spectacle ensues—the presence of the empty zinc coffin is a bad omen in Chechen culture, we are told. Removing the empty zinc box from their plane, the Chechens place it in the center of the runway. A large truck belching blue smoke arrives, and the Chechens proceed to drive it over the zinc box, over and over, until nothing remains but a mangled hunk of twisted metal, evidently satisfied that the lurking evil spirits inhabiting it are now destroyed.

Next begins the haggling between the Georgian government delegation and the Chechen undertakers over what to do with Gamsakhurdia's coffin. The Chechens, led by their vice president, Zelimkhan Yandarbiyev, insist it be immediately loaded onto his plane and flown back to Grozny. The Georgians insist on verifying, unscientifically, that it is actually Gamsakhurdia lying inside. The Chechens resist, saying opening it would be sacrilege. One of the Georgians responds by pointing out that Gamsakhurdia was an Orthodox Christian, not a Muslim Chechen. The Georgians refuse to allow the coffin to be loaded into the plane. Zviad Gamsakhurdia's corpse, now almost an afterthought, lying in the middle of the cracked asphalt runway as the officials argue.

The Chechens finally relent, and agree to a brief opening of the coffin for verification. Several of us crowd around it, its pale wood now damp and earthen colored after almost two months in the winter ground; there is something of a morbid anxiousness to it all.

The Georgians begin carefully prying the cover off with chisels, and slowly the lid slides open. Without formaldehyde or other embalming agents, biological processes have taken their course. Zviad is gaunt. But although I am "meeting" him for the first time, there is no doubt it is Gamsakhurdia, his unique, chiseled facial features still unmistakable. He is dressed in a black and white suit, his simple dark tie blotched with specks of green. Perhaps most curiously of all, the ousted president wears no shoes. (This elicits rumors of all fashions, noteworthy among them that Gamsakhurdia, an Orthodox Christian, converted to Islam before his death. Which makes no sense. Had he converted to Islam, he would have been buried in a shroud, not a coffin.)

A Georgian official lowers his head toward Gamsakhurdia's, like a man checking a diamond for authenticity, and squints. It's the bullet hole he's interested in. Indeed it is there, on the right side of the president's head, partially obscured by some sort of mold, but still clearly visible. The viewing is over within a minute or two. The Georgians put the lid back on, as if putting the cover back on a tub of margarine. The corpse takes off into the sky.

IN GROZNY, THERE was a splendid state funeral for Gamsakhurdia. He was then interred in the garden of the stately Chechen guest mansion where he had spent a year in exile. A white stallion led the cortege, which was wholly appropriate because the white horse is linked with Persian and Zoroastrian mythology and was a constant in the Zviadist iconography of light against darkness and good against evil. After his 1992 ouster in Tbilisi, no fewer than twenty thousand of his supporters marched along a riverbank, a woman riding such a steed, and those devotees who refused to believe in his indisputable death continued to insist he would return one day, of course atop a white stallion.

I have already described his pedigree—the son of Georgia's most famous writer and philosopher—his acts of anti-Soviet defiance, and his explosive personality, all of which earned Zviad Gamsakhurdia his credibility as national-savior-to-be.

Zviad's vision of Georgia's unique role in the world certainly played a role in his mystique. His supporters peddled a pamphlet called *The Spiritual Mission of the Georgian Nation*. It was based on an erudite, obscurantist 1990 speech Zviad gave at Tbilisi's Philharmonic Hall in which it was suggested that Georgia was meant by God to serve as a link between Occident and Orient, thus fulfilling its supposedly unique destiny.

But there are other reasons, far more intoxicating, for the often maniacal degree of devotion one found among Zviad's hard-core supporters—again, a disproportionate number of them middle-aged and older women, spinsters in a land where ordinary outlets of passion were greatly constrained at the time: a *psychosexual* appeal, a surrogate for unrealized desires.

Zviad's sometimes reserved, sometimes bombastic, enigmatic personality, prone to seeing provocations and blackmail, added to the mystique.

For many years after his death, on Zviad's birthday or that of his literary-giant late father, large crowds of those devotees, these insurgents who believe in Zviad's return or resurrection, gathered at the Gamsakhurdia family compound—a very large brick home in the center of Tbilisi. Often there were well over a thousand of them. They marched along the narrow streets, pushing and shoving to get closer to the shrine. Again, most were women, disproportionately middle-aged and older, dressed in black, most in long skirts, and slightly frumpy, flat black simple nylons. So ubiquitous are the nylon-wearers that the dead Gamsakhurdia's army of female devotees are known as the Shavi Kolgotebi (the Black Stockings).

A MAN IN wire-rimmed glasses rants through a megaphone about what they called the "junta" (Shevardnadze) running Georgia and about Gamsakhurdia, who many here still insist is alive, one day to return on that white horse. Some of the Black Stockings appear to be in a trancelike state, eyes fixated on the podium, hands clutching umbrellas used as parasols to parry a searing sun. Listening intently, one of the women teeters. Her eyeballs roll back in her head briefly, facial muscles twitching and then relaxing, eyes becoming placid again. Orgasm, or the cusp of one.

BUT WHY HERE? Why Gamsakhurdia? Why Georgia?

The corset of Oriental love rites applied here, stoked no doubt by centuries under Persian and Ottoman rule.

Westerners knew little about the complexities of Soviet Russian sexual mores. We were hoodwinked by the prudish facade of Communism. But those who spent significant time in Moscow or Leningrad knew firsthand about the hedonism and promiscuity afoot. It was not for nothing that late Imperial Russia's ladies of the court equated copulation with Rasputin as communion with the Almighty, or that Soviet theoreticians in the 1920s propagated that sex was "a drink of water." These notions found fertile soil.

And if Soviet Russia was difficult to understand, Georgia's erotic essence was practically unfathomable to the outsider. Here was the confluence of Occident and Orient, patriarchic mores, and mountaineer traditions. Even during Soviet times this included bride stealing, meaning simply gathering a favored female off the street and keeping her away from her family for a night. Even if there is no physical contact, the night away can technically negate her virginity, virtually ensuring marriage to the wife rustler. The practice continued many years after the Soviet collapsed and was not technically made illegal until the early 2000s.

"Chained libido, political repression, virginity," said Eka, an artist, explaining the deity-like, erotic Zviadist phenomenon. She pronounced "virginity," using the Russian word *destvennost,* as if it were a profanity—for Eka was an exception, a maximalist, one of the few who embraced her sexuality openly. She illustrated the Georgian tendency to excess by pointing to the scores of people who preferred to dart in between speeding cars along Tbilisi's main Rustaveli Avenue, as if getting a thrill from nearly being mowed down, rather than walk a few yards to use a nice, safe underground walkway.

Eka was definitely an exception. Or was she? When I first arrived in Georgia to live in 1992, the Oriental Persian-Ottoman-influenced mores meant that young women should avoid accidental eye contact with a man, often by quickly turning away, as if avoiding a sin. My first cameraman for Reuters, Gigi Mdivani, one day noticed me observing young women as we drove down Rustaveli in his very used Opel. There was no doubt I was looking out of physical interest, but there were also pure aesthetics involved. At the time, many Georgian women dressed extremely well, often in elegant hand-tailored dresses from good-quality cloth. It was a stark contrast to the cheap-looking, acid-washed, East German—inspired jeans I often saw in places like Moscow. Cleavage, however, unlike in Russia, was a big no-no.

"You spend too much time looking at 'our women,' " scolded Gigi. "You can't look at them like that."

"Why not?" I asked. "I'm just looking."

"We are Asiatics," replied Gigi, putting a halt to the conversation, but not to my gawking from the open window of the Opel. "Our women are not like Russian women," he said with a sneer.

Gigi pointed to the ruins of the Intourist hotel on Rustaveli Avenue, then gutted and blackened after the war that had driven Gamsakhurdia from power a few months earlier.

"You see that hotel? In the Soviet period, all summer it was full of Russian women. They came here, and our men surrounded them with attention. Flowers. Wine. Feasts!" It was a story I came to hear often. Legions of relatively well-off married Russian women were known to frequent Georgia for requisite week-or-two flings in the subtropical summer.

Outwardly more libertine than their Georgian sisters, the Russians came for an early version of female sex tourism. Georgian women would not have been caught dead alone in the lobby of the Intourist hotel without a male escort or "brother"—as Georgians referred to any male cousin or even distant relative. The freewheeling Russian women used Georgia as a place for guaranteed action: Georgian men were legendary for their chivalry, but casual dalliances with Georgian women were almost unheard of—well, at least they went unreported. A trip to Georgia for middle-aged Russian women indeed meant wine, bouquets, the endless Georgian feasts known as the *supra,* countless compliments, and, of course, furtive sex. The Russian ladies went home north happy. The Georgian men wore their conquests as feathers in their caps.

It was the perfect combination, at least for the Georgian males and the Russian females. If the Georgians had wives, the infidelity was expected to be accepted—grudgingly or not.

THERE WAS NO doubt that Gigi's proclamations of Georgian female chastity carried some truth. Brides were indeed expected to be virgins, or at least be known as virgins, at marriage. Of course, this would have been the case in the United States or many other Western countries just a half century prior as well.

There were whispers about the doctors who did *gakerva* (literally, "sewing up"). In other words, hymen restoration.

The doctors expert in this art fulfilled an important function, no doubt. Not only did they do "repair jobs," enabling new husbands to rest easy after their wedding nights, they also issued postexam "certificates" testifying that a woman was a virgin, to ensure that her groom-to-be would not return her after the nuptials, like an ill-fitting pair of shoes. This avoided not only scandalous embarrassment but relegation to the purgatory of permanent spinsterhood.

I searched for such a doctor.

After considerable giggles and hesitation, my assistant Nino found me just such a physician. "She's willing to talk to you, but only on the condition of anonymity," whispered Nino. Even then, the conversation was an elliptical one, with the doctor describing her "work" in the third person. (It was obvious that she was the one doing the sewing, but, technically, the practice was illegal, I was told.) So shrouded in semiexaggerated secrecy was my visit that I agreed not to even ask the name of the "doctor."

I had prepared, on Nino's advice, warm-up questions on broader medical issues. Of course, the doctor, whose name I never did learn, knew what I was there for. After the requisite mutually understood bluffs, we got down to business.

"It is extremely delicate work—*a jeweler's craft*," she softly told me, without ever admitting directly that she was one of "four doctors in our city who are real experts." Her eyes lit up with the pride of an eagle, with the mystery of a shaman. "You must understand . . . it is not like taking out an appendix, *es saiuveliro samushaua* . . . a jeweler's craft. . . ."

Less admirable defilers of her craft, "in it only for the money," she said, preferred simply to issue bogus "virgin certificates." "Quacks," she lamented. Even so, said the mystery hymen doctor, this was of "social benefit." A young girl could be "scarred for life with the stigma of a harlot" for not producing blood or pain for her new husband. "Of course, our men are too backwards to understand that the hymen can be broken by nonsexual means as well."

I was gratified to hear her note this basic medical reality, which would not have been acknowledged by quite so many people a half century ago in the United States either.

The virgin doctors were a viable recourse for those having encountered premarital sex, but so male-dominated was the social scene that many young women I managed to talk to about the situation were convinced that Tbilisi's legendary gossip machine meant they could not risk any perceived impropriety.

"I don't want to, but I have to be," said a doe-eyed acquaintance, Lika, of her virginity—still intact at age twenty-six. "If I am not a virgin at marriage, no man will have me. My parents will be forever shamed."

"But they don't have to know," I replied, "unless you tell them."

"You don't understand. They will just know," sighed Lika. "There is a general saying that if two people know a secret, everyone knows. Here in Tbilisi, we say if one person knows a secret, everyone knows."

As such, it was nothing to hear of thirty-something, forty-something, even fifty-something virgins. Hence the widespread theory about pent-up erotic passions, Zviad Gamsakhurdia, and the Black Stockings.

There were, of course, the sexual miscreants, but they fell into two broad categories: If they were Georgian and unmarried, the women were branded as sluts. If they were ethnic minorities, say, local Jews or Armenians or Slavs, then they were given a green light to mess around.

Divorce was the other way to sexual freedom. One friend, Medea, said that at age nineteen, she married a guy as just such a path to liberty. It lasted six months," she said. "And then I was free.

"There is no stigma for divorced women who want to have liberty, to sleep with whom they want. I know lots of girls who got married and then divorced just so they can have sex."

And then there were those young women who simply shunned all the rules and regulations, like Eka.

At nearly six feet tall, stunning, and often clad in sheer black dresses, she was unmistakable passing down Rustaveli Avenue.

When Eka described the Georgian tendency toward maximalism, she was of course describing herself. A talented young painter, she did nothing to less than excess. At the ripe age of eleven, she addictively read and reread Bulgakov's *The Master and Margarita,* like my Leningrad extortionist buddy Vova and just about everyone else in the former USSR. Instead of doing a few illustrations based on scenes in the book, she painted in excess of 150.

"The problem here is that young men don't understand that some of us really want to explore. They assume all we want is a husband.

"Our problem is that we have been at war too long," she said, trying to explain what she considered the Georgian approach toward love and intimate relationships.

When she meant war, Eka meant not only the four wars in four years that Georgia had endured—two wars with ethnic overtones and two short but brutal civil wars—but hundreds of years of being tossed around between different empires—Greeks, Mongols. Ottomans, Persians, Russians.

"So love is war—a matter of survival, of cunning. For instance, if a woman is single, she will play the coquette, putting her virginal qualities at the forefront. If the girl is married, she will taunt her prey, demonstratively but delicately playing with her wedding ring, slowly sliding it up and down her finger. She will torture the prey through temptation."

THE GENERAL STATE of anarchy in Georgia meant increasingly frayed psyches. Extreme behavior was the norm. Even in the mid-1990s, armed paramilitaries still roamed the streets with grenade launchers and AKs. At the entrance to Georgia's Parliament Hall, there was a sign with a pistol with a red slash through it and a written note asking deputies to check their guns at the door.

Hard drug use among men skyrocketed, becoming so endemic that even the teetotaler president Eduard Shevardnadze announced that all parliamentary deputies would be scanned for possible narcotics use. Shevardnadze proudly announced on national radio, during his weekly address, that he had been the first to submit his urine for analysis.

THE DISORDER DID have another side—a nascent, barely noticeable sexual "revolution" started to take root. One bar, called Kazbegi, after one of the country's highest mountains, was a hot spot for quick encounters. Our tape editor at Reuters, David, bragged to me that so many condoms had been tossed into the toilets there that the plumbing had to be completely ripped out and replaced. To him, this was a sign of progress. Shevardnadze had other ideas. During another radio address, he noted that many parents had called to complain about the bar as a den of sin. The bar was eventually closed down under unclear circumstances.

Fifty meters from my house, a brave soul opened Georgia's first sex shop. A sandwich board advertised "sex toys, vibrators, artificial phalli." A gang with guns (ergo the police) came and ordered the innovative enterprise closed within a week or so. Guns and hard drugs were OK, but there were evident limits to the science of disorder as a method of governance.

From Eka, I got occasional cognac-induced telephone calls. It was clear she was rotting amid Georgia's chaos and still-Oriental ways. At last, she elected to vote with her feet: She joined the flood of those leaving the country, ending up in France, where she finally flourished.

Georgians, unlike their neighbors the Armenians, never had much of a diaspora. Perhaps it was because of the country's beauty, and the traditional ties to the land, but "for Georgians it is very difficult to live abroad," one friend told me.

By the late 1990s, the government announced that 1 million people, or nearly one in five of the entire Georgian population, had left, seeking better futures elsewhere, and the uncertainty behind.

• • •

GIVEN THE GENERAL mayhem, few had time to wonder what had become of Gamsakhurdia's grave. I was one; another was Thomas Goltz, my writer friend whom I had met in Sukhumi in 1993. Now it was April 1995, and we were in Chechnya, determined to find Zviad, or what remained of his grave.

We set out in search of the mansion. It had been located in the very heart of Grozny, but that area now resembled a torn-up football field rather than a city. Parts of walls or half-intact walls stood here and there, and orientation was difficult. Finally, we located the remains of the mansion. A scorched outside wall of the building was still standing, but the inside was gutted and looted. Was this really the place? Then there among the rubble we found it: a headstone, half blown away by bomb shrapnel, but with an epitaph written in Chechen and Georgian.

However, it turned out that Zviad's corpse had moved on again, before our discovery and visitation. Suspecting Russian troops might desecrate the site, a group of Chechens and Georgians had spirited his corpse a few hundred meters away to a secret location and buried him again.

War washed over Chechnya, receded in 1996, and then rolled over that sad land again in 1999. Years passed before most people thought about Gamsakhurdia's resting place. It was not until 2006 that Russian troops in Chechnya announced they had found the whereabouts of his secret grave. Once again his corpse was exhumed and, at the insistence of his family members, whisked off to a Russian laboratory for a postmortem—more than ten years after his death.

Meanwhile, back in Tbilisi, the passage of time had brought in changes. In 2003, a brash young former minister in Shevardnadze's government had gone into opposition, calling election results corrupt and demanding Shevardnadze's resignation. The brash young man, of course, was Mikheil Saakashvili, and the movement he led to depose Shevardnadze became known as the "Rose Revolution." In an act of national reconciliation and to finally get beyond the hot-and-cold state of civil war that had existed virtually from the time of Georgian independence in 1991, President Mikheil Saakashvili called on Russia to send Zviad back to Georgia so that he could be reburied on Mtatsminda Mountain, a sacred area near a cathedral in Tbilisi. Tens of thousands of mourners marched in the procession for this, the fifth burial of Georgia's first president.

A WORD ABOUT WAR

I never planned to become a "war correspondent." I'm not even sure I knew what one was. There are no "war reporter" schools. There are reporters who cover places that happen to be strewn with conflagrations. I was one of those.

There are, of course, those who choose the designation willfully and with alacrity, for many reasons—ranging from a sense of duty to inform the world of the latest massacre, injustice, or other outrage—to the addictive high from that first rush of adrenaline after narrowly missing being hit by a tank round.

As I said, my "inclusion" into the profession was not premeditated and can be traced to a first bloody dustup—in ex–Soviet Moldova, early 1992, pitting the "pro-Romanian" government forces against the Slavic "pro-Soviet" separatists of "the Transdniester Republic." Mission completed, my editor deduced (incorrectly) that I had an inborn proclivity for covering wars and whatever human stupidity accompanied them. Given this set of "qualifications," I was sent on to Georgia for the next round of bloodletting, then back to Russia, where ethnic Ossetians—aided and armed by the Russian army—and Muslim Ingush died by the hundreds in a nonsensical week-long melee over a piece of Ingush territory Stalin had given to the Ossetians, who as Orthodox Christians were natural Russian allies. This all happened by chance or pure stupidity—I was asked to go, and I agreed to do the job. Then it was back to Georgia, and a host of other places, for more. Slowly, covering wars or bloody conflicts becomes completely normal, or one convinces oneself of this—that one can always stop, always leave, go back to whatever one was doing before "this," no consequences to mind, spirit, or health.

By the spring of 1993, I was supposed to be making plans to leave Georgia and to return to Moscow—that was the agreement, actually— but my editor would have none of it: for I had in his estimation somehow now qualified as a "war correspondent." I was not going anywhere soon, except to the next post-Soviet dustup, and amid the empire's ashes there were any number to choose from.

PART III
(1993–1996)

AZERBAIJAN AND ARMENIA AT WAR

Chaos at Kelbajar helicopter field, Azerbaijan, April 1993.

AZERBAIJAN: LIFESAVING CARPETS

It was hard to fathom that we were nearing the site of battles and an un-folding humanitarian emergency. Driving deeper into Azerbaijan, there were no signs of war: no army transports, no armed columns, and no sense of alarm. Moving closer to the point where refugees were re-portedly pouring out, we saw only the occasional car or farm tractors, tilling fields. It was not until we got to the base of the mountains, near the town of Khanlar, that I saw the large crowd gathered in a clearing.

A woman among hundreds flailed her face with dirty fingernails the size of small daggers, blood squirting as she ripped flesh from her own cheeks. Her delirious screams were soon joined by others in a cacophony of ritual mourning, reaching a peak with blood streaming from scores of self-gouged faces, turning patches of melting snow scarlet.

The Azerbaijani woman had just walked three days through the icy passes of the Murov Mountains, together with thousands of her fellow townsfolk from Kelbajar, which had just been conquered by Armenian forces. Kelbajar Province had once been home to sixty thousand. But now all who survived were on the move over the still snow-covered mountains. The first wave of refugees had been able to jam themselves into overloaded trucks that inch along through the icy passes laden down with everything from goats to refrigerators. Another small batch was plucked to safety by overloaded Azerbaijani helicopters, with minimal possessions, on the day of the final Armenian assault. The third wave—like the hysterical woman gouging her face into a cratered valley of scars—had been forced to flee on foot, hiking over the treacherous Mu-rovs, while dropping virtually everything of value when it became too heavy to carry as exhaustion set in. The least lucky were the unknown numbers of people who fell into snowbanks and froze to death along the way, or those taken hostage, to be used as future bargaining chips for everything from fallen bodies to fuel.

THE MORNING HAD begun languidly enough; part of what made living in the conflict-strewn Caucasus Mountains in the early 1990s was Tbilisi, with its sad, but elegant, decrepitude. The Georgian capital then was essentially lawless, but there was still that casual tranquility to it all, another paradox to its "war zone" label.

The dawn hours in my unheated (and usually electricityless) apartment were deceivingly peaceful. I lived in the heart of the city. The pace of Georgian mornings is deliciously slow. Only Kurdish women sweeping the streets broke the silence, alighting with their straw brooms before dawn and disappearing quickly, rendering themselves seemingly invisible during daylight. Men on horseback trundled by the window occasionally. They barked, *"Matsoni!"* to advertise homemade Georgian yogurt in glass jars covered with scraps of old newspapers, jangling in rough-hewn satchels at the side of their mounts. Muffled arias wept from the windows of the Tbilisi State Conservatory across a narrow lane. It was all in vivid contrast to the standard Tbilisi night noise of squabbling drunks, the fighting packs of feral dogs, some rabid-looking, and the occasional rapping of random, unexplained gunfire. (The bursts of bullets bred frequent morning speculation, focusing on the question of whether there had been a very real shoot-out, or just celebratory volleys from a drunken wedding reception or party.)

Tbilisi lies at the rough geographic center of the Caucasus, and those few reporters living there were thus never more than a few hours' drive from any number of ethnic and civil wars or upheavals: Abkhazia, Chechnya, Russia's violent North Caucasus region, the South Ossetian—

Georgian conflict, and the war between Azerbaijan and Armenia over the mountainous territory known as Nagorno-Karabakh.

One early April morning of that year, my rickety rotary phone began clanging away.

I hesitated to pick up the receiver, wanting to believe it to be maybe just another wrong number. It rang and rang, and I began to fantasize that I could hurl the phone across the room or rip it out of the wall and no one would ever know; telephone connections from anywhere to Georgia were by now notoriously unreliable. At one point, the entire country had exactly eight international phone lines (we wined and dined two of the international operators—sisters by the names of Nato and Nanooka, who thus allowed us to jump our turn, which was indispensable as even calls to Moscow had to be ordered up to two days in advance).

The ringing subsided. But as I drifted back to sleep, it began to rattle again, this time not stopping. This was not the typical short ring of an inner-city connection, but the telltale nonstop bell-hammer that in the USSR indicated a long-distance call. This was never a good sign, because it was almost certainly some Reuters editor in London demanding news from another conflagration, battle, explosion, or other calamity in a place that he or she couldn't pronounce.

I picked up the phone. On the other end of the line, speaking through an echo chamber of static, I heard the voice of an apologetic young British woman calling from the central Reuters desk in London. It was about Nagorno-Karabakh. There were reports of thousands—no one knew how many—of Azerbaijani refugees fleeing an Armenian offensive, and Reuters wanted me to check out fact from fancy, and fast.

Nagorno-Karabakh ("Black Garden") was the first of many long-dormant ethnic disputes to erupt as Gorbachev loosened the reins over the empire. The Azerbaijanis and Armenians had been quietly disputing control over the technically autonomous Azerbaijani region for decades.

Armenians claim that the region is an indelible part of the Armenian motherland, and thus part of the first self-declared "Christian" state in the early fourth century. Many Azerbaijani historians maintain that it was part of the ancient Alban state (not Albanians!), most of whom converted to Islam in the seventh century and Turkified themselves in the eleventh and twelfth centuries; the remaining Alban Christians, the Azerbaijanis maintain, were forcibly "Armenianized" in the nineteenth century—a notion utterly rejected by most Armenian historians as complete delirium.

And that is the easy part.

The trigger was set off by the low-level violence going on in and around Nagorno-Karabakh since the late 1980s, anti-Armenian pogroms in Azerbaijan, and a plea by the local Supreme Soviet, dominated by the majority Armenians there, to be transferred to Armenian control (they contended Stalin had "illegally" transferred the region to Azerbaijani control), partially as a divide-and-rule tactic.

I hung up and started dialing contacts for more information, the sum of which was that the Armenians had attacked a particularly strategic and vulnerable part of Azerbaijan called Kelbajar, which was a "pure" Azerbaijani province—not part of the Nagorno-Karabakh autonomy. This raised the specter of a total war between Armenia and Azerbaijan, not just over the relatively isolated mountain region—a situation that might provoke Azerbaijan's ally Turkey to get involved, or Russia on the Armenian side, others speculated. Just as ominously, then there were the reports of the thousands of Azerbaijani refugees fleeing through the few icy passes of the Murov mountain range, which peaked at 3,700 meters, or 14,000 feet, and which bottled up Kelbajar to the north. Some reports suggested that hundreds might have frozen to death.

Only a few media outlets, the BBC, for example, and the veteran war reporter Thomas Goltz, who was based in Azerbaijan, had gotten hold of a crisis emerging in Kelbajar. Given the tiny foreign correspondent contingent in the region, Nagorno-Karabakh was a war competing for shelf space with a host of other tragedies—most notably in Bosnia and Afghanistan. Still, rumored reports of "tens of thousands" of refugees pouring out of a place few could pick out on a map demanded attention.

Wearily, I prepared to drive toward the calamity. I called Nodar, my nicotine-fingered, cigarette basso profundo–voiced driver. Good spirited but unenthused, he set us off south toward the border with Azerbaijan in his moving chunk of scrap metal, a three-speed 1972 Soviet Volga.

Even though there was a "border" post in those early post-Soviet days, it was a casual one, to say the least. On the Georgian side, two or three men sat in an old traffic police booth, rarely bothering to stop anyone except the drivers of Turkish- and Iranian-plated long-haul trucks from whom bribes could be extracted. The barrier was a dirty rope, which, from inside the booth, the ever-smiling Georgians simply let droop down to the ground so we could pass. The Azerbaijani side was more formal, crawling with customs bureaucrats. Despite the legions of them, there was nothing that could not be brought through for the right informal "fee." There were layers and redundant layers of border police asking the same questions—often scouring passports to check whether one had visited Armenia—a red flag meaning a possible "spy" had been nabbed. Likewise, Azerbaijani stamps could elicit suspicions at the Armenian frontier.

An Azeri guard let us through, entranced in the importance of raising a red and white steel bar rather than lowering an old rope, as on the Georgian side. We entered Azerbaijan at war.

The road scenery was deceivingly majestic. The sun was coming over the spectacular mountains in the distance, as if the war we knew to be ahead were a mirage. We passed shepherds driving herds of sheep, like they did every day. Smoke drifted from chimneys as teahouse keepers by the side of the road stoked fires to prepare shish kebab for customers.

After two or three hours of driving, we finally came to the clearing with the woman digging bloody trenches into her face and screaming. At least she had made it to the bottom of the mountain.

ONE STILL MISSING, stuck in the high ranges of the Murov pass—was one of our local reporters, my friend Khalid Asgarov.

Himself a native of Kelbajar, his father, Shamyl, was the acknowledged head of the Kurdish community in Azerbaijan and the chief of the prized local carpet museum. While Khalid had for several years been living in the Azerbaijani capital of Baku, he went home to Kelbajar as a reporter. Khalid stayed because his father had refused to leave, believing that the Azerbaijani garrison would stand and fight, and that reinforcements were on the way. An Armenian *grad* rocket ripped a hole in the roof of his house. Even then, sensing he would never see his homeland of Kelbajar again, Khalid's father insisted on gathering up whatever represented his life's work—the library, the carpets—before escaping when it was almost too late.

Khalid's father, Shamyl, was not the only one to choose those painstakingly handwoven, naturally dyed carpets to carry over the bone-chilling mountain passes, rather than their old family cars or abundant flocks of sheep and goats. The carpets would be the surviving shards from their fragmented lives. Sentimentalism was not the only driving force for choosing carpets over livestock.

Khalid and his family set out over the pass together with some of the last refugees to get out, on foot, snow and wind at times blinding. Many did try to drive their goats and sheep up the mountain, only to see them collapse and freeze to death along the way.

"There were no guarantees a sheep or a goat would make it through. We knew the carpets could," Khalid later told me, after the ordeal ended. A thoroughly gentle person, he somehow managed a smile.

At the summit, as the temperatures and wind turned lethal, the carpets, stars shining overhead, were unfurled right there, in that moonscape, and put on like robes, those struggling toward safety wrapping themselves, their offspring, and their elderly safely away in them through the pass.

The carpets, spun from the same wool as the sheep left behind, literally saved them.

The carpets would then perform another mini-miracle—serving as sustenance at the end of the road, when the hellish trek ended in homelessness—the cherished fabrics a form of hard currency to restart their fragmented and homeless new lives as refugees. A single one could cost hundreds of dollars. Even in those threadbare days, an extended family with enough of them could trade them for cash, enough to eat for a while, with maybe something left over to start a tiny business.

WITH NO SIGN or word from Khalid, I looked around for any indication of the usual "international relief effort" associated with conflict zones.

It was timid, to say the least. What I had seen so far had been a single Azerbaijani man with a megaphone shouting himself hoarse in the throat trying to instill some sense of order at the makeshift camp near Hanlar.

News about the catastrophe, as it were, consisted of the decision of the government of President Albufaz Elchibey to declare "Emergency Law" throughout the land—the Armenian conquest of Kelbajar, the people freezing to death in the mountains buried at the end of the story, almost an afterthought.

Later that evening, I bedded down for the night in a fleabag hotel in the nearby city of Ganja. In the grim, tacky bar in the hotel's first floor, blaring with unlistenable Soviet pop music and decorated with cheap disco-style lighting despite tragedy all around, I met Billy Nordstrom, a stocky, lonely, and lone logistics coordinator from the UN High Commission for Refugees (UNHCR).

"This is the most challenging situation I've ever faced," he said grimly. He knew that people were freezing to death in the mountain passes, but using Azerbaijani helicopters to try to pluck people from the side of the mountains was simply an invitation to the Armenians to shoot them down, military helicopters being indiscernible from those ferrying refugees. The UNHCR man spoke of organizing a "humanitarian corridor"—an internationally backed agreement to allow a more aggressive rescue effort. But time was short, organizational details daunting. Nordstrom's limited ability to achieve results had him frustrated and angry; as a "logistics man," he assumed there were dozens of bureaucrats between him and decisions that determined who might live and who might die.

Just getting news out that the exodus was continuing was maddening;

the people manning the phone at the hotel made halfhearted attempts to dial the operator and hand me the phone, the operator indifferently responding that all the lines to Moscow were busy and that I should try again in the morning. Finally I lost my temper, mixing expletives with a half-coherent ramble about the crisis afoot and people freezing to death in the mountains and nobody—in their own country, what's more—caring. The operator kept up her outer indifference, but evidently at the expense of some of her conscience; after five minutes, I was on the phone to Moscow, relaying new information to the desk from the UN man that tens of thousands could be trapped. The story was getting bigger.

The next morning I ventured up the road leading back to Kelbajar, where I met more frozen-to-bone refugees coming out, straggling to safety, some holding babies, others with a few possessions or their beloved carpets, now their only currency and nest eggs for starting over.

"I am a new refugee; I will give you a good price on my family rug," one mumbled, tugging at my arm.

Others, like a farmer in tattered clothes, were more philosophical:

"Where is the help? We were left to die up there in the freezing mountains. Yesterday I was walking next to an old man. He finally could go no farther and just collapsed in the snow," he said, adding, "I don't know where the international community is looking," revealing sophistication as to how the international system (and Azerbaijan) worked (or did not).

The war over Nagorno-Karabakh had already created hundreds of thousands of refugees on both sides and widespread destruction. Amid the hundreds of battles, Kelbajar was just another previously unheard-of dot on the map.

BUT THIS BATTLE was very different in two ways.

The first was simple treachery.

On this, a day after having arrived in the area, I still failed to encounter a single Azerbaijani soldier. This, I thought, was extremely odd; if the Azerbaijanis were being driven out of Kelbajar, then I thought it certain that troops would be sent in to at least reinforce what remained of Azerbaijani positions or to help with the rescue effort. Instead I saw nothing.

The reason for this, it quickly emerged, was that Surat Huseinov, the former Azerbaijani "generalissimo" recently stripped of his overall command because of the Azeri military collapse in recent weeks, had ordered his troops back to barracks, leaving the defense of the front lines up to policemen and green national army troops under a different (and incompetent) command.

A wool merchant who had managed to amass a fortune in the declining days of the USSR, when access to state-subsidized goods mixed with a little entrepreneurial imagination could lead to quick and substantial gain, Huseinov had committed this act of brazen self-interest out of a political disagreement with Azerbaijan's Popular Front president, Albufaz Elchibey. (His surname was self-adopted, intended as an important-sounding moniker meaning "Mr. Ambassador.") Huseinov had essentially chosen to cede Azerbaijan's most strategically important regions in order to humiliate and bring down the Elchibey government before promising oil deals with foreign petroleum companies could be signed and implemented, evidently so greedy for a cut that he was ready to help effectively sell off part of his country for it.

Weird and wicked, yes—yet such clan-based intrigues plagued Azerbaijan throughout the war and were ultimately a major factor in what would turn into an astonishing defeat at the hands of the numerically smaller but highly motivated Armenians.

The fall of Kelbajar marked another turning point in the war. The conflict had started as a battle over Nagorno-Karabakh but now washed outside that territory as defined on maps. Thus it was the start of a long and painful process that would last another full year, and which would see Azerbaijan lose vast tracts of territory while gaining hundreds of thousands of refugees as its leadership bickered over responsibility for each tactical defeat. At the end of the process, represented in a poison-chalice cease-fire agreement in May 1994, Armenian forces would occupy some 14 percent of Azerbaijani territory, including all of Nagorno-Karabakh and more, an accurate demonstration that the often Kremlin-designed borders of USSR republics held little sanctity.

Khalid Asgarov and his relatives miraculously did finally reach the capital, Baku, where Khalid had been living since student days and his career as a photographer. At one point, twenty-two relatives were living with him in an old rented house, miles from the city center. He pleaded with me to buy one of the carpets from his aunt. I said I couldn't do it, that I didn't want one, but I eventually relented, Khalid insisting that the deal was vital to the family's well-being and fair. He refused my offer of cash with no carpet as compensation, offended with me, disgusted with the idea.

Each of the intricate, spectacular multicolor rugs was eventually sold off in this way, until finally they were gone, their roles and destinies fulfilled.

ARMENIA: A FADED TINTYPE
OF MOUNT ARARAT

The night landscape after crossing the border from Georgia into Armenia changes almost immediately, pine forests warping into a rocky, harsh, and often treeless terrain of severe mountain slopes covered in snow. With little foliage to absorb the bright moonlight, the earth takes on a surreal appearance, and the icy cold takes on a strange sense of lunar warmth.

I set out with Alexis Rowell of the BBC, a notoriously irreverent, bespectacled, sharp-witted hooligan of a young correspondent. He was one of the first to report on the capture of Kelbajar and the biggest shift in the undeclared war between Armenia and Azerbaijan.

After crossing the new international frontier, we reached Stepanavan—a grim Sovietesque splinter of a town hugging the bank of the Dzoraget River. The main point of interest was a spot near the center of town. On this freezing morning, a gaggle of men had assembled around several dozen twenty-gallon jerry cans of precious gasoline.

We haggled first, not over the price, but over the source of the fuel; it was well known that some suppliers watered down their product with water. When asked if this was the case, one of the merchants shrugged, an answer translating as "there are no guarantees." This could mean anything from our buying 72 octane—a smuggled Azerbaijani grade that would gum up an engine faster than cotton candy sticks to your beard—to jet fuel, which would fry the pistons in most Soviet-built cars such as our Niva.

I advised rolling the dice and filling up—we had only a quarter tank left. But Alexis—evidently trusting some hidden sixth sense—vetoed that. "Let's drive on," he said, sneering at the knot of dubious gasoline hawkers and confident we would not end up petrol-less in the middle of a frozen landscape.

We passed through the desolate southbound road toward Yerevan, winding a downward trajectory through Spitak, the epicenter of Armenia's 1988 earthquake. It was littered with the remains of dozens of shoddily constructed Brezhnev-era high-rise buildings that had collapsed, killing twenty-five thousand people. Adding to the sense of gloom, we saw almost no lighted buildings. Occasionally a candle or an oil lamp flickered in a window. Azerbaijan had cut natural gas supplies to Armenia for the obvious reason that the two countries were at war, and a second gas line though Georgia was regularly sabotaged by Georgian citizens of Azerbaijani descent in acts of solidarity with their ethnic kin. To top it off, Armenia's Metzamor Nuclear Power Plant had been shut down as a security precaution since the 1988 earthquake. In a word, Armenia was darkened into a brownout lasting years.

This was the infamous 1992–93 winter when park trees were felled in the capital, Yerevan, for firewood and scavengers allegedly burned parquet flooring to keep from freezing. Much of the suffering was real; but some stories—such as dog owners eating their pets to ward off famine—were most likely hyperbole. Still, hyperbole can be useful in galvanizing a sense of bitterness and victimization and tapping in to the omnipresent feeling of oppression, struggle, and survival through which many Armenians identify their national historical experience.

We approached Yerevan. At one windswept road, crossing under an inert stoplight, we espied another group of unshaven men hawking gasoline from large jars. The merchant claimed his product had been brought in from Russia and was "Super" grade. Alexis sniffed it with a discriminating twist of his nose, as if degusting a rare Cabernet, and told the man to fill up our tank. We paid him and sputtered into Yerevan, the engine backfiring only a dozen times or so.

• • •

ARE YOU ON our side or for the Turks?" screeched the reception woman
at the grim Dvin hotel. It was the first thing she said, before anything
about the keys or telling us what time breakfast would be. Pointing out
that Armenians were fighting Azerbaijan and not Turkey was pointless.
In this woman's mind (and those of many others), it was all part of the
same pattern: The Karabakh war was just another Turkish effort to exterminate them, a logical extension of the almost-impossible-to-fathom
Mets Yeghern (genocide) of an estimated 1.5 million Armenians at the
hands of the dying Ottoman Empire (present-day Turkey) during World
War I.

I asked for coffee. "Turkish coffee, if you have it," I said, biting my
tongue a bit too late in requesting the thimblelike small cups heated in
copper urns. The woman scowled. "Armenian coffee, you mean."

The corridors of the hotel were dank and dark. Even when the power
was on, the voltage was dreadfully low; lightbulbs glowed as if tarnished
with wood stain. I caught myself hypnotically staring directly at the dim
filaments, experiencing no discomfort.

Our floor woman, a busybody Soviet holdover who distributed room
keys and kept an eye on guests, slowly prepared the coffee over a makeshift spiral heater that barely seemed to emit any heat at all. Attached
to it was a piece of metal spiral plugged into a socket that seemed to be
falling out of the wall, two misshapen holes between shards of copper.
The death-trap sockets, the power outages, the pervasive feeling of dep-
rivation and darkness, the stories of hunger, the stories of the shelling of
Karabakh, and the siege mentality—all seemed to conspire to re-create
the essence of the Mets Yeghern, echoes of excruciating pain.

Indeed, no other city I had been in conveyed the same sense of heavi-
ness and a certain depression as did Yerevan in those days. A Muslim
trading post turned into the happenstance capital of a rump Armenian
empire, Yerevan could brood like no other city. The buildings projected
a gloomy sternness; tufa rock facades with their hands on their hips, all
defiantly facing in one direction: Mount Ararat.

It is doubtful that there has been a national symbol sadder or more
compelling than the old volcanic cone where Noah and his ark allegedly

found terra firma after the biblical flood. For centuries it has been regarded as the center of the Armenian experience. But since the 1921
Treaty of Kars between the USSR and present-day Turkey, this most res-
onant symbol of Armenian-ness has been just over the border in the land
of the enemy and is thus thrust into the face daily, a symbol of national
loss. Such is the importance of the mountain that apartments having an
"Ararat view" in Yerevan go for 30 percent more than ones that do not.

After coffee at the hotel, Alexis and I set off to find out more about
the official Armenian insistence that it was not officially involved in the
Karabakh war, or in the forced exit of Azerbaijani civilians from Kelbajar. The official line was still that the conflict was purely between the
Karabakh Armenians and Azerbaijan, and that the armed forces of the
Republic of Armenia were not involved at all, aside from the participa-
tion of "volunteers." Now that official line was starting to change, with
pride starting to take the place of discretion.

"Taking Kelbajar was the only way to save Karabakh," Tigran
Naghdalian, the young, unflappable spokesman at the HQ of the nationalist Dashnaksutiun Party told us. The "Dashnaks" were the central
champions of the Nagorno-Karabakh cause. "Without having created
this 'security zone,' Karabakh would be reliant on a tiny strip of territory [the so-called Lachin Corridor] connecting it to Armenia and facing
strangulation," he emphasized.*

We pointed out that as a result of the Armenian actions, hundreds of
non-Karabakhi Azerbaijanis were left to potentially freeze to death in
the mountains. Naghdalian held his expression steadily, as if to say "I
know . . . but war is war. . . ."

International condemnation of Armenian behavior, including a new
Security Council resolution demanding the "immediate withdrawal of
occupying forces" (which Armenia chose to interpret as meaning only
"local Karabakh forces"), was starting to grow.

---

* I met Tigran Naghdalian many times over the ensuing years, and we eventually became friends. He went on to a stellar if short career, rising to the post of head of Armenia's state TV network before he was killed in late 2002 by an assassin's bullet—one in
a string of unsolved political murders in the country.

Of greater concern in Yerevan was saber-rattling in Turkey about a response to the Armenian offensive, and what could be done to aid Azerbaijan. The first act by Ankara was to close the frontier between the border towns of Kars and Gumri, which had been enjoying a lively trade since the border opening in 1991, but which remains closed as of this writing, two decades later. Predictably, Yerevan was rife with rumors that the Turks would do more than just seal the frontier and were planning to pour over the border and finish the eradication of Armenians begun in 1915.

"The Turks are coming to slaughter us again," declared our receptionist upon our return to our cold and dark hotel. "But this time we won't let them!"

We decided to go check the border for ourselves, climbing back into Alexis's rattrap Niva, and headed in the general direction of Mount Ararat. It was partially obscured by clouds and mist until we came to a monastery complex called Khor Virab, when the glory of the famous mountain exposed itself to us. Khor Virab was also a deeply revered site, as it is believed to have been the site of the dungeon where Saint Giorgi the Illuminator spent thirteen years imprisoned for his faith before curing the pagan Armenian king Trdat from a bout of insanity. Trdat then declared Armenia to be the world's first Christian "state" in AD 301 and spent much of the rest of his days building Christian churches on the sites of former pagan shrines.

Even though the monastery is just a few dozen meters from the barbed-wire border with Turkey, we saw no trace of any grand Turkish armies ready to sweep across the frontier. Instead, we were treated to one of the ritual animal sacrifices (*matagh* in Armenian) at Khor Virab that take place on a daily basis and which are a holdover from the pre-Trdat pagan epoch. This time, a rooster was being slaughtered as part of a traditional wedding pilgrimage to the site. A crowd of women in long dresses and men in leather jackets enthusiastically followed behind the bride and groom, the war in Karabakh, the prospect of the Turks pouring over the border, and the grim state of the country—for a few moments, at least—distant thoughts.

We got back into the vehicle and headed south along the empty road, thinking we might find some "real" activity in that direction, such as a more militarized area. Long shadows cast a melancholy air onto the brutal rocky, winter landscape. Why did people live here? I asked myself. In search of Turkish troops, we meandered down a back road toward the frontier. Ahead of us, on the right-hand side, was an unmanned sentry booth. Down in the gully, we could see barbed wire—and in the distance, the red and white, star and crescent–emblazoned Turkish flag. In the border guard huts on the Turkish side, nothing moved. We took out our cameras to take a picture of a silence so deep it seemed to breathe.

Suddenly, a short squat figure appeared in the distance on the Armenian side of the frontier. With one hand, he tugged on the strap from which his Kalashnikov was dangling and started to march toward us, reaching a jog and almost a gallop while dangling the AK behind him.

"NE FOTOGRAFIROVAT!" he shouted. "NO PICTURES!"

We laid down our gear.

"What are you doing here?" the now ex-Soviet (but still Russian) sentry snorted, with an equal mix of reproach and bewilderment.

"Hiii!" said Alexis, in his lilting, disarming London accent, blissfully unaware that that word of greeting in English means "Armenian" in Armenian. . . .

The sentry stared emptily at the glib Alexis as if he were from Planet X.

Just as the sentry started to mutter something, another, taller and thinner border guard appeared, tucking in his shirt as he approached us, yawning slightly.

"What do you want?" asked the taller one. By his epaulets, he appeared to be a captain.

We explained that we were reporters. There was talk in Yerevan, we explained, about Turkish troops massing on the border, and that we had come to check it out.

The captain looked at us curiously, smirked, and then opened a gate and waved us inside a barrackslike building.

The structure was perched on a promontory above the border area behind a maze of barbed wire and sinister-looking radio towers. We stopped to take a look. The captain told us to keep walking. "The border comes later," he said.

Once inside the barracks, he led us into a larger, comfortable room with sofas and coffee tables. He slowly examined our passports and accreditations.

"Now, what is it you want?" said the captain.

"We want to see the border crossing," I said.

The captain rolled his eyes. The border was closed, he said, emphasizing that there had never been a fully functioning crossing point here, not even in peaceful times. This has been a rare spot where NATO member Turkey met the USSR.

The captain's wife and two more border guards entered the room. They sat down and urged us to do the same. Then the captain went into another room and returned with a bottle of vodka. His wife, a tall woman who took pains to look city-stylish despite her isolation on this rocky, lonely border raced off and roared back, her arms bursting with candies, bread, and some sausage, words flowing ceaselessly from her smiling lips.

"You boys must be so hungry. You know, it's so quiet around here. No one to talk to. Nowhere to go, to have a good time. My girlfriends back in Russia can't understand what I'm doing here. You know, there are some things you have to do in life. . . ."

Her border guard husband sized her up quizzically, then dismissively. My talk involving rumors about the Turks and paltry ruminations about the starkness of Ararat clearly did not interest him. He told us he was Russian and not Armenian and hailed from Sverdlovsk, in western Siberia. He lamented the breakup of the Soviet Union, and he let us know it in the form of melancholy vodka toasts. He said he had never met an American before. Now he was a man marooned on a distant, foreign border post in the middle of nowhere and did not know why aside from a lingering sense of Communist-era duty, which meant nothing anymore.

"*Vy ponimaite?*" he asked rhetorically and repeatedly. "Do you understand?"

He poured the vodka around, asking us questions about where we were from and what we were doing. It seemed to be his first human communication in months. His wife tugged at her kinky hair and nodded, adding a feeling of exaggerated importance to our impromptu encounter.

"This used to be the border between NATO and the Warsaw Pact," he related. "Now I am guarding the border of a country that doesn't exist anymore, my country, the USSR. It is difficult for me even to look at it that way."

Alexis and I nodded in a kind of sympathy.

"Soon we will be humiliated into leaving here as well," lamented the captain, muttering to himself.

We stayed for over an hour as the captain toasted to peace, love, and friendship between nations—the usual stuff. But as the vodka began to gain its hold, underneath he was clearly still preoccupied over the loss of the empire, and his new role as a foreigner guarding a border with another foreign country.

It was pretty sad, actually.

Finally, as we prepared to leave, the captain pulled me aside.

"I have something I want to discuss with you," he said in a low tone.

"Yes?" I asked.

"Perhaps you and your friend would like to go into business with me."

I thought for a split second. Drugs? Weapons running? Loose nuclear materials?

"We're not businessmen, we're journalists," I said, but curious about his proposal nonetheless.

"Listen, what I have access to is rare stuff."

"What do you have?" I asked, playing him like a trout, while remembering the would-be gem smuggler I had met back in Leningrad, years earlier.

"*Snake venom,*" whispered the captain, coming closer to my ear.

"Snake venom?" I asked, incredulously.

"Top quality," he whispered. "The best."

I tried to emphasize that I knew nothing about snake venom or how to maximize its commercial potential, but the captain seemed deaf to my words.

"Davay . . . ," he cooed. "C'mon! It is really good venom. If not you, then maybe you have some friends who we can do business with. . . ."

So far, our quest to capture the outbreak of hostilities between Turkey and Armenia that might lead to Russian intervention (and thus, theoretically, possibly to World War III) had been less than productive in raw news terms. We'd traveled up and down the border on wild rumors about Turkish troop movements but had only seen a rooster getting its head ripped off at a monastery and drunk warm vodka with a marooned Soviet border-guard-cum-snake-venom-peddler. Yet the day's fragmented images made sense in a way—under the absurdity of it all, the war afoot, the political doublespeak on both sides of the front lines—people went on with their lives, adapting however they could. Another basic truth: journalists wandering around in conflict zones spend more time chasing after wild leads about nonexistent troop movements than actually seeing them.

WE SET OFF back in the direction of Georgia, making a special stop along the border between Armenia and the part of Azerbaijan where Kelbajar is situated. The road leading from the Armenian town of Vardenis was nothing but dried mud ruts. There had been reports that Armenian units had entered from Armenia itself, but this was officially denied in Yerevan, in keeping with the official but implausible line that the war was solely between the 100,000 or so Karabakh Armenians and 7-million-strong Azerbaijanis.

Escorted by several local officials who had intercepted us, we headed toward the zero zone on the actual frontier, and there we found our story.

The ground was damp, and clearly imprinted with telltale signs of moving war machines.

"BMP tracks," said Alexis, using the Russian acronym for armored personnel carrier, or APC.

"Tractor tracks," said our escort from the local administration.

"A tractor? Why would a tractor drive into enemy territory?" asked Alexis, rhetorically. "To harvest snow-covered wheat during the middle of a war?"

THE MEN GRINNED, sharing with us the silent inside joke of the Armenian government's complicity in at least this part of the ghost war with Azerbaijan over Karabakh.

Officially, the Armenians justified their conquest of Kelbajar and areas surrounding Nagorno-Karabakh as the need to establish a "security zone" around Karabakh that would be given back to Azerbaijan when it recognized Nagorno-Karabakh's independence or when some sort of permanent peace plan was arranged.

The man who imagined the offensive on Kelbajar on the Armenian side had other ideas. He was a newcomer to this war but a seasoned veteran of other guerrilla conflicts. An erudite, ascetic archaeologist by training, he had fought as a volunteer on the pro-Palestinian side in the war in Lebanon and against the Israelis during their invasion in 1982. Then he had taken up the cause of the Kurdish Peshmergas, and greatly admired the Bekaa Valley–based Kurdish Workers' Party, or PKK, the Marxist organization fighting for Kurdish rights in Turkey. But at core, his cause was Armenia, and his stated goal that of reestablishing control over what he considered historic Armenian lands, including Mount Ararat and much of present-day eastern Turkey. In the mid-1980s, he became a key figure in ASALA (Armenian Secret Army for the Liberation of Armenia), which engineered bombings against Turkish government targets in Europe and the assassination of Turkish diplomats. He traveled under fake Cypriot and other passports for years, finally ending up spending three years in a French jail on weapons-related charges and the possession of forged documents. To his enemies he was a terrorist; to his supporters, a national icon.

His nom de guerre was Commander Avo, although at birth in distant California, his Armenian-American parents had named him Monte, with the family name Melkonian. He was later killed in action at the age of thirty-five in June 1993 outside the Azerbaijani ghost-town city of Agdam, and his funeral was attended by thousands, including the president of Armenia, Levon Ter-Petrossian.

But all that would happen later.

Back when the Soviet Union was unraveling, it was natural that Melkonian would find his calling in the Karabakh cause. Within only a few months, he developed a reputation in Karabakh as an extremely disciplined commander. As a nondrinker, he was a rarity among his fighters and had ruffled more than a few feathers by insisting on absolute sobriety among them. When he did find them imbibing a bit of homemade moonshine, he was known to demonstratively pour the contents onto the ground, eliciting rage from his subordinates.

He also raised many eyebrows among Armenian fighters for a far more serious reason: Those under his command were given strict orders not to harm noncombatants or even Azerbaijani military captives, despite the grisly habit of the locals—on both sides—of senseless, gruesome revenge killings of civilians and soldiers alike. This set of ethics earned him real enemies among his own men, according to a biography about Melkonian's life written by his brother, Markar. He relates the circumstances about a massacre, in which several dozen captives—including some noncombatants—were tossed in a ditch, stabbed to death, and some burned alive after ethnic Armenian forces took the Azerbaijani-held town of Karadaghlu in 1992:

> By the time Monte came across the ditch on the outskirts of town it was a butcher's scrap heap. Monte had given strict orders that no captives were to be harmed. The veins in his neck stood out like braided hemp, and he hollered until he was hoarse. . . . More than 50 Azeri captives had been butchered at Karadaghlu. But it was not the butchery that damaged Monte's reputation among the Karabakh mountain people. On the contrary, vengeance ran deep in the mountains, and the loudest voices on both sides demanded blood for blood. What damaged Monte's reputation, rather, was the fact that the butchery at Karadaghlu had

taken place *against his orders*. . . . Karadaghlu only confirmed what . . . everyone else seemed to know: Avo, the new Headquarters Chief, was a weakling.

But whatever his lesser-minded underlings thought about him, Commander Avo was a master tactician. He had spoken months before about the importance of taking Kelbajar, but the idea was regarded as unrealistic. For Monte, Kelbajar was not an end in itself, nor was Karabakh. It was the natural action that would lead to the recovery of what he considered control over "historic Armenian lands." As Markar writes:

> But why advance into Kelbajar? No Armenians lived there. Monte claimed they "*had* to take Kelbajar" because Azeri gunners in the area had launched artillery barrages against Armenian villages. But to him, the operation was not purely—nor even primarily—based on security considerations. "This is a historical issue," he told Baghryan: current demographics and political boundaries notwithstanding, Kelbajar was part of the Armenian homeland. "Of course this is historical Armenia!"

Monte cited the presence of old Armenian monasteries in Kelbajar as justification for his "historic lands" argument.

Monte Melkonian's moment came during early April 1993 when the Azerbaijanis, having been deserted by "commanders" like Surat Huseinov, had collapsed all along the Karabakh front. It was then that he decided to launch a lightning strike from Karabakh into Kelbajar from the east—only to discover that he and his men had been beaten to the prize by another Armenian attacking force under the command of a French Armenian ("Shishko," or "Fatty") coming from the west, meaning Armenia itself. It was the tread tracks of Shishko's armored vehicles that Alexis and I had seen near the border.

For Melkonian and Shishko, Kelbajar and other soon-to-be "occupied territories" of Azerbaijan were not bargaining chips or even part of a temporary security zone, but part of a once-mighty, now-fragmented ancient Armenian empire that they were reconstructing. Not long after the conquest of Kelbajar, Melkonian pointed out to a British journalist that this was "the first time in a thousand years that Armenians had 're-captured' land," rather than losing it. The logic was clear.

IN THE EARLY 1990s of Armenia, one of the most popular, and indeed few, souvenirs on sale was a map illustrating "Armenia, 2104 BC."

The cartographical fantasy was one of many indicative of how the aspirations of small, former "empires" can be fueled by the collapse of a giant one like the USSR.

The map included all of present-day Armenia, Karabakh, much of present-day Turkey and Azerbaijan, and parts of Georgia—a land stretching from the Black Sea to the Mediterranean to the Caspian.

To be fair, in Tbilisi I also saw maps of ancient and medieval Georgia that included lands long since lost to other countries (mainly Turkey and Russia), and in Azerbaijan I had seen maps of that nation that included much of northern Iran ("Southern Azerbaijan") as well as chunks of to-day's Iraq. But in Armenia, the "Greater Armenia" maps seemed to be everywhere, and believed. It was only a matter of time—and faith—until the stolen heritage—what some detractors have called the "Greater Armenia" project—would be restored and ancient glory revived. And Kelbajar was the first step in that direction.

Indeed, three years later I found myself in Stepanakert, the capital of Nagorno-Karabakh, which by then had been stitched to Armenia from top to bottom after the conquest of additional Azerbaijani lands and the expulsion of hundreds of thousands of Azerbaijanis. There I met an ethnic Armenian fighter who himself hailed from Lebanon, had fought in the Karabakh war, married a local woman, and was now living in an old Soviet-style apartment building in the town.

He was a gracious host, and jugs full of local wine were consumed as the fighter and his Armenian guests sang songs while he strummed a guitar.

We began talking about Commander Avo—the late Monte Melkonian—and the official line that the "occupied territories" would be given back to Azerbaijan once Nagorno-Karabakh's independence was recognized by Baku.

"Oh, that is naive," our host said with a warm smirk. "OK, perhaps a few chunks—but nothing strategic."

Then he pointed to what, in the dim candlelit apartment, looked to be a faded tintype on the wall.

"That is what keeps us Armenians going," he added with another smile, pouring more wine.

It was an image of the indelible Armenian symbol, Mount Ararat.

Surely, I interjected, Ararat was an understandably painful symbol, but no one realistically thought present-day Turkey would ever relinquish it.

"Yes, perhaps you are correct," he said calmly. "But it is like a beautiful woman you desire. Deep in your heart, you know perhaps that she is totally unobtainable. But you keep fighting for her nonetheless."

AZERBAIJAN: THE SHISH KEBAB WAR AND EASTERN DEMOCRACY

I am sitting on an ancient Baku balcony—a spit of space barely big enough for one along a wide avenue, just down from the shores of the Caspian Sea. The scent of crude oil washing up on the bay from outdated, leaky Soviet oil rigs lingers in the air. Hanim, the henna-haired mother of my cameraman, Adil Bunyatov, serves me never-ending cups of steaming, slightly bitter Azerbaijani tea. (As she and others swear in these arid parts, this is a remarkably effective way to "calibrate" one's body temperature to the heat and obtain "equilibrium.") We need it. It's over one hundred stifling degrees Fahrenheit.

The street below me looks serene, old men in teahouses gathering to share the latest gossip, groups of teenagers kicking an old soccer ball around.

Yet Azerbaijan is still at war. Now not only with the Armenians. Azerbaijan is now at war with itself. "The country is falling apart," says Adil, despairingly.

The wool-merchant-cum-warlord Surat Huseinov, high on battle fumes from his act of treachery in pulling his troops off the front and practically gift-wrapping territory to the Armenians, is not satisfied. His legion of mutinous, motley "rebels" march toward the capital, meeting little resistance. They quickly force President Elchibey to quit—Huseinov's original "goal."

Not enough for the semiliterate Huseinov, who now smells real blood and riches. Elchibey flees into internal exile. Elchibey "temporarily" brings in Azerbaijan's former Communist-era strongman, the wily Heydar Aliyev, the onetime Soviet Politburo member. It's predicted this will lead to some reconciliation with the "rebels."

Now it isn't even clear what Huseinov wants, except some warped form of power. He obviously considers this more important than fighting the Armenians, who are (to no one's surprise) taking advantage of the chaos in Baku by chopping off ever-greater chunks of Azerbaijan.

We head for the front, which is wherever Surat's column of mutinous tanks and APCs have parked for breakfast, lunch, or dinner, or just broken down because of low-octane fuel. We flag down a taxi and head north, along the main road between Baku and the old Azerbaijani capital of Shemakhi, four hours north, to see what there is to see.

Adil Bunyatov had been working as a photojournalist and a TV cameraman for several years, more often than not in the former USSR's myriad conflict zones. This was pre–oil rush Azerbaijan, and working for foreign media outlets was one of the few ways to make a decent living (aside from government-related corruption). By now, he was frustrated with the "business" of news gathering, which was increasingly coming to mean documenting the descent of his homeland into chaos and comic-opera wars, like Surat Huseinov's "campaign" to take the capital.

ALTHOUGH THE MAINSTREAM international press was terming this a "civil war," most of the action involved Huseinov's rebels moving their armored vehicles a few kilometers closer to the capital, and then parking again while the government forces pulled back to the next bridge or hedgerow. There seemed to be no thought of taking territory not directly adjacent to the two main roads out of the capital. The "battles" were thus relegated to holding or giving up a chunk of asphalt and then going home for the night. Indeed, in the outdoor cafés of Baku, we sometimes saw the same "government" officers we had seen on the nearby front lines during the day, eating shish kebabs and speaking of the day's brave deeds. Thus, the Civil War or Internal Conflict or Surat Huseinov Putsch or Elchibey Ouster became known for what it really was, namely, the "Shish Kebab War."

Adil waxed cynical as we puttered along the road. If I expected war-bravado talk from him, I was to be disappointed. With the Soviet downfall, "democracy" was an abstract concept, but was embraced as a promise that the USSR only needed to inject a bit of it to find the promised land of justice and easy consumerism. In Azerbaijan, this feeling was even more palpable, given the hopes the country's untapped oil reserves represented.

Adil Bunyatov, tweaking his thick black mustache, ceased talking about the war altogether and, completely out of the blue, launched into a missive about doing something "real" instead of covering ceaseless, crazy conflicts.

"I want to open a ketchup factory," he said, talking mostly to himself, our car rattling away though the desert.

"What?"

"You heard me. I want to open a ketchup factory. The problem is, I can't."

The collapse of the Soviet economy and the poor quality of merchandise in the USSR meant that nearly all finished consumer goods in Azerbaijan were imported. In the case of ketchup, this was almost economically insane. The country was a veritable hothouse and tomatoes cheap, tasty, and in great abundance. Salt, vinegar, and bottles were readily available. The problem with the dream project, Adil noted with irritation, was that the country was flooded with ketchup made in Turkey. The reason for this was that the Turkish ketchup, along with everything from German UHT (ultra-high-temperature) milk to cheap Chinese candy bars, was imported, and that meant that the Department of Customs folks were working in consort with the Ministry of Economic Development folks to make sure that no ketchup (or milk or chocolate bars) would be produced in Azerbaijan and were dividing the fat tariffs slapped on the imports between them. By Adil's calculations, a bottle of ketchup from Turkey cost upward of ten times what he figured he could sell Azerbaijani ketchup for and still make a profit. Perhaps such savings didn't matter much to the expense-account oil men starting to seep into Baku, but it drove Adil up the wall. The ketchup talk was part of Adil's broader monologue on "Eastern Democracy."

Democracy is what Azerbaijanis were promised. Instead, their country was falling apart, losing territory to the Armenians, getting caught up in comic-opera wars like the one we were covering, corruption, warlords, crime. Therefore, "democracy" was increasingly associated with simple anarchy.

Adil lamented all of this. He did not believe Communism was a better model for Azerbaijan, and yet neither did he believe that the country was ready for "real" democracy. Ideally, Azerbaijan would have an "Eastern Democracy"—a kind of temporary, benevolent autocracy, headed by a type of "father figure"—similar to those running the new sultan-type states emerging in Central Asia. Most of their leaders were busy building sultanate-type regimes, often based around elaborate if still whimsical cults of personality. As the 1990s progressed, the whimsical part fell off and an overt, heavy sense of dictatorship and repression took over in almost all of them.

Adil had just returned from Turkmenistan, across the Caspian Sea from Azerbaijan. "There is something I would call Eastern Democracy," said Adil. He gave an example, noting that the quirky leader of Turkmenistan, Saparmurat Niyazov (who had renamed himself Turkmenbashi, or "Head of All Turkmen"), provided his four million subjects with free natural gas, salt, and other basics. (These were the early "soft" years of Turkmenbashi's post-Soviet reign; however, later he would evolve into one of the most erratic, repressive leaders in the world.)

"It is a kind of social contract," Adil added. He obviously found the sense of order familiar and comforting in a way, compared with the constant battlefield losses to the Armenians and the ongoing, ludicrous "civil war" we were observing in the steppe and desert north of Baku.

"In Eastern Democracy, the strong man takes care of the needs of the people. There is law and order," argued Adil. "It is a transitional way to democracy, because we are in a transitional situation. Our people are used to a patriarchic system, to having a 'big man,' and that's what they want now."

While Adil's ketchup monologue continued, we saw the first APCs parked along the road to Shemakhi and a few dozen soldiers. We stopped the car in a dusty clearing at the side of the road and asked which side of the war they were on. These were government soldiers, it turned out.

"Where's the front line? Where are Surat's people?" asked Adil.

"Right up there." One of the government guys pointed to a nearby hill. There were no more than a hundred yards separating the two sides. No trenches. No real fortifications. Nothing but a hundred yards of air.

There was also a conspicuous lack of any noticeable tension between the sides, at least in this place. Aside from one government type taking a quick peek though some binoculars at the "rebels," the sides didn't seem to be paying much attention to each other.

Having nothing much else to do, the government group decided to show its hospitality by giving us a ride on their APC through the rocky, desertlike terrain so that we could get a look at the lay of the land. We left the roadway and started down an incline. Soon we were cruising down a dusty trail. I sat atop the APC while Adil filmed through a periscope from inside.

We drove for about three miles before we approached what looked like some sort of old collective farm building. Nearby there was a square, cement-type block structure. It was a natural well, used for outdoor bathing. The cement slabs blocked our view, but under the fountain of water pouring from a spigot bobbed a woman's head—she was taking a shower.

Our government soldier friends became instantly distracted and began whistling and hollering. Evidently the driver of the APC was not immune to the charms of the lady's head of hair, for he had apparently taken his eyes off the terrain in front of him.

There was a gentle jolt, a wiggle of the wheels, and then the right side of the APC gradually began to elevate in a way I knew it should not. As the vehicle started to lurch, I scrambled to get on the high side, grabbing toward one of the wheels now spinning in the air. Then I felt myself falling off, losing consciousness as I hit the ground. When I came to, I could see the APC teetering on its side above me, rocking slowly toward me. The armored vehicle was about to roll over onto my legs.

At the last second, I felt two hands pulling me by the arms along the rocky ground just as the multi-ton hulk of military metal slowly somersaulted over exactly where I had been lying, its turret digging into the sand. Now on my feet, I embraced the soldier who had saved my life—or at least my legs.

But the soldiers were less worried about me (or doing battle with the rebel foe) than the reaction of their commanding officer should they return to "base" without their APC.

There were eight or nine of us, but I am still amazed at our achievement. Grunting and groaning, we pushed and shoved until finally we managed to prop the APC on its side, and then with another herculean effort, righted it back on its wheels. Rather than congratulate themselves on our success, however, the soldiers then began cursing one another over the damage, waving their fingers and assigning blame. When one seemed to take too much interest in a Kalashnikov propped on a bush, we knew it was time to go.

"Let's get out of here," Adil said.

It was a good idea, and I still had my legs.

Leaving our friends and the APC behind, we ascended a sandy ridge and kept walking in the general direction of the road, eventually finding it several miles away from where we had left our driver.

"You Americans don't really understand. We're not totally ready for democracy, as you call it," Adil said, wiping APC soot and sweat from his brow. "I'm not saying we won't have it eventually. But right now it's too early. This is chaos, not democracy."

What Adil really wanted was just a normal life for himself and his family.

Prophetically, Azerbaijan would in the coming years take on some of the elements of an "Eastern Democracy": The former Communist strongman Heydar Aliyev conceded to some demands of the wool-merchant-cum-warlord Surat Huseinov, including making him prime minister. Within two years, however, Aliyev outmaneuvered Surat, who ended up in prison for several years on charges of coup plotting.

The Heydar Aliyev clan, helped by new oil money, then built an authoritarian system with all the whistles and bells—handing off power to

Heydar's son Ilham before Heydar's death, holding sham elections, and engineering the total dominance of the state over most aspects of life.

We got back to the car and continued to the ancient town of She-makhi, the former capital of Azerbaijan, probably crossing the front several times without knowing it because the sentries were asleep or something. There were a few gun-toting men hanging around the main administration building, and we met a city official inside, who said merely that he "was on the side of peace." But we had no idea who was in control, and no one seemed to want to tell us.

"Let's go back to Baku to see who is in power today," Adil suggested, sarcastically.

"OK," I said.

Aside from my near death by APC, it had been an enlightening day. A "civil war" that was barely one, the lone government casualty the wrecked piece of military hardware.

INDEED, THE REAL war was elsewhere, and receiving almost no news coverage because one had to cross the lines of the Shish Kebab War to get there. That real war, of course, was being fought over Karabakh, and during that white-hot summer, Azerbaijan's battlefield losses to Armenia continued unabated. The most notable loss came in July, when Azerbaijani troops lost the frontline city of Agdam, once home to seventy thousand souls, but already largely abandoned by civilians. The Armenians then carted away doors, window frames, and even the white bricks used to build the houses as war booty.

I made it to within a few miles of Agdam the day after it fell, and saw it burning in the near distance—the fate of all fallen cities in all the Caucasus wars. There, I met the last Azerbaijani unit along the road, a platoon of twenty or so. The commander, distraught and on the edge of a nervous breakdown, insisted on digging up a dead comrade to show me. There was no corpse; only a perfectly flattened head remained, which the by now inconsolable commander pried up with a stick and displayed to me. He claimed it had been intentionally run over by an Armenian tank as his forces retreated.

I thought of my own narrow escape from getting crushed by the flip-flopping APC outside Shemakhi.

I listened to the commander wail and wave around the head of his friend with Agdam burning in the background, the requisite wave of refugees, cars loaded down with rescued refrigerators, blankets, and mattresses pulling away from the area.

AND I WOULD have to file again from the chaos of Azerbaijan a few years after the fall of Agdam and the Shish Kebab War, and this time the subject was Adil Bunyatov, my friend and cameraman.

Less than two years after Adil's dreams of opening a ketchup factory and his soliloquy about "Eastern Democracy" and speculations about whether Azerbaijan might be better off with a little benign dictatorship instead of the chaos that came with gradual moves toward broader political freedoms, the autocratic government of Heydar Aliyev was faced with a new rebellion. Adil went forth to do his job of finding and filming the "front," which this time took the form of a suburban military barracks in Baku. But unlike the Shish Kebab War of the summer of 1993, this was an all-too-real confrontation pitting Azerbaijani against Azerbaijani, and when the guys with guns on either side of the politic divide fired their weapons, it was in anger and with intent to kill.

When the smoke cleared, dozens of soldiers lay dead; the rogue officer behind the rebellion was allowed to bleed to death on his way to the hospital.

Adil was no longer there to report it. He was killed in the opening blast when a stray bullet struck his jugular. The doctors tried to reassure his family, which included a wife and a son, that his death had probably been very quick and almost painless.

He was the first of my close reporting friends and colleagues to be killed in action.

He would not be the last.

PART IV (1993–2004)

CHECHNYA: ECHOES OF THE DEPORTATION

Dudayev addresses rally in Grozny, June 1993.

The most tragic thing about the first Chechen-Russian war was that it took place at all. Until just before it began, almost no journalists or political pundits believed there would be a war—those who had even heard of Chechnya assumed the embattled separatist leader Dzhokhar Dudayev would eventually be toppled by his own people, saving the Russians the trouble.

The reasons that it erupted were, at charitable best, human stupidity on a protozoan level; at worst, they were heinous and recklessly criminal. The decision by the Russian Federation to send in troops was made in a bathhouse by naked, drunken men during a birthday celebration for the country's defense minister, Pavel Grachev. At first the Russians relentlessly bombed airports around the Chechen capital city, Grozny, to establish a no-fly zone.

Someone forgot to tell them that the Chechen separatists had no planes, except some old Czechoslovak training craft that were practically incapable of getting airborne, let alone dropping a bomb. Once the ground war began, thousands of fresh-faced Russian youth in armored columns without infantry were sent into Grozny without even city maps, getting lost in the maze of sixteen-story residential high-rises in the city center. This made them easy targets for the ragtag Chechen militias, who, armed with grenades and RPGs (rocket-propelled grenades), often laughingly ascended idling Russian tanks, flipped open the hatches, and dropped the explosives inside, turning the crews into shreds of human flesh. The Russian reaction was to carpet-bomb the city, using levels of tonnage that had not been seen since the Allied bombings of Dresden during World War II.

I first came to Chechnya during the summer of 1993, covered most of the war that broke out in 1994, and would return dozens of times over the next decade. Many of the central characters included in the following chapters were killed during the carnage. I often wonder why I am not among their number.

GRENADE, LIGHTLY TOSSED

It was a sultry summer day in 1993. Two old men in a Moskvich sedan picked us up at the side of the road after we crossed the "frontier." This was my first foray into Chechnya, a tiny (the size of Connecticut) place it took the czars' armies longer than any other to "pacify" in the nineteenth century. As the empire reeled, Chechen activists wasted no time in declaring independence from the Russian Federation.

Despite the searing heat, our two driving hosts wore Chicago 1930s–style black fedora hats, popular in Chechnya at the time, but totally incongruous with the surrounding countryside, dotted with flocks of sheep and newly constructed mosques. I sat in the back along with my traveling companion, Liam McDowall of the Associated Press, studying the fedoras. I couldn't escape the feeling that we were being driven to Grozny by members of the rap group RUN-DMC or some Prohibition-era gangsters. In the ex–Soviet Union, the fedora was a strictly Chechen accoutrement, the favored headgear of the renegade former Soviet nuclear bomber squadron commander General Dzhokhar Dudayev, president of the Chechen Republic of Ichkeria, a state recognized at the time by no other country on earth.

We entered Grozny and asked the two fedora-topped gentlemen to drop us at the best hotel in town.

"There's only one hotel—the Kavkaz," they laughed, and brought us to a menacingly rundown shack across from Dudayev's presidential palace on Grozny's massive central square, which would later assume a legendary role as the heart of the resistance during the war.

The hotel lobby was teeming with armed men milling around. One was lightly tossing a live hand grenade, detonation ring intact, into the air repeatedly, as if it were a lemon or a small ball. "Hey, which room are you guys in here?" he asked. We answered that we hadn't checked in yet. We inquired about rooms. A rail-thin man at the front desk said that he had only two left, and that the door lock on one was broken. After no deliberation we deposited our things in the room with the lock and left the grenade-tossing young man and his companions behind.

The city was tense, but in the then-jovial, chaotic Chechen way. The Russian-backed opposition had tried to stage a referendum on Dudayev's rule, but not through diplomatic negotiations. An armed clash erupted down the street at the state drama theater. Several people were killed in a melee a couple of hours before our arrival. Dudayev's forces celebrated their "victory" by discharging every type of weapon they had into the cloudless sky and performing a *zikr*, a Sufi dance of remembrance for the dead.

So loud was the volley of fire that my editor in Moscow couldn't make out what I was dictating when I tried to file a dispatch from the press center of the presidential palace. I finally got off a few stock quotes and told him not to worry—the gunfire was only a celebration. He laughed, hanging up the phone, evidently getting more "color" than he bargained for from the nonstop gunfire than I could give him in a million words.

The next day, tens of thousands began assembling on the square in front of the presidential palace. Dudayev was coming to address the masses. Bravado-happy bodyguards pointed AKs at different angles into the crowd below, but any real sense of security was mythological; there were so many in the crowd openly armed with everything from Kalashnikovs to old hunting rifles. Then Dzhokhar emerged and mounted an old pickup truck with a loudspeaker.

It was the first of dozens of times I would see him. Short, dressed in a black suit and tie and the obligatory fedora of the time, he exuded a powerful, even mesmerizing presence, despite his rusty Chechen-language skills after so many years of speaking solely Russian in the Soviet military. His message was clear: The Chechen opposition to his rule was being financed and directed by Moscow, and war with Russia was just a matter of time. Moscow, Dudayev argued, was going to "invade" this tiny republic of 1 million people, which represented only about a half percent of the entire territory of the Russian Federation, of which the Chechen Republic of Ichkeria had never really been a voluntary part.

Dudayev then reiterated the grim litany of Chechen history seared into every Chechen soul, from fifty years of resistance to Russian conquest in the nineteenth century under Imam Shamil to the *vysyl*, or deportation, of February 23, 1944.

"Never again!" shouted Dudayev at the end of his speech.

When the mass demonstration was over, a man from the presidential administration named Kazbek led me down to a memorial that the separatist government had constructed to explain the national psychosis.

It was an eerie, chilling monument, dedicated to the hundreds of thousands of Chechens deported en masse by dictator Joseph Stalin nearly fifty years before. There were no graves; rather, only *reclaimed* grave markers belonging to Chechen elders. After the forced send-off of the Chechens, the markers had been summarily ripped from graveyards and blithely used as building materials for paving sidewalks or roads in the now totally Sovietized Grozny, devoid of anything Chechen.

February 23, 1944, is the day of the Chechen deportations. Ironically and perhaps sadistically, February 23 was and is to this day "Red Army Day."

The previous night, every Chechen had been told to show up in central village squares early the next morning to celebrate another victorious battle against the Nazi foe. Instead Stalin's People's Commissariat for Internal Affairs (NKVD, the precursor to the KGB) quickly bundled more than 400,000 people into cattle cars and sent them—with almost no provisions—into exile thousands of miles away into the arid steppe of Central Asia on charges of collaborating with the Germans. (The Germans never made it to Chechnya, and only a tiny minority of Chechens actually had sympathized with them in other areas under Nazi control, but Stalin obviously feared that the Chechens were a security risk, given their long, poisoned history under Russian colonial rule.) A third of the deportees are estimated to have perished along the way of disease, dysentery, and dehydration; those who died were thrown out along the tracks.

"This is what the Russians have in store for us again," said Kazbek. Here was the key to understanding the upcoming dynamic. Dudayev was far from universally popular; he had many detractors in Chechnya, perhaps well over half the population. Thus the war to come would be one of *resistance*, not formal *independence*. The memory of the deportation distilled this into a potion.

Regardless of what they thought about Dudayev, his often erratic behavior, and evidence that after a life in the Soviet military he had little knowledge of the Sufi-type Islam practiced in Chechnya, the overwhelming majority of Chechens would fight for their homes and land, the deportations still fresh as yesterday in their minds.

There were repeated flare-ups throughout 1993 and 1994 between Dudayev and his detractors. Each attempt by the Chechen opposition to topple Dudayev ended in failure, his supporters far more motivated than his Moscow-financed and more Russified foes.

Finally, in August of 1994, I attended a sizable Dudayev press conference in his presidential palace. He had called the gathering to announce, asserting complete certainty, that Russia was planning a "large-scale aggression" against Chechnya, an intervention. Although it was widely reported in the press, the claim was generally scoffed at as another one of Dudayev's incoherent ravings. And, anyway, what kind of a war could a few thousand lightly armed Dudayev-loyal Chechens expect to wage against the mighty, thousands of times larger and better-equipped (as was thought at the time) Russian military machine?

The answer turned out to be a mind-bending war to make one's hair stand on end, unequal as the two forces were.

It was about to begin.

GROZNY

It was evening on November 26, 1994, in the Azerbaijani capital, Baku, when the phone rang. It was the desk in Moscow.

"Grozny has fallen," the editor told me. Battles had raged all day, the Moscow-backed Chechen opposition had taken the presidential palace, and Dzhokhar Dudayev had fled. At least that is what the Russian government information agency TASS was telling the world.

There was no independent confirmation, and cell phones did not exist at that time. So I phoned Eldar, our Azerbaijani driver. Together with Adil Bunyatov, the Azeri cameraman killed a year later filming an army mutiny in his homeland, we sped away from Baku, up the Caspian Sea coast toward Grozny, an eight-hour drive.

We arrived in the city well after dark, but it was clear something bad had indeed taken place, and we drove right into the middle of it. Flames spewed from broken overhead gas mains. There were no civilians silly enough to be on the streets—only men with weapons, some injured, delirious, or aggressive. We slowed at an intersection on the main avenue, heading toward the presidential palace. Two fighters forcefully stopped our car, ripped opened the rear door, and lifted in a wounded pro-Dudayev comrade, whose leg was bleeding profusely. They shouted, steering us toward a hospital, where we delivered the moaning man to the front door, his comrades dragging him inside.

A destroyed Soviet-vintage T-55 tank adorned the yard of the presidential palace, its turret blown off and lying upside down on a lawn. The palace windows were missing, but the lights inside were glowing.

I entered, not sure what to expect. On the first floor I found Aslan Maskhadov, Dudayev's chief military commander, calmly giving a live televised update from an improvised studio. He was denying the reports that the "rebels" were in control: That was clear by his mere presence.

Clearly, the TASS report cited by my Moscow editors was wrong, and no doubt willfully so. Next I ascended the stairs to find Movladi Udugov, Dudayev's information minister (sometimes dubbed the Chechen Goebbels), gun in holster, casually stepping over smashed glass, and followed him into his office. "TASS says that the city has fallen to the opposition," I told him.

"What are you, some sort of idiot?" Udugov barked. "Does it look like to you that the opposition is in control?"

He then offered to let me call my desk in Moscow on the single phone line that still functioned.

"Where the hell are you?" shrieked desk man David Lundgren upon hearing my voice.

"Grozny, inside the presidential palace," I replied.

"But that's impossible!" he shouted. "TASS just ran a bulletin saying the presidential palace is on fire and the city has fallen to the opposition."

"I'm telling you I'm standing inside the information minister's office as we speak," I said. "Nothing is on fire. There aren't any opposition guys around."

The information minister, Udugov, then grabbed the phone and spat out random figures, telling Lundgren that one hundred opposition fighters had been killed and two hundred captured during the day's fighting. (Just minutes later, he rehashed those numbers, telling me that two hundred had been killed and one hundred injured. Udugov, a rabble-rousing opportunistic propagandist with a known penchant for beer and bacchanalia, despite a later "conversion" to strict Islamist piety, was never much for exact numbers.) He finished with an admonition: "CANCEL YOUR SUBSCRIPTION TO TASS!" he shouted to the desk man in Moscow, slamming down the phone.

"But what about Dudayev?" I asked. "They reported he fled."

Udugov sighed, picked up the phone again, and dialed a number, handing me the receiver.

"Ask him yourself," he said.

The phone rang twice, and then a male voice answered with a simple *da* (yes).

"Hello," I replied in Russian, introducing myself and explaining the reason for my late-night call to the supposedly ousted president of the outlaw Chechen Republic. "Where are you and what are you doing?"

Dudayev calmly said he was at home, about a mile away, and eating a bowl of soup.

"My wife, Alla, makes very good borscht," he said. "Do you have any more questions? If not, I'm a bit busy, as you can probably imagine."

I might have asked when the real war was to begin, but that was days away, when Russian planes began bombarding the city. As Chechen elders in the square performed the *zikr*, furiously prancing in a circle chanting the word "Allah," Dudayev held an impromptu press conference on the top floor of the presidential palace, his facial expression unchanging as the bombs began to fall in midafternoon, hitting the main airport, among other targets. Press counselor Udugov seemed almost amused as we terrified journalists hit the floor or crawled into the corners of the room. "All right, journalists into the basement," said Dudayev matter-of-factly as he closed the press conference.

Despite the Chechens' confidence, not many believed they would stand and fight, given the incredibly long odds. The Russians could blow the city to smithereens. A few days before the Russians formally intervened, I found Udugov speaking on an open telephone line in his office, cracking jokes and cheerily ordering money paid for some unspecified weapons and military-type radios.

I asked him in my pragmatic Western train of thought: Is it not far-fetched to believe the Chechens could win, with just a few thousand lightly armed fighters against the mighty Russian military machine?

"If you fight and lose, you still have won," he smilingly told me, showing absolutely no signs of worry, let alone irritation with my question.

The response from many Chechens was similar. Among them was their bizarre "foreign minister," a Jordanian Chechen diaspora re-émigré by the name of Shamsuddin Yusuf. On his office wall, a poster proclaimed: CHECHENISTAN: VACATION PARADISE. Outside the presidential palace, there was a handwritten note next to the main entrance, immeasurably telling in its against-all-odds spirit of defiance:

> All volunteers arriving from other regions of the CIS: Please go to the General Staff of the ChRI [Chechen Republic of Ichkeria]. Volunteers are needed for the following specializations: 1/ Tank operators of all types 2/Artillerymen a. Mortar-firers b. Experience with BM-21s, GRAD-RC30 of all types.

THE WAR had begun.

The Russians formally sent in troops on December 12, 1994. They continued to bomb targets in and around the city. The Chechens engaged them in several battles in the north of the tiny republic, in hit-and-run, delay-the-inevitable actions. As the fighting got within a few kilometers of the city, most journalists pulled out, given the level of danger and having no way to file stories from Grozny in the pre–cell phone era, satellite phones being an extraordinarily expensive luxury then.

Our lifeline to the outside world was "The Elephant"—a first generation, Norwegian-made satellite telephone and the lone one belonging to Reuters. It cost $55,000 and up to $40 a minute to use. It weighed nearly a hundred pounds, and took as much as a half hour just to set up. It worked only on electricity, not batteries, but it allowed us to continue reporting when we came across a generator—or a power line not already taken out by the war.

The Elephant was designed for ship-to-shore communications—and thus it included a Telex attachment, which turned out to be something of a curious curse. I always left the thing on at night, pretending to sleep between the shelling and bombing around Grozny. The phone was zeroed in on a satellite that covered the western Pacific Ocean. All night, the Telex printer spewed out reams of thin rolled paper. I would get up, thinking it could be an urgent message from London or Moscow. Instead, I typically found the following type of dispatch:

> MAYDAY, SS Perth, South China Sea, emergency on board, crew member injured while using chainsaw, intestines hanging out of his guts. Immediate assistance required. END.

THE CITY WAS emptying out, forlorn except for Chechen fighters milling about. "When someone breaks into your house, you shoot to kill, whatever we think of Dudayev," one of them told me behind the presidential palace. He and other fighters were overseeing a group of captured Russian troops as they tried to repair a few tanks the Russians had either lost in combat or abandoned as they broke down.

The Chechens behind the palace were cooking up a meal—in this case slaughtering a lamb for supper. I marveled as one of them, with extraordinary gentleness, held the lamb by the head, carefully but quickly slitting open its throat, and then pouring water into the open slit, the lamb's eyes still wide open with a mixture of amazement and fear. "What's the water for?" I asked naively. "It's to reduce his thirst, so there is less suffering," he answered matter-of-factly.

I headed back into the presidential palace to gauge the mood. The only high official around was Vice President Zelimkhan Yandarbiyev, an aloof, bearded, ideologue poet.* Above his desk was a birdcage with two parakeets inside, their contented chirping occasionally drowned out by shelling.

"You're still here?" he asked. "You might want to think about getting out. The real bombing may start tonight," he told me, saying that negotiations to head off a full-scale war had gone nowhere.

---

* In 2004, Yandarbiyev was killed in a car bombing in Qatar. A Qatari court tried and found three Russian intelligence agents guilty of his murder. They were eventually extradited to Russia, where they received a hero's welcome.

That night, the dwindling group of reporters among us sat in the lone open eatery, a misleadingly named restaurant called and spelled "Lasagnya" (the menu bore no relation to anything Italian or Mediterranean) on Grozny's main street. We engaged in that journalistic specialty—speculating and pontificating with audacious assuredness.

The Chechen government television station blared from a screen plopped onto the bar, offering a wild mix of local music videos, self-help programming, and battle cries. One segment featured a commander in fatigues giving lessons, using a pointing stick and a diagram of a tank, calmly instructing fighters-to-be about the most vulnerable places on a tank's armor for an RPG or grenade launcher and how to go about this very possibly suicidal mission.

Later in the broadcasting evening were battle scenes of a Russian-language version of the Peter O'Toole classic *Lawrence of Arabia*.

Then more Chechen music videos, mostly about love and featuring makeshift backgrounds amid rosebushes and other romantic touches.

On went the journalistic pontificating.

"There is no way the Russians are going to carpet-bomb this city," said one reporter from London.

No sooner did the words slide from his mouth than did we hear the roar of a fighter jet overhead. Then the doors to the restaurant were blown open by a huge explosion down the street, and the blitz began.

After reporting the air strike on the center of the city to the desk that night, my reporting partner from Ukraine, cameraman Taras Protsyuk, and I fielded a frantic phone call.* We were ordered out of the city at

---

* Eight and a half years later, in 2003, I was back in St. Petersburg when a call came through on my cell phone: Taras Protsyuk had been killed in Baghdad, the very first journalist to die in the American war to oust Saddam Hussein. A US tank had fired a round at him as he stood on a balcony of the Palestine Hotel—where practically all foreign reporters were based—filming the first American troops arriving in the city. The tank round blew off his legs, and he bled to death. To this day, there is no concrete explanation as to the motive for having mowed down Taras with a tank round; speculations range from the fog of war to a mistaken impression that his tripod-mounted camera was in fact some sort of weapon, to more sinister theories that those who fired the tank round knew he was a journalist and simply did not care.

once by our boss in Moscow. Taras, a fiery, idealistic, and witty character who regularly scoffed at obvious threats to his personal safety, protested vigorously. We reluctantly, and with a sense of guilt, agreed after being threatened with being fired for insubordination.

But as we pulled out of Grozny in our Niva, we met hundreds of cars, headlights hazy through a driving snow and filled with silhouettes of men with guns. Unbelievably, they were heading *into* Grozny, not out like us, most visible in their cars armed with nothing but Kalashnikovs or other light weapons to confront the inevitable Russian tank and MiG fighter plane onslaught. It was almost as if they were enthusiastic about getting another chance to take on the Russians, and seen through the prism of the deathly deportations of 1944 and their associated privations, it was understandable.

We bedded down for the night in Nazran, the muddy capital of the tiny neighboring Russian republic of Ingushetia. Taras was livid about having been sent out of Grozny, where there was a war to cover. I told him to settle down. "You just don't understand. You can't, because you're an American," he told me. "I know that I am going to die sooner or later doing what I do" (which was covering every conceivable war there was). "It's just my fate!" Taras shouted at me in bitter irritation.

The next morning, Taras called the Moscow desk in the morning with some half-baked story that we would just approach the outskirts of Grozny to take footage of the oil-storage facilities that had been hit by aerial bombing and were now spewing black smoke into the air. We promised to stop and turn back if we saw any "front lines." We crossed at least three, but I told Moscow that we had simply encountered groups of Russian troops by the side of the road. After all, how does one define a "front line" in a guerrilla conflict?

By the first days of January 1995, following the disastrous New Year's Eve assault on the city, there were dozens of foreign journalists covering the Chechen war, but none remained permanently based in Grozny, the bombing and shelling having become incomprehensibly intense. There was no place to stay except in dark basements, and venturing outside even briefly was extremely risky. Despite the exercise of caution by most of them, about twenty foreign, Chechen, and Russian journalists were killed or disappeared in the first year of the war alone, in an area about the size of Rhode Island.

Though the press corps was formally no longer "based" in Grozny, "commuting" to the city was equally or even more hazardous, because it meant making two-hour car treks along snow-covered roads, almost randomly controlled by columns of nervous Russian troops or jumpy Chechen fighters.

This was a typical "day at the office":

I SET OFF for Chechnya with cameraman David Chikhvishvili from a muddy town in Dagestan, the mainly Muslim "autonomous" republic to the east of Chechnya. Along the way we meet a column of Russian APCs and tanks that train their guns on our car, an old BMW driven by a local driver who is taking five hundred dollars for the hair-raising round-trip to Grozny and back. The way into the city is blocked in three directions by Russian troops. But there is a dirt road that leads to the city limits and avoids Russian checkpoints. I can never figure out why the Russians are so sloppy in their "blockade" of Grozny other than sheer incompetence. There is always some way in, even if often laden with hazards. On the way to this "access road," we hear the telltale drone of fighter planes bearing down. The driver slams his foot into the brake pedal, and we throw open the doors in the middle of the road and jump into a drainage ditch. The fighter plane roars so loudly that our eardrums pop. Then there is a tremendous flash and a split second later a huge explosion as the bomb goes off less than a hundred yards away. Were we the target? It is hard to say anything other than this is another close call survived. Then we are back in the car and on our way again, southbound toward Grozny. The mud track ends and we are now back on the main asphalted road, taking a right at an enormous sign that reads G-R-O-Z-N-Y in concrete letters standing about ten feet tall. The name means "threatening" or "menacing" in Russian, as if one needs to be reminded that the town was originally established as a forward encampment for the czarist conquest of the Caucasus.

There is a flat open space in front of the sign that has been cleared out to make way for an impromptu morgue. Someone has taken an enormous roll of material, evidently from a textile plant, and placed it upright. Thus those who recognize the corpse of a loved one can wrap them up and take them home for burial in the backyard in town, or in the ancestral village in the mountains if the bereaved family can make it there. The corpses are in varying degrees of decomposition. As badly rotten ones are taken away to be tossed into mass graves, fresher ones are deposited and lined up.

One is a Chechen fighter, recognizable as such only because he's still dressed in fatigues—otherwise it's difficult to tell who he is. His head is missing down to the lower jaw, and the lower part of his skull is soup bowl shaped—the inside of the skull bone shimmers as if a car wash man buffed it to a high shine. Next to him is a woman, who looks to have been anywhere from forty to sixty when killed, her hair long caked into a lumpy form, like an old rag doll. People search for their missing by circling around the line of corpses, trying to find any discernible feature, and we begin filming the grisly ritual. But the war is getting to people's nerves, and the deference reserved for foreign journalists during the first days of the war is already fading. For some, we are at best a nuisance; at worst, perceived fabricators or spies. A middle-aged man aggressively approaches us.

"What are you reporters here for?" he growls. "You film all of this and then you don't show any of it. Nothing changes. You just need it for your own purposes."

My cameraman, David, at six foot four and with an expression that projects a readiness to pounce on anyone who insults him, is a man with a notoriously short fuse.

"We need this?" he shouts at the man, barely able to restrain himself. *"We need this?!"*

The man berating us shuts up. David finishes filming, and I snap a few photos and take some notes. Then we move on into the heart of the city, getting to the heavily bombed Chernorechiye ("Black River") suburb before the driver balks and refuses to go any farther. We randomly meet a rebel fighter who, after a full-speed sprint along a wall, leads us through a courtyard and into the cellar of an apartment building. We expect nothing more than a shelter but instead discover ourselves inside an elaborate, underground hideout—and a beehive of activity. Below the lifeless steam pipes are rebel commanders, a field hospital, a "deputy Chechen foreign minister," and many women volunteers, some in their sixties, working as nurses.

"Tell the West to send humanitarian aid," chortles one aging nurse. "Send us bullets and bombs," she jokes.

It is now time to reverse our running steps along the wall and get back to that place in the Chernorechiye District where we left the car and driver and then get out of town and back to Dagestan in time to file for the nightly news cycle—and then wake up in the morning after a restless sleep without dreams (or at least none that I can recall) to do it all over again, albeit with a daily variation of danger.

It was inevitable that the Russians' superior firepower would eventually allow them to take Grozny. It was simply a matter of destroying the central parts of the city block by block, gradually driving out the cellar-dwelling Chechen fighters, and this is precisely what happened. In early February 1995, in the last district they still had a toehold over, I met the chief Chechen commander—Aslan Maskhadov, driving with a lone bodyguard in an unarmored jeep. Renowned for his almost meek, mild manner, he placidly told me that the loss of Grozny was nothing to be overly concerned about. I was surprised to hear this.

"The main thing is that people now know how to dig a trench, how to handle a gun," he said. The fighters withdrew into the mountains; the Russians kept up their attacks, taking village after village and pushing what was left of the resistance deeper into the southern part of Chechnya. Some began predicting the demise of the rebels. International interest in the story waned.

This of course did not mean the war was anywhere near an end. A massacre by Russian troops in the town of Samashki, population ten thousand or so, in April 1995, again attracted the world's attention, but unfortunately only after it was too late. The war correspondent Thomas Goltz and I spent a week trying to somehow get into the town, which Russian forces had blockaded and were shelling and bombing. After failing to subdue a small band of fighters inside, a large group of Russian troops went on a rampage in the village. When we were finally let in, we found house after house where people were gathering burned bodies to bury; the Russian troops had used flamethrowers, or grenades tossed into basements, to "pacify" the inhabitants. More than 100 and as many as 250 civilians were killed.

The Russians had also taken Grozny by destroying it, but the rebels fought on the mountains, where they were subject to relentless, but often ineffective, artillery and air barrages.

THEN, ON A lazy, hot June day in 1995, there was a seminal event in the world of guerrilla tactics and terrorism.

Two military-style trucks, escorted by several apparent police cars, rolled northward through the wheat fields of the Stavropol Territory, one hundred miles north of Chechnya, finally reaching the outskirts of the town of Buddyonovsk. There the column finally met a roadblock its leader, the by now legendary and notorious Chechen Shamyl Basayev, couldn't bribe his way through. He decided to make what he thought would be a last stand.

Shamyl Basayev, a onetime builder, Moscow student, and computer salesman, was already a registered terrorist/separatist ideologue: In November of 1991, he and a comrade hijacked a plane to Turkey in a publicity stunt to draw attention to the Chechen independence cause. In June 1995, he and his men engaged in the most brazen act of the war to date— making good on his threat of bringing the conflict outside of Chechnya and into the Russian heartland.

(Basayev's exact destination may never be known. Some speculated Moscow, or perhaps a chemical weapons complex not far from

Buddyonovsk. More than likely, Basayev and his band stopped in Buddyonovsk only because that's as far as they were able to proceed without
detection [or as far as they got before actually stumbling on a cop or two
who wouldn't take a bribe]).

Complete bedlam filled the streets as Basayev and his gang fought
their way through the provincial town, with events broadcast on live
Russian state TV. First they struck the main police station, then took
over a couple of other buildings before finally deciding to make a last,
suicidal stand at the local hospital, a sprawling old complex of buildings
that had once housed an Orthodox monastery. The Chechens herded together over a thousand hostages to use as human shields.

I arrived late the next evening on a flight from Moscow, via the main
regional airport. As we reached the outskirts of Buddyonovsk, trigger-
happy Cossack volunteers with shotguns had only minutes before shot
to death a female Russian journalist who apparently failed to slow down
quickly enough at their checkpoint. The center of the city was a chaotic
mix of burned-out cars, hysterical locals with relatives inside the hospital, and Russian troops and police, who were helpless to do anything lest
Basayev make good on his pledge to blow the hospital to kingdom come
should they storm it.

Basayev's demands were bold and basic: a cease-fire, the withdrawal
of Russian forces from Chechnya, and direct peace talks with Boris Yeltsin's government. But Yeltsin was in Canada at a G-8 summit, and his
lieutenants dragged out negotiations, telling Basayev at one point that
they had gathered over two thousand ethnic Chechens from the area
around Buddyonovsk and would slaughter them if he didn't release
the hostages. To show he meant business, Basayev responded by ordering half a dozen Russian servicemen hostages shot in the courtyard of
the hospital.

As dawn broke on the fourth day of the test of nerves, Russian Special
Forces tried to storm the complex. The Chechen terrorists held up some
hostages as human shields in the hospital windows. The fighting raged
on and off all day, punctured by periodic telephone exchanges between
Basayev and Russian negotiators, now led by Russian prime minister

Viktor Chernomyrdin. (President Boris Yeltsin had dropped out of sight with a supposed ailment.) Faced with a mounting toll of over a hundred civilian deaths and the fact that the Chechen suicide squad still held hundreds more hostage and with live world television coverage, Chernomyrdin caved in, which probably saved hundreds if not thousands of lives, for the time being at least.

As a precaution against Russian duplicity, Basayev demanded and was given some one hundred of his hospital hostages—including some who went voluntarily, among them several Russian reporters—to take with him along his homeward journey, to be released once he and his men were safely back in the mountains of Chechnya. The convoy consisted of a couple of buses and a refrigerated truck with about a dozen bodies belonging to his fighters inside. Cameraman Zhorra Vardzelashvili and I followed behind in a jeep.

The column moved slowly, rarely faster than forty miles an hour, passing through the golden wheat fields of the Stavropol Territory. The sun began to set. Mosquitoes pranced in the dimming light. Russian military helicopters constantly trailed the convoy overhead. Every once in a while, we would stop, allowing the would-be suicide squad and their hostages (many probably suffering from Stockholm syndrome) to stretch their legs, and me to set up my satellite phone and call in the latest details of the progress of the odyssey after talking with the fighters. They all said the same thing: They had fully expected to die during their mission, and had never expected to return to Chechnya.

Shamyl Basayev snoozed most of the way back, slumped in one of the bus seats, catching up on some one hundred sleep-deprived hours of staring certain death in the eye.

Basayev had plans to drive through central Grozny in a show of bravado once the convoy arrived back in Chechnya, but the idea was vetoed by Chernomyrdin on the logic that Grozny was full of humiliated and liquored-up Russian troops, and a shot from one could spark another round of uncontrolled bloodletting. The Chechen commander apparently agreed with this wisdom, and instead of heading straight for Grozny, the column took a circuitous route though the deserts of northern Dagestan. As darkness fell, warplanes replaced the tracking helicopters, pouring out a constant stream of flares, illuminating the desert night sky like fireworks.

We finally parted ways with the convoy in the middle of the night during a rest stop in the desert.

CONTRARY TO PREDICTIONS that the Russians would ignore the agreement, peace talks did begin, with international diplomats arriving to mediate in Grozny. The Russians also symbolically pulled some troops out of Chechnya. But they left others intact, which meant the fighting slowed but did not stop. Haggling over a proposed peace deal lingered for months before breaking down.

To complicate matters, Dzhokhar Dudayev, the separatist leader, was assassinated on April 21, 1996, while speaking on a satellite phone from the foothills of the southern Chechen mountains. The Russians had homed in on his satellite phone signal and launched a missile. It exploded a few yards from where he had been speaking, killing him almost immediately.

Meanwhile, I continued to make rotational reporting trips into Chechnya as the months dragged on, living in private homes that had somehow escaped destruction and paying the owners for room and board. My host was Rosa, a huge Chechen woman with a screeching laugh who professed to be a member of a "women's fighting brigade" and thus an implacable foe of the Russians. Who knows whether she ever really saw any battle, but she was making quite a windfall on the war correspondents staying at her cramped one-story house that lacked indoor plumbing. (Her rebel credentials came into question when I accidentally discovered a stack of papers under my bed—Rosa's forms, requesting financial compensation for war damage to her undamaged house, from the Russian-installed authorities in Grozny. At the time, taking money from the Russians was considered treasonous among the fighters.)

Rosa did seem to have a good ear for information, and a nonstop mouth to broadcast it with. "I'm telling you, Basayev is going to retake

Grozny within a month with every fighter we've got, or his name isn't Shamyl Basayev!" she shouted at me.

I wonder who else heard, because the prediction seemed odd. The Russians and Chechens were negotiating again, and this time it was President Boris Yeltsin himself who had given the go-ahead for peace talks. The war was terribly unpopular in Russia and threatening to ruin Yeltsin's reelection chances, bringing the possibility of a return to power by the Communists. It did not make tremendous sense to me that Basayev would be planning some suicidal assault on Grozny, which was still jammed to the teeth with Russian troops and checkpoints.

But Rosa's words made me curious. I set out to find Basayev. He was, predictably for a very wanted man, not easy to locate, especially after Dudayev's death-by-sat-phone. He moved from one mountain hideout to the next. Along for the ride across boiling rivers and broken roads in our old Niva driven by our Chechen driver, Musa, was Carlotta Gall, now with the *New York Times,* collecting ever more information that would establish her as the Martha Gellhorn of the early twenty-first century.

We spent one night at a safe house in the mountains, friends of Musa's. Our hosts seemed nervous, and I soon figured out why: Musa whispered that they were embarrassed at not having any meat to serve their guests; so embarrassed that they could not bear telling us themselves. Still, they tried to put as festive a face as possible on the situation, serving us long green boiled wild garlic shoots collected in the forest, a diet that had kept fighters hiding in the mountains from going hungry.

The next morning we set out again in the jeep, heading for Basayev's ancestral village of Vedeno on a rutted road with a steep incline. The town (really just a collection of farm-type houses) went back and forth between Russian and Chechen control during the war. Now it was in Chechen hands again. Musa meandered through his network of contacts, and eventually we were taken to Basayev's family home. Its windows were all blown out, the dwelling rendered inhabitable by bombing. Russia's "Enemy Number One" was, wisely, not hanging around at home. But arrangements for a rendezvous were made.

We drove up to the house. Shamyl Basayev, some comrades-in-arms, and Basayev's father, a small, taciturn man turned bitter by the war, were waiting.

Basayev, looking clean and dressed in blue camouflage, ordered some chairs pulled up to an old wooden table in the yard outside his bombed-out family home. We began talking over tea warmed in a kettle over an open fire.

Years later, Basayev became perhaps the first terrorist to actually *embrace* his label as a "terrorist," saying he was no different from the Russian army—whom he also called terrorists for killing Chechen civilians. Basayev always had a wry sense of humor, but as the war years wore on, it seemed to become more forced, sardonic, tired, and bitter.

He railed against the peace talks with Moscow, saying they would bring nothing.

"It's just another fiction," he snarled. "They don't want peace. They're just using this period as a chance to bring in fresh troops and break our momentum. Now we Chechens are basically helping Yeltsin get elected," he told us.

Nonetheless, Basayev said he would "accept orders" from the Chechen separatist leadership.

"But I'll insist on taking harsh measures," he added, hinting of "something to come," leaving me wondering if it was just a bluff or if he was pondering some new Buddyonovsk-style attack. About that event, Basayev was adamant.

"Buddyonovsk wasn't terrorism," he rebuked me sharply. "It was a 'coercion to peace.' Is it not terrorism when the Russians deliberately target Chechen women and children?"

Eleven members of his extended family had reportedly been killed, he said, several of them just before his raid on the Russian town of Buddyonovsk. He had yet to take on the cloak of hard-line Islamism that he adopted in later years, or even come close to embracing the label of being "Russia's Enemy Number One," which he would wear like a badge of honor until his death, blown to bits while riding a truck piled with explosives in 2006, on its way to another attack. He was a hardened man, but one still capable of delivering an impish message with a wink as we finished our tea.

"You'll probably want to stick around Grozny this summer," he said slyly.

Something big was up.

A MONTH LATER, Shamyl Basayev and his Chechen forces surrounded Grozny and the twelve thousand Russian troops bivouacked there. One version had it that part of the advance posse had entered the city disguised as part of a wedding procession. Then groups of fighters pinned down the Russians at their command posts. Reinforcements were rebuffed and entire columns destroyed in elaborately well-planned ambushes that resulted in huge Russian losses due to "friendly fire," that is, tricking Russians to fire at Russians. Meanwhile, panicked Russian TV reporters trapped in the city called in over live TV, telling the country that official claims that the situation was under control were a "dirty lie."

I was almost as unprepared for events as the Russian General Staff. In Tbilisi at the time, I caught a flight and headed to the area as soon as I heard the news, along with cameraman Sergiy Karazy. Even approaching the outskirts of the again-besieged city was preposterously risky. The Chechens had blocked road traffic from all sides as they closed the noose on the surrounded Russians.

Sergiy and I decided to try to get into Grozny by foot, all the roads closed to traffic by either the Russians or the Chechens, who had them pinned down. In stifling heat, we walked through a surreal and ugly landscape of modern urban warfare. Discarded Russian uniforms and body parts still lay around the city bus terminal as we passed, having already covered three miles or so. The stench of rotting flesh was everywhere, but more was in store.

From the smoggy, smoke-filled burning oil installations, we could hear Russian helicopter gunships overhead, signaling danger and Russian control of the air. But every time we heard one pass, it was followed by a whooshing sound from the ground—Chechen fighters firing make-shift ground-to-air "Stinger" missiles fashioned from air-to-ground rockets salvaged from previously downed attack helicopters. Known for uncanny resourcefulness, the Chechen fighters affixed wooden handles to the base of the rockets, attaching to them improvised ignition devices powered by nine-volt transistor batteries, the kind a cheap radio requires. To guard against the flames emitted when these "Poor Man's Stingers" soared skyward, the fighters had fashioned vulcanized masks from old car tires.

I was invited by a fighter to try one but passed up the opportunity to experience how effective the rockets and masks were. I don't regret this fleeting moment of lucidity.

Fighters we met said a command center had been set up near the heavily damaged central market area, and so we went there to cadge a quote or two. Word had it that the area was littered with Russian corpses and that local kids were using the heads of decapitated soldiers like soccer balls, kicking them up and down the streets.

I never saw or filmed that. Instead, as we approached the market, a familiar face emerged from the twisted metal of the market stalls.

There he was again.

"What brings you here?" asked Shamyl Basayev sarcastically. No answer was needed or expected.

I asked him if the Russians could retake Grozny.

His expression instantly changed, becoming stern. "Of course they can retake it. But it will cost them ten thousand dead and three months."

While Basayev jumped in a jeep with some of his armed comrades, Sergiy and I continued on foot. The Chechens had established their ambush positions; the Russian units were waiting for reinforcements that would never arrive. It was time to go.

We had walked for several miles when we passed a half-destroyed fire station. Chechen fighters swarmed about. They were skittish, dirty, and aggressive after almost a week or so of urban warfare and demanded that we follow.

We were led into the remains of a courtyard, where a wiry, thinly bearded man demanded our documents.

I immediately recognized him as Abu Musayev, the Chechens' feared counterintelligence chief and the man who was reported to have authorized the execution of my friend Farkhad Kerimov, the Azerbaijani cameraman, in May 1995. According to witnesses, Farkhad was approached by some Chechen fighters in the rebel-held south, who offered him a ride. Rather than an escort to Grozny, they marched him to a field, pronounced him a spy, and pumped his chest with twenty-two bullets. The accusation was paranoid hogwash.

Now Sergiy and I were standing in front of the man who likely ordered Farkhad killed on the basis of his war psychosis.

"We've been far too liberal in letting you journalists wander around our republic," Abu Musayev, oozing suspicion about our presence, remarked. He kept leafing through our passports and ID cards as if looking for some secret symbols.

"We know that you relay our positions to the enemy," he said.

I blurted something along the lines of "Why would we want to do that?"

It was pointless. Sergiy and I were at his unhinged whims. Unlike a fighter bomber raking our car with deadly rocket fire, or our happening to be in a building hit by a random bomb, this situation was specific and very personal. The "Hanging Judge" master of Chechen security was about to decide our fate.

Musayev was known for something else—some investigative journalists alleged he was also involved in giving orders to kill Fred Cuny, a legendary humanitarian activist from Texas. Cuny disappeared at almost the same time as I had been near the site of the massacre in Samashki in 1995. Theories abounded among the Chechens that he could have been a CIA spy—or that they may even have been deliberately fed such disinformation by the Russians. Cuny disappeared in those early days of April 1995 and was never seen again—just a month before Farkhad's disappearance and execution.

After pondering on that subject for what seemed to me an eternity, Musayev sort of smirked, looked around the burned-out firehouse, and handed us our documents back, obviously disappointed that he had no place to hold us or hide us—we'd only be a liability.*

"Get out of here," he said.

The day, however, was not over.

A Russian hard-line air force general, Konstantin Pulikovsky, had issued an ultimatum that he would bomb the city into oblivion if the Chechen fighters did not surrender. This set off a panic among the remaining, now-tiny number of Grozny residents. They scrambled to get out through the only exit—a rarely used road out over a ramshackle steel-plate bridge in the southeast of the city.

The morning of the day of the ultimatum for the Chechens to surrender, the day the city was to be incinerated, I awoke and Sergiy and I set off for the center of Grozny again, crossing the treacherous bridge in a car while wave after wave of refugees streamed out on foot.

With us again was my driver Musa, the Chechen with one lame arm. Before we crossed the rusty bridge, he stopped, gravely withdrew a piece of paper he had stashed in his vest, and began to recite verses from the Koran. He was not particularly observant (he drank alcohol copiously and smoked like a diesel locomotive). It was the first time I had ever seen him appeal to the Almighty.

Musa knew the back roads, which meandered around the city's refineries, exceptionally well. The only problem was that most of them were deserted and dusty and thus perfect places for laying homemade mines. A decade before IEDs (improvised explosive devices) became a household word of terror among US military personnel serving in Iraq and Afghanistan, the Chechen resistance to Russian occupation had started fashioning early forms of the deadly item in Grozny from glass jars of gasoline set with detonators. We both laughed nervously, and Musa uttered the standard mantra heard throughout the war.

"*Inshallah,*" he breathed. "[We'll only die] if God wills it," he said.

---

* Musayev was killed in 2000 during the second Russian-Chechen war.

The Lord allowed that we drive the gauntlet in safety, and we returned to Basayev's makeshift HQ in the market, where we had seen him the day before. With Russian shells raining down, there was almost no one around. We shot some footage of a couple of young fighters trying to get a captured Russian tank running and then drove down the street where my former landlady Rosa lived. I knocked on the door. She'd gone, like most others.* Just as we started to pull away, one of her neighbors, a tiny, birdlike Cossack woman we called Aunt Nina, ran out into the street. Aunt Nina was well known for her feisty tirades against both Chechen fighters and the Russian troops who had destroyed her Soviet-style satisfactory life. Already in her seventies and with no place to go, she had vowed to stay and guard her tiny house in Grozny no matter what. Now, with the still-intact parts of the once 400,000-strong city under threat of being leveled, she begged us to take her out. We piled her and one suitcase into the back of our jeep and headed back out of the city.

We were stopped just short of the rusty bridge by a group of fighters led by a man who identified himself as Commander Magomed, which is how "Muhammad" is pronounced in Russian. He checked our documents, showing particular interest in mine, before squeezing himself into the jeep and ordering us to drive to "headquarters." HQ was a shattered apartment block about a half mile away. Magomed got out and started talking in staccato Chechen with another fighter while Musa strained to eavesdrop. He did not like what he was hearing.

"They're talking about using us as human shields," he said softly.

Musa got out and approached the men. He threw around names of Chechen commanders he knew. Then another couple of fighters emerged from a basement, and one embraced Musa. It was difficult to determine the fulcrum moment, but something had changed. After another extended exchange of words, Musa wrapped his arm around the back of the apparent real commander in the odd gesture that served as the Chechen handshake, and we were allowed to go free. Magomed looked disappointed.

---

* Rosa was reportedly killed in Grozny over an unclear disagreement in the late 1990s.

The day was still not over.

When we got to the rusty bridge leading out of the city, we got out to join the stream of refugees and walked so as not to test fate and overload the creaky structure. At the far end, however, we met with an unpleasant surprise. A large force of Russians on APCs had arrived, evidently to cut off the last remaining road out of the city before General Pulikovsky's planned incineration. We drove up slowly as a group of five soldiers trained their guns on our vehicle. A few dozen yards away, an open-top jeep was burning. Two blackened bodies sat upright in the backseat, as if the flames would somehow die out at some point and they would just continue on their journey.

"Why are you defending these black asses?" seethed one Russian Rambo, using the ugly word *chornie-zhopy* to describe all Chechens, including Musa. "Don't you have enough blacks in America?"

Just then one of his drunk or doped-up comrades became distracted by a group of two or three cows in the distance and opened fire on the animals, felling them with ease, the cows moaning and writhing on the ground for a bit before expiring. To ease the tension, I delicately suggested that I had a few bottles of Orange Fanta inside the jeep and offered them to the soldiers. They guzzled them down as if they hadn't drunk for days and, friendlier now, let us pass.

In the end, the threatened firestorm never materialized. The ultimatum came and went, and it was clear that great divisions had opened in Moscow. Alexander Lebed, the tough-talking former general who won fame for his heroics during the Afghan war, won the upper hand, and another truce took hold. This one lasted, a peace accord was signed, and the Russians pulled out of Chechnya over the next few months.

I always wondered if the threat to level what was left of the city had been real or just bluster, whether the Russians would really go through with it. Why not, I thought, they'd subjected the city to everything else. Then I thought of the old saying that some men get a bigger kick out of knowing they could have killed someone than out of actually murdering.

The Russians would not be gone for long. They would be back again in three years to avenge their losses. By this time Chechnya had reached medieval standards of barbarism; killing, kidnappings, and the "independence" movement had taken on a decidedly radical Islamist hue. At the same time, a certain Vladimir Putin began his rise to the Russian throne.

THREE LIBERTINE SABOTAGE WOMEN

Yes, by December 1996, the last Russian soldier had left Chechnya. The impossible had become reality: David had defeated Goliath: the Russians' historical power humiliatingly vanquished by a few thousand Chechen guerrillas. Or so it seemed at the time. What the Russians also left were large parts of a capital, Grozny, flattened, tens of thousands dead or maimed, a steadily growing radical Islamist movement (since money and ideology had poured into Chechnya during the war), and warped psyches.

But if one could look past the rubble, there was still an atmosphere of victory-high, a belief in a new start. The wretched city came to life, renamed Dzhokhar-Kala (Dzhokhar City) in memory of the war-hero late president Dudayev. There was also residual revenge: The bizarre, ZZ Top look-alike warlord Salman Raduyev (he wore an enormous red beard and triple-sized sunglasses to mask the fact that half his face had been blown off in a wartime explosion) announced "Operation Ash" and promised to blow up a dozen Russian cities. Few took him seriously, and fewer thought he had the slightest thing to do with a series of bombings in Moscow years later—Raduyev had the bravado habit of taking credit for all sorts of explosions, even ones that later turned out to be no more than natural gas leaks from leaky ovens.*

---

* Raduyev was captured by Russian forces in 2000 and died in prison in mysterious circumstances, reportedly killed by other inmates or guards.

There was not only an election, there was a fair one (a major rarity in the former USSR of that time), conducted and approved by studious-looking European observers in expensive winter parkas. Former "suicide brigade" members put fresh-cut glass in a few pane-less window frames and festooned burnt-out storefronts with flashy campaign signs.

Shamyl Basayev, the terrorist, ran for the high office too. His campaign brochure trumpeted his personal accomplishments. "Shamyl made the only proper decision—he hijacked a plane," it read. Movladi Udugov (the "Chechen Goebbels") ran on a ticket of "Islamic Order"—though Udugov had never been considered observant until he reportedly became a middleman for cash from radical Islamist circles in Saudi Arabia and Pakistan. He played up the fact that he'd taken a second wife (and personally urged me to follow his example) in accordance with the Koranic injunction to protect widows and rebuild the population base.

In the end, it was the moderate Aslan Maskhadov who racked up a landslide victory, though I considered Basayev's 25 percent or so of the vote impressive for a self-described terrorist with no political background. Basayev accepted defeat more or less graciously and declared he would ascend into his mountains and turn to beekeeping. (The honey gig didn't last long.)

I stayed behind in Grozny to work on a few features, and out of a desire to explore the concept of "aftermath." My host was Musa, who had graduated from being our driver to having become our local "stringer," who called Moscow with occasional quotes.

On the night before I prepared to leave Grozny, Musa announced it was time to celebrate. Accompanying us was Ivan, a quiet, sensible ethnic Russian reporter friend of ours and Grozny native who had stuck it out though the war and then stayed behind after most ethnic Russians had left along with the Red Army.

"Celebrate?"

I wondered what Musa meant by the word. By six p.m. the streets of Grozny were deserted.

"Where are we going?" I asked Ivan. "Nothing is even open."

"You'll soon find out," replied Ivan with a smirk.

"*Zhirus!*" Musa grinned.

A *zhiru* is a divorced or widowed Chechen woman, or one considered past "marrying age," one who is exempt from all the traditional Chechen conventions of female chastity. But to call a woman a *zhiru* is not to call her a whore; it simply means that she has a social license to engage in sex.

Musa used his good arm to pull his coat over his lame one. "I'm going to my second wife," he barked at his first one, who in her gentle but vapid way looked neither surprised nor disappointed and kept sweeping the floor with an old broom. We headed out the door and got into his sputtering Lada, driving down Avturkhanov Street into town. Leafless trees, many with mangled or missing limbs from the months of bombing the city had endured, lined the median, while on either side of the street stretched row after row of windowless, burned-out early-twentieth-century neoclassical buildings—an occasional candle flickering behind thick plastic sheeting in place of glass in the odd apartment still semihabitable. The main square—always vast but now much larger due to the "removal" by bombardment of most structures that had once defined it—boasted the remains of Dudayev's presidential palace on the right and the pile of concrete rubble that was once the parliament building on the left.

We ended up in a neighborhood of the single-story homes that seemed to have gotten through the war more or less intact, and pulled into the courtyard of one. There was little sign it was anything more than a simple single-family dwelling. An electric generator hummed outside. Once inside, I realized it was a private restaurant-hideaway—probably the only one functioning in postwar Grozny.

We were ushered toward a corner of the one large room surrounded by plastic curtains with floral patterns. A waitress threw the draperies back. We entered and sat down, and the curtains closed again. Two bottles of vodka adorned the table, along with another of Russian champagne and a small dish of black caviar. The three of us—Musa, Ivan, and I—sat down; there were three other seats. Musa grinned like a Cheshire cat. Ivan played sheepish but quickly warmed up.

Within a few minutes the curtains were snapped open again just long enough for three women to be ushered through. In their twenties and thirties, they were stylishly but not provocatively clad in long, nearly ankle-length dresses, the hair of each adorned with the traditional Chechen female half-scarf worn loosely from the top of the head and ending in a knot at the back of the neck.

With the curtains now between them and the prying eyes beyond, the women doffed their head scarves and made it clear they had come to "relax."

Musa's female companion was a tall, attractive woman with reddish-brown hair by the name of Zina. She was twenty-eight years old, divorced, boisterous, and obviously headstrong. That a woman was going to drink alcohol at all was provocative enough in increasingly Islamifying Chechnya. She did not even wait for Musa to pour, grasping a shot glass and demonstratively projecting it in his direction. He obliged her.

Next to Ivan sat Fatima, a chirpy woman of about thirty with short brown hair. And placed across from me was Louisa, who gave off a warm, reserved air. I didn't ask, but she was also probably in her late twenties or early thirties.

Musa proposed a first toast to our female companions. Zina twirled her shot glass between her red-enameled fingertips. Fatima and Louisa complied with equal alacrity.

"Lawrence, there is nothing more powerful on Allah's earth than the beauty of a woman, and here we are blessed by three of the most beautiful women in the world. But I want you to know something else. Just because a woman is beautiful and feminine does not mean she is any less valorous or brave as the most fearless fighter or man of the gun."

At first I did not completely understand the correlation between the toasts and our female guests. Musa elaborated.

"All three of the women seated around you played a great role in the campaign," Musa said gravely, referring to the war.

I had met a few Chechen women among the fighters. Others had helped out as safe-house nurses or aided the fighters in other ways, cooking or keeping a lookout for the *federali*, or "federalists," as the Russian troops were known. One field commander, Doki Makhayev, whose hideout house I had frequented, had several female fighters in his entourage, but most of them had battle-hardened demeanors and mannish features. (Makhayev was later killed by the Russians while trying to escape his village hidden in a truck under a crate filled with watermelons.)

These female companions, in contrast, projected a kind of war-tinged elegance. It was hard to believe they had been taking potshots with AKs or lobbing grenades.

Zina explained that she had worked as a secretary at an iron and cement factory in Grozny that was later bombed into bits of concrete and twisted metal. With her feminine bearing, who would have believed that she was a sabotage woman? Zina went on, saying it was easier for her to go unnoticed carrying a handbag that contained a homemade bomb; she claimed, in once such instance, that she left the cheap Chinese Gucci-type knockoff filled with explosives and a detonator along a rail line used for Russian equipment transports. The cheap exploding bag had done some expensive damage, she proudly announced.

Fatima and Louisa, who had worked in various Chechen businesses and government departments before the war, used their charms to "move" explosive materials around the country. This meant employing a bit of cleavage to engage notoriously corrupt Russian officers and agreeing on prices for anything from RPGs to ammunition. They would later be left in a designated location, and the rebels would then pick them up. "The commanders find doing business with a babe more palatable, for some reason," Musa joked. I felt like I was in the middle of a scene out of the 1966 classic film *The Battle for Algiers,* except I imagined Algiers looked like Club Med compared to pulverized Grozny.

Musa and the three "sabotage women" raised their glasses to *touolum* (victory) in Chechen.

There were more toasts, a dinner of fish and chicken was served, and the bottles of vodka were quickly emptied and just as quickly replaced with fresh ones.

Zina eventually suggested that we all head back to her place. We piled back into Musa's Lada, six of us in a car meant for four, heading into a district close to the epicenter of destruction that was once the center of Grozny. We passed a long-since-burned-out tank with its turret blown off in the median, and turned right. Zina's building looked to be about half habitable; the front had taken artillery hits and it was possible to see into the apartments, opened like tin cans. We parked and marched up a pitch-black flight of stairs. Zina took out a key and opened a penitentiary-style metal door.

Considering the building's battered exterior, the apartment was comfortable, with a table, sofa, and an unexpectedly elegant hanging lamp. There were only two rooms, one large living room and a little room off to the side that served as a bedroom. Zina produced a bottle of cognac and tea, and Musa said something about "going to take a rest" in the little room. Zina followed him in and closed the door. Ivan and his girlfriend kissed passionately on the couch, gearing up for their turn. Louisa looked at me and smiled.

Suddenly, loud banging on the metal door erupted. Someone was beating on it with the butt of a gun, and loud male voices ordered us to open up in the name of the law, or specifically, in the name of the newly minted morality police.

Zina was there in a flash, almost in anticipation of the bust.

It did not go the way the two baby-faced officers anticipated.

"Who the hell do you think you are, *molokososi* [literally, "nursing babies"]?" screamed Zina. "*I fought in this war.* And where were you? Do you have any idea who I am?"

The two boys looked stunned at this rare reproach of Chechen male (even adolescent) authority, but still demanded to know who we were.

"None of your fucking business!" snarled Zina. "This is my apartment, and I will do whatever the hell I want with whomever I want." Then, as Musa, Ivan, and I looked on, Zina attacked, kicking and clawing and punching the morality squad boys, who were now thoroughly stunned. They backed away slowly, silently, glaring menacingly until Zina slammed the door in their faces, livid with having to prove anything to anyone.

The appearance of the morality squad at her *zhiru* door underlined a trend in postwar Chechnya. What had started as a secular conflict had become more infused with elements of religion, and a more radicalized, militant form of imported Islam was replacing the tolerant, Sufi-based traditions in the country, and this meant that Zina, who believed she had fought for Chechen freedom, was already much less free.

All the commotion had taken an unfortunate toll, with Zina and the other two "sabotage women" loudly denouncing the audacity of the morals police punks and Ivan's trying to settle them down. Time was now running out, it was getting late, and postmidnight was not an advisable time to wander about Grozny. We piled, all six of us, into Musa's tiny Lada to drop off the girls. Louisa's long dress became shorter with her sitting down on my lap. I'd never again come even remotely close to a self-described sabotage girl.

I never saw her again.

IT TOOK VERY little time for the more radical interpretations of Islam to begin to be institutionalized in Chechnya.

During the war, I witnessed the first "Sharia court" proceedings in the village of Komsomolskoye, where a well-known commander was given twenty lashes for "insubordination." It was much more political theatre than punishment. The commander may well have been insubordinate, but the lashes were not of a particularly vigorous nature—they were staged for the TV cameras. When the "lashings" were over, the commander proudly stood up and flashed a broad smile, showing no sign of physical discomfort.

But the theatrics soon gave way to sobering new realities.

In September 1997, less than a year after I had seen the three sabotage women, Chechnya's first public execution took place. Hundreds watched as a man and a woman convicted of murder were gunned down by firing squad in central Grozny.

The crowds of spectators grew as more executions followed: Later that same month, several thousand spectators assembled in Grozny's Square of People's Friendship. Half a dozen Chechen fighters, or by now "soldiers," lined two manacled men up against a wall in the square, and a firing squad raked their bodies with volleys of automatic-weapons fire.

Chechen officials said it was the only way to deal with a massive crime wave sweeping the land, explaining Chechens were not afraid of secular courts and would have sought blood revenge against secular judges. The names of the condemned and those of their clans were displayed in front of them to shame their relatives into "correct" behavior.

The three sabotage women, their war credentials increasingly worthless, soon fled Chechnya for Europe, where they are today.

A DISAPPEARANCE

Now "Independent Chechnya" became synonymous with a literal industry of kidnappings for ransom and random killings. Joining the several hundred thousand people already displaced by the war were tens of thousands more—those who had somewhere to go—escaping the medieval-quality anarchy. There were, of course, those odd exceptions: Those who could have fled but chose not to for one reason or another. One was a friend of mine. Her name was Galina Nizhelskaya. I met her during the war. She was working as a translator for the medical charity Merlin, which brought doctors to Chechnya from abroad.

Galina, in her twenties, was trying to complete her studies at the Chechen State University, which were regularly being interrupted by the war. She didn't have a high opinion of journalists, and she started with an aggressive but predictable sideswipe, no doubt fueled by the constant pumping for information aid workers face from them, as well as her precarious life state. "You are all so self-important, haughty, conceited, you hacks. You just want information to sell; you are all nothing more than speculators." I simply listened. I understood her need to vent. She was stuck in Grozny. I was not.

I noticed something else unusual about Galina. Her features were distinctly Slavic, round cheeks and a curly head of hair, vaguely resembling a younger version of the Icelandic rock star Björk. At the same time, her accent in Russian was imbibed by the giveaway staccato Chechen.

"You don't look Chechen," I told her.

"That's because I'm not. I'm Russian," she said.

Grozny, of course, was full of Russians before the Soviet collapse, but the ones left behind now were almost all elderly people with no place to go. There were very few young Russians, let alone ones studying at the Chechen State University. Galina explained matter-of-factly that Chechnya was where she had begun her education and that Chechnya was where she would finish it, even though she could transfer to another Russian university. I wondered what kept Galina behind in the smashed city.

The answer was a defiant independent streak. And the fact that Galina was—in a way—a woman without a country.

I asked about the tediousness, not to mention the danger, that life in Grozny meant for young people. Going out after dark was almost unheard of, and "there is no place to go anyway," she said. Galina agreed to a longer interview, at her grandparents', with whom she was staying, another reason to endure Grozny, despite the dangers.

It was a typical Russian-style house that had escaped damage thanks to being near the outer edge of the city. Galina explained that she stayed in Chechnya throughout almost the entire war. During the worst days, as Grozny was being pummeled, she moved to a village with a group of ordinary Chechen women, washing clothes, cooking for men, and waiting to go home.

This was even more unusual for a Russian in wartime Chechnya. I asked if she didn't feel somehow different, being one of the few young Russians left in pulverized Grozny. "No," she said. "People are people." But there was something uneasy in her eyes, a fatigue and a knowledge that she did not completely fit in anywhere.

One of the less noticed effects of the empire's collapse was the creation of all sorts of left-behind types who defied easy categorization. Galina was Russian, but not fully accepted in the rest of Russia as Russian. It was that Chechen accent, a *certain gesture*, a certain look. "They treat us completely differently," she sighed. "As if we are not Russian enough."

I saw Galina a few more times during trips to Chechnya. After the war ended, she sent a couple of letters with Grozny postmarks—the war destroyed the entire phone system, and Internet connections didn't exist.

I marveled that she was still staying behind. Grozny was getting more dangerous by the day. Under the separatists, kidnappings for ransom replaced Russian bombardments as the main danger; an entire industry of private jails cropped up, run by warlords. Grisly extortion demands—in one case accompanied by a film showing a foreign hostage with his finger being chopped off—were common. In one famous case, the heads of four British telecommunications workers held hostage for several months were placed neatly along the main highway running through Chechnya, placed upright like freshly cut jack-o'-lanterns, warnings that refusals to meet ransom payments would be costly.

In the spring of 1997, Galina unexpectedly called me from the nearby Russian city of Pyatigorsk. She had finally decided to try to transfer and finish her studies there. "Finally you got some sense in your head," I told her. With only six months to go, Grozny was getting so treacherous that her grandparents were going far away to live with distant relatives.

But there were two glitches. One was that admirable but dangerous defiant streak. The other was her Chechen accent, despite being Russian.

University authorities were supposed to help get Russians from Chechnya transferred to other institutions for free. "But I wasn't Russian enough for them," she told me again.

"They asked for six hundred dollars tuition." I said something about helping her with the cost. She violently rejected the suggestion. "Who do they think they are, Harvard or something? I've only got a few months to go. I'll make it, don't worry about me." Determined, back she went to her shattered Grozny.

Galina never called or wrote again. I hoped she had graduated and moved on. About a year later, I started to get a strange feeling. Finally, I called a number Galina had given me in the town of Buddyonovsk, where her mother lived, since there were no land or cell lines in Grozny yet.

"Lawrence, Galina disappeared in early May, a year ago," said the unknown voice at the other end.

Her mother recounted the all-too-familiar details: Witnesses said she had left the university building in midafternoon and headed for a mini-bus taxi stand. Two or three young men called to her from a car nearby; Galina seemed to know them. She got inside. The car sped away. Galina was never seen again.

She would have graduated in less than a week and was planning to leave Chechnya forever within days, her mother told me.

I promised to try to find out more. I called our Reuters man in Grozny, Musa, who had good connections with individuals in the Chechen government at the time. He had also known Galina from her aid work. He listened gravely, but clinically, as if it were a story he had heard too many times. "I'll get on it right away," he promised in a low voice.

Musa spoke with an overworked prosecutor who claimed to be working on the case. He told Musa that according to his information, Galina was alive. But there was no ransom demand, no phone calls, nothing.

I relayed the information to Galina's mother by telephone. She remained patient, but with each phone call her resignation deepened.

I made repeated calls to Musa. He went to the prosecutor's office several times. "They say they are working on the case." It was clear Musa had no more ideas. I kept Galina's mother informed, but she was no stranger to the dice roll that postwar life in Grozny posed. With each telephone call from me, none of them offering much reassurance, she responded with increasing and predictable resignation.

Almost another year passed. No information, no ransom demands. When it was clear that Galina was not ever coming home, I asked Musa exactly what he thought might have happened. Kidnapping was a business in Chechnya, after all. Why would the culprits not at least demand a ransom? Galina had even worked for an international organization, typical targets for extortion.

Musa paused. "Don't you understand? Human life has no value here right now."

Then he said: "Pretty girl like that, they could have just kidnapped her, used her, and thrown her out by the side of the road," he said somberly, and with the knowledge that even his inquiries were putting him in danger.

"Lawrence, I could keep asking, but I have a wife and children."

Almost ten years later, I called Galina's mother again, just to ask how she was getting on. Her voice had not changed, as if the disappearance had occurred yesterday. It was the shattered but collected voice of a mother whose lone child—a child of the empire, accepted neither as fully Chechen nor Russian—had disappeared into the thin air of anarchy and violence.

THREE BOYS SEEKING MARTYRDOM

It would be several years—2002—before I returned to Chechnya. By 1999, the place became such a no-man's-land of grisly crime, chaos, and kidnappings that very few outsiders, journalists included, dared visit. Reuters still had Musa reporting the occasional line from Grozny, but the situation was so treacherous—even for him—that he sent his entire family away from Grozny and into their home village at the foot of the Chechen mountains, where things were quieter and there was less trouble. I mulled a trip in early 2000 and rang Musa to tell him I was planning to drop by.

Musa was livid. "Lawrence, I'll kick your ass if you come down here and kidnap you just to teach you a goddamn lesson. You'd be sold ten minutes after you set foot in this place," he warned. "Just last week, one of my neighbors was kidnapped the day after she got here. She was nobody—just came to visit relatives and was Chechen herself."

THE TALK OF Chechen "independence" had by now faded away. The elected president Maskhadov was far too weak to rein in the gangs that had taken over under the banner of radical Islam. Shamyl Basayev, who had originally claimed to have abandoned his warrior ways and political ambitions to go into beekeeping, now fully embraced the so-called Wahhabi, or radical Islamist, movement, as did the "Islamist" Movladi Udugov—despite Udugov's reputed love of booze-soaked parties. Islamic "camps" opened, often staffed by Saudis and Pakistanis, to educate the Chechens in the ways of "true" Islam and wean them away from their traditional Sufi beliefs.

, Slowly but surely, the largely secular Chechen independence movement became infused with jihad ("holy war") and the creation of an Islamic caliphate across the whole of southern Russia, from the Caspian Sea to the Black Sea. The vanguard of this jihad, of course, was to be the Chechens under Basayev and his ilk.

The moment of truth came in August 1999 when a band of rebels led by Basayev invaded the neighboring Russian republic of Dagestan, proclaiming it the start of the campaign to create the "caliphate." With the exception of a few local Islamists, the Dagestanis (composed of some forty ethnic groups) did not support the unwelcome guests, who retreated to Chechnya after a few weeks of Russian bombing.

Then came a series of unsolved, mysterious apartment bombings in Moscow and another Russian city that killed almost three hundred people. The Chechens denied responsibility, and many suspected FSB (the Federal Security Service, the main successor to the KGB) involvement, but together with the invasion of Dagestan, the bombings were enough for Moscow to justify another war in Chechnya.

The Russians did not make the same mistake they had in the first war—instead of using infantry and sending underfed, confused conscripts to be cut to shreds, they bombed what was left of Grozny after the first Chechen war by air, block by block, with long-distance artillery and aviation. Musa stayed around for as long as he could. One day he sent Reuters a video of an eyeball in its socket lying on the driver's seat of a car that had been caught up in the bombing.

"This is really nightmarish," he told me, in an understatement that for Musa represented, even in his battle-hardened mind, deeply disturbed emotions.

In Chechnya War II, the Russians were also more cunning in another way—they banned reporters from the war zone altogether. Most news organizations forbade their reporters to go in anyway, given the security risks. The few brave ones who did make it in were often detained or deported.

Within weeks, the Russians, with their new policy of bombing even more intensely and engaging troops even less, pummeled the Chechen fighters into the mountains and took over Grozny.

Within a few months of the (second) Russian takeover of the city, journalists were relegated to weathering dog-and-pony shows organized by the Russian army. Highly scripted, they usually were full of glitches and unexpected events. I went on one. One day a Russian "handler" took me to a kiosk selling Coke and smokes in central Grozny. An irate woman so scorched the handler with anti-Russian epithets that he scurried away hurriedly, me in tow. "No point in this," he said.

The alternative was to take "unofficial" trips with dodgy Chechen characters who charged immense sums to smuggle us over the administrative border into completely uncharted waters; it was like journalistic Russian roulette, avoiding checkpoints, traveling in disguise, and always hiding from Russian troops or anyone else who could pose a danger.

I embarked on several such clandestine trips in 2002 and 2003 and made my last one with a character named Isa. The usual form was cloak-and-dagger stuff, hushed discussions about how much I needed to pay for my "tour" amid sworn oaths (if they meant anything at all) that I would not leave any information about how to find me while I was away in Grozny.

We met as arranged on the border of the Russian republics of North Ossetia and Ingushetia, which itself borders Chechnya. All I knew was that I was to find a car whose license plate number I was given. It approached and I got in, and the driver took a circuitous route down back roads to avoid roadblocks.

"Where are we going?" I asked.

"Someplace safe," came Isa's vague and unreassuring reply.

Isa was a small slender twenty-eight-year-old with a droopy eye who wore a solid green baseball cap and had the habit of constantly checking over his shoulder.

"It's too dangerous to take you to Chechnya today—it would be dark by the time we got there," he informed me. "We'll spend the night here in Ingushetia and head off in the morning."

We pulled up to a two-story building, the car passenger door coming so close to the building door that I could barely squeeze out and slip inside. Isa looked around nervously.

"Make sure no one sees you get out of the car," he whispered.

It was soon clear that we were in a building converted for use as a temporary center for refugees from Chechnya. Isa introduced his mother, Aina, who happened to be the director of the facility. It obviously doubled as a safe house for Chechen insurgents during the winter months, when life in mountain hideouts became unbearable.

We crept down a corridor and ducked into a room with a wood-burning stove and a cheap, steaming old kettle warming itself on a coiled wire heater. Isa switched from Russian into Chechen and gave Aina what sounded like a detailed set of instructions. Then he told me he had "business" to attend to. I was led into another tiny room with two cots and a mattress thrown on the floor. "Do not leave the room under any circumstances, do not to speak English, do not use your cell phone," he said sternly. "If you need to urinate, you will just have to wait until it gets darker. Too dangerous to go outside in the daylight." The thought crossed my mind that I had volunteered to be ransom bait.

Within a few minutes Arbi, a twenty-six-year-old fighter, walked in. He recognized me immediately, saying he remembered me visiting the house of Doki Makhayev, the Chechen field commander who was killed by the Russians after being found hidden under a load of watermelons. That had been years earlier, during the first war. I remembered Arbi as well, but he had changed. Then he had been a jovial lookout for the insurgents; now he was gaunt and had sunken, empty eyes. He was a shell of his former self.

A second, younger man named Ruslan sat on another cot. He was muscular and square jawed. We engaged in some small talk in Russian, and it soon became clear that neither of them fully trusted me. Many hard-core fighters thought journalists sneaking into Chechnya were FSB spies.

I turned on a miniature shortwave radio. Arbi asked if he could look at it. Slouched on a cot, he tuned in to a Koran reading on a Saudi short-wave station and drifted off listening to it, as if in a kind of trance.

Ruslan, meanwhile, paced the tiny room. He pressed his hands on his sides, as if something hurt. "It's my kidneys," he said. Ruslan explained he had spent several weeks in a Russian "filtration camp"—notorious places into which young Chechen men were routinely rounded up, inter-rogated, or tortured in an effort to net possible fighters. Ruslan said he'd been hung up by his hands and beaten repeatedly in the kidneys.

Both of the boys asked what I was up to. I told them I was mostly interested in getting to Grozny to interview an "emir" to whom Isa had pledged allegiance. Since the Chechen insurgents had essentially lost control over any significant territory to the Russians, the remaining fighters had split into groups of thirty to fifty or so, each overseen by a supposedly secret "emir" who coordinated what was left of the active fighting—mostly hit-and-run attacks on Russian troops or small sabo-tage operations, like the laying of primitive mines.

I asked them about their thoughts on religion, and the fact that all fighters were now considered Islamist fanatics by the Russians and many in the West.

Arbi distracted himself from his Koran broadcast to explain that ear-lier, he had not been religious at all, not even during the first war. It was during the second war, he said, after seven members of his extended fam-ily, including two brothers, were killed in one week of Russian bomb-ings, that he fully embraced Islam. He said his goal now was to become an Islamic martyr.

"What kind of Islam," I asked. "Like in what country. Saudi Arabia? Iran? Iraq? Kuwait?"

"Real Sharia hasn't been accomplished anywhere," Arbi replied.

Ruslan took several hours to loosen up, but once he did, he agreed to talk. Arbi, obviously the more radical of the two, left the room.

Ruslan told me of the miserable winters fighting in the mountains and said more insurgents were dying of tuberculosis than from combat, of eating tree bark to stay alive. He admitted he had been only nominally religious until he was put through an indoctrination camp in the town of Serzhen-Yurt, where "Arabs taught us" how we should live, how to be a real Muslim. "But I'll tell you a secret. It will never be possible to make a truly Islamic state out of Chechnya," he said. "We have our own Sufi traditions. There are different types of fighters. Some are sincere; some are just using the banner of Islam as a cover for their criminal activities."

I found this a stunning statement from a supposed resistance fighter.

"The truth is, I don't much care whether I live or die anymore. My life means nothing to me. So I fight for my own reasons. Of course I want the Russians out. Of course I fight in the name of Allah. But mainly I fight from a sense of rage at all the injustice." He paced the tiny rectangle of a room nervously and incessantly, back and forth.

Ruslan and Arbi openly stated that they had drifted into the ranks of the insurgency for personal reasons—revenge and rage.

Isa finally returned. He asked if I wanted to use the toilet, which was a hole in the ground a good distance from the building. First he went out to scout and then told me to move quickly outside, shadowing me right up to the outhouse door, where he then stood guard.

In the morning, another "contact" arrived to pick us up for the ride to Grozny. The exercise at the front door was the same. The car crammed up close to the entranceway, and I slid in again, unshaven, grubby in a cheap Chinese parka and a simple cap. There was a driver by the name of Said—who evoked the first inkling of confidence I had encountered since arriving. He was of even demeanor, smiled, and held a Kalashnikov rifle. Nominally at least, he was a member of the pro-Russian administration in Grozny. Isa obviously had some sort of deal with him.

"We'll be safe once we get to Grozny," he said. "If we get there," I thought to myself.

"Listen carefully. If we encounter a checkpoint, stay quiet. The Russians manning them are as nervous as we are, and they want to stay alive. They don't want to get mowed down either," Isa instructed. "So they keep a low profile. It's an unwritten agreement."

Said had documents that identified his position in the Moscow-backed Chechen justice ministry. This, transporting me, was a side business. "I've got government documents and a registered weapon; there shouldn't be any problems—they are bound to let us through right away. But if they question you, you tell them that we are on our way to the government HQ in Grozny and that we are doing a story on the new system of regional constables being established in the republic."

We took another circuitous route out of Ingushetia, across rolling hills dotted with small farms. Although the Ingush are extremely close to the Chechens ethnically and linguistically, there was now considerable bad blood between them.

Tens of thousands of Chechens had taken shelter in Ingushetia—some in a maze of refugee tent camps, squalid places plopped in the middle of unused fields, endless stretches of muddy lots where a modicum of order had emerged for aid-distribution activities.

Thousands more were "private sector" refugees—those who had taken up residence inside Ingush homes. The Chechens accused their Ingush hosts of profiteering from the war business by using them for the most arduous menial tasks and paying them nothing—instead of giving them rations and shelter in exchange for farm labor.

Isa looked out over the landscape, which was covered in low-hanging fog, and announced it was time to move. Traveling for six hours over a territory that should be navigable in one, we finally reached our destination in the northeast of Grozny, which had more one-story homes and was less damaged than much of the rest of the still-gutted city.

We screeched to a halt. Isa triumphantly got out of the car, borrowed the Kalashnikov from Said, and, laughing uncontrollably, unleashed at least ten rounds into the air in an act of ridiculous defiance before sprinting into the safe house. We were standing in broad daylight, no more than a kilometer from the main Russian-installed Chechen government complex.

Said's wife was making dinner. We tuned in to Moscow-backed Chechen TV. First came "cartoons" of a uniquely Chechen variety. Cuddly animals were instructing Chechen children not to play in abandoned and damaged cars (the streets were littered with them), not to pick up things that looked like grenades or unexploded cluster bomb munitions, and not to play with trip wires across the roads that might set off booby-trap bombs. Next up was an hour-long broadcast called *Missing*. There was no commentary, just announcement after announcement detailing how this or that person had disappeared in the middle of the night, often taken away by armed men driving armored personnel carriers. Sometimes there was a photograph of the victim, other times not. The predinner prime-time programming gave an ample sense of the unimaginable traumatization of Chechen society.

We spent the next two days darting around Grozny, me keeping as low a profile as possible while talking to as many people as possible. Isa never produced his vaunted "emir." Then he said something "undesirable" had come up and that it was too dangerous to stay in the city.

We sped out of Grozny. Isa popped in a cassette tape. The musician was Timur Mutsarayev, a shadowy fighter based in the mountains. He had become a kind of national bard for the insurgents.

During the first Chechen war, there had been a similar bard, Imam Pasha. But Imam Pasha sang of independence, Chechen pride, and the beauty of the Chechen mountains. Imam Pasha rarely touched upon Islamist themes in his songs, and I once attended an alcohol-soaked birthday party where he had been invited to perform. No radical Islamist would have played to a boozed-out crowd.

Mutsarayev was illustrative of the shift toward radicalism produced by the brutal wars. Isa sang along to the gritty guitar ballads, with lyrics like "twelve thousand mujahideen marching all the way into Jerusalem."

We passed one checkpoint on the way back to the border where I was to be dropped off, but the Russians waved us through with only a cursory check of Said's government-issued documents.

Isa turned to me and calmly said: "You know what, Lawrence? I have one dream in life. I dream of lugging a huge bomb to one of these checkpoints, detonating it, and killing as many Russians as possible."

As we got closer to the border, Isa confessed to me that he earlier harbored suspicions that I was a Russian agent with the FSB. "But we now know you're not.

"I also have to tell you something else. We had to leave Grozny early because some 'bad people' had gotten wind that a foreigner was in town. They were ready to pay $25,000 to 'buy' you."

"Thank you for not selling me, Isa," I said, wondering if it was just bravado talk, or a real case of the by now war-eroded Chechen tradition of *adat,* or deference and protection of guests.*

---

* Ironically, Isa himself disappeared a few months later. I received numerous calls from his relatives as to when I had seen him last. It eventually emerged that he himself had been "bought" or kidnapped for the same sum he was allegedly offered for me: $25,000. The ransom was paid and he was released, but his whereabouts today are unclear.

PART V (1998 – 2005)

RESURRECTIONS: THE ABDICATION OF ATHEISM

T he Soviet Union was an atheist country. Officially, that is. With the triumph of the Bolsheviks, Orthodox Christianity was either crushed or co-opted. Many cathedrals turned into toolsheds or grain silos. But for those who continued to imbibe the "opiate of the masses," the window was still left a crack open, even if the priests who presided over their flocks were often informers. In 1990, when newly unsealed KGB archives showed just how deeply the church had been corrupted, even dissidents and archivists who dug into the piles of documents were stunned at the scale of the miscegenation. Islam was no different. Mosques were shuttered, and the few that were allowed to reopen were usually staffed with the "Mullahs of Marx"—there to keep an eye on the faithful, or in other words, keep the "faith" to a minimum.

With the demise of the empire, countless cathedrals reopened. Millions were spent on constructing mosques, sprouting up like mushrooms in those areas of the former empire where Islam held sway. Even Judaism made a remarkable revival, despite the departure of over half of the former USSR's Jews to Israel (and the United States).

The 1998 reburial of Czar Nikolai II and his family, assassinated, soaked in acid, and thrown into a Siberian pit eighty years earlier, showed just how morally conflicted those in power were over this unfortunate history of deception and dishonor. The Russian Orthodox Church, evidently not wanting to admit the scale of its complicity in substituting Marx for Moses, even cast denial on DNA evidence that these were the real remains of Russia's last czar, Nikolai II and his family.

A NAMELESS BUNCH OF BONES

None were a complete set and all were missing something—a clavicle here, a rib there, chunks of pelvic bone there.

Each of the nine semiskeletons, charred by burning and soaking in sulfuric acid, lay under glass covers with metal handles, looking like so many steam tables at a buffet.

It was July 17, 1998, exactly eighty years to the day since the last of the Romanovs were lined up against a basement wall and executed by firing squad. For those not killed by the hail of Bolshevik bullets, bayonets awaited use.

The room is silent. City coroner Nikolai Nivolin identifies each bag of bones for me. In the center is the last czar, Nikolai II. Next to him is Czarina Alexandra ("Alix" until her marriage to Nikolai and conversion to Orthodoxy following her German Lutheran upbringing). Then there are the children—Olga, Marie, and Tatiana. The remains of son Alexei, the hemophiliac whom the czarina credited the mystic Rasputin with curing, had not yet been found. Neither had those of daughter Anastasia, whose absence had fostered a cottage industry of charlatans over the twentieth century who claimed to be either the princess or one of her descendants, often in the most unlikely of places. (Several years later, both bodies would be found in a nearby mass grave; routine DNA testing then put the claims of self-convinced pretenders to the Russian regency to permanent rest.) Finally, and perhaps saddest of all, we are shown the remains of the really unlucky ones: the family physician, Dr. Eugene

Botkin; the maid, Anna Stepanova Demidova; the family cook, Ivan Kharitonov; and lastly, a servant, Alexei Trupp, loyal to the last breath.

But the 99.99 percent certainty established by multiple teams of forensic experts that these disinterred bones are those of the Romanovs is not enough for the Russian Orthodox Church hierarchy. Their motivations seem obvious enough. They had publicly kept quiet about the regicides for eighty years. The church hierarchy, many of whom served under Communist rule (and collaborated with the Soviet regime), felt an obvious complicity in the murders of the Romanovs. Days before the reburial, His Holiness Patriarch Alexius II launches into a public tirade, saying there is no "proof" that these are the remains of the czar and his family. The church's official position is that once the bodies are shipped out to the former imperial capital of St. Petersburg, they would be blessed not as those of the last czar of Russia and his family, but as a bunch of nameless bones. The country's patriarch would not be there to confer the reinterment in the Romanov family crypt.

And the politicians? They are bickering too, hesitant, as if the scorched bones of the Romanovs might jump out of their glass cases and impale them.

Many of these are former Communist officials, and though the blame for the regicides can hardly be transposed onto them generations later, neither had the country or its leadership come to terms with what happened that dark day eighty years ago. While a cult of the murdered innocents and certain nostalgia for the imperial family have always existed in Russia, there are still many unreconstructed hard-liners who consider Czar Nikolai II to have been a bloodthirsty, incompetent tyrant and a blunderer into lost-cause wars. What is more, it is thought that his family was nothing better than a bunch of greedy gem- and gold-obsessed miscreants, hooked on the ravings of the likes of Rasputin.

The scene before my eyes in Yekaterinburg, in those days before the czar's bones were reinterred, resembled a sort of morbid circus.

The local governor in Yekaterinburg has hastily convened a press conference, emphasizing that he has always and steadfastly argued that the remains should be put to rest right here. The pugnacious mayor of Moscow, Yuri Luzhkov, perhaps smelling tourist dollars, has made his own heavy-handed pitch for them to be buried in Moscow. Finally, there is Boris Yeltsin, the unpredictable, sometimes playful, sometimes self-destructive president of the reborn Russian Federation. Over the course of weeks, the Kremlin makes contradictory statements about whether or not he will attend the reinterment. Yeltsin will come, he'll send a representative. He will, he won't, he will, he won't.

DR. NIKOLAI NIVOLIN, chief coroner of the city of Yekaterinburg, is a man of relatively few words. He is a scientist through and through, and the ecclesiastical and political bickering over the remains of the last czar clearly tests his nerves. Nivolin has spent eight years on this work. Yes, he is a scientific man, and yes, this is a forensic exercise. But for him it is also undoubtedly an emotional one. In fact, he cannot hide the livid scorn with which he regards the tawdry debates about the authenticity of the bones.

"How dare people with no competence in these matters call the results of our investigation into question!" he sputters.

Across town, in a simple cafeteria-style watering hole near the center of Yekaterinburg, I meet up with Alexander Avdonin, the ethnographer who has spent half his sixty-odd years first pondering, plotting, and then secretly excavating the czar's remains. The small bespectacled man slumps back in his chair as if he'd just completed a long journey through the muggy central Russian July heat. His eyes are weary, and he is drinking a cold beer to mask his impatience and boredom with my questions. Many of my inquiries seem sophomoric to him, and his bored facial expressions let me know that. I try to apologize by saying that I have been spending most of my time in the Caucasus Mountains, covering contemporary killings in places like Chechnya and Abkhazia, rather than investigating slightly older murders, such as took place here in 1918. With this he relaxes. Two of his historian companions pull up chairs, and I listen while they rehash technical details dealing with the work Avdonin has undertaken so far, and theoretical questions about the whereabouts of Anastasia and Alexei. Avdonin says he is more than confident in the information he has that will eventually lead to the uncovering of those remains as well. (Years later, they were recovered.)

IN 1976, FIFTY-EIGHT years after the Romanov regicides, Avdonin was approached by an unlikely partner in the hunt for Russia's royal bones. Gueli Ryabov was not only a well-known Soviet film producer, but a Communist Party member as well. More to the point, he was a man with access to secret archives about the extermination of the imperial family. A sense of intrigue that transforms itself into an obsession soon bonds the two—find the bones! They know the basics: The Romanov bodies were burned and doused with sulfuric acid and thrown into a temporary pit before being moved to another hole some distance away, a mass grave that was then covered with earth and railroad ties. But what if the burning and sulfuric acid destroyed all of the evidence? What if there are buildings on the site? And what if the Soviet government has at some stage secretly reexcavated the site and removed the remains in order to leave absolutely no trace that could ever serve as a shrine?

But Ryabov has stumbled onto what he believes is the key to unearthing the remains: a lengthy, highly detailed account of the burial given to him by the son of Yakov Yurovsky, the Bolshevik functionary who served as the chief executioner of the imperial family. Written in 1922, it would not be published until 1993, three-quarters of a century after the murders. The following is a slightly redacted version to give a sense of time and early-Soviet-era grammar and style:

On 16 July 1918, about 2 o'clock in the afternoon, comrade Filipp came to the house and presented me with the resolution from the Executive Committee to execute Nikolai. . . . He further stated that during the night, a comrade would arrive with the password "chimneysweep," to whom the corpses must be given, which he would bury and liquidate the job. . . .

Yurovsky then goes on in excruciating detail about how he vetted the executioners; how some had qualms about shooting the girls; how others wanted to use their bayonets to finish the job, but how the blades would not penetrate the blouses because diamonds had been sewn inside; how some soldiers tried to steal the gems once discovered; how he had to get the stones out of the soldiers' pockets; how their transport got stuck in a swamp on the way to a mine shaft to dump the bodies, until finally a second mine shaft is selected:

> Exhausted. Without sleep. Began to get agitated: Any minute we expected the Czechoslovaks to seize Ekaterinburg . . . [so] I decided to make use of the swamp. And burn some of the corpses. Unharnessed the horses. Unloaded the corpses. Opened the barrels. Placed one corpse to test how it would burn. The corpse charred relatively quickly. Then I ordered the burning of Alexei. At this time [the men] were digging a pit in the swamp where the cross ties were layered. [It was] about 2½ *arshins* deep, three *arshins* square. It was just before morning [and] burning the rest of the corpses was not possible because the peasants had begun coming out for work, and for that reason we had to bury the corpses in the pit. Laying the corpses in the pit, [we] doused them with sulphuric acid, and with this ended the funeral for Nikolai and his family and all the rest. . . . The initial burial spot, as pointed out earlier, was 16 *versts* from Ekaterinburg, and 2 *versts* from Koptyaki, the latter place being located approximately 8–8? *versts* from Ekaterinburg, and 1? *versts* approximately from the railroad line.
>
> Yakov Yurovsky,
> April–May 1922, Moscow

Despite Gueli Ryabov's ministerial pedigree and Soviet-era filmmaker fame, the work he and ethnographer Alexander Avdonin have cut out for themselves is highly sensitive, even dangerous. And it is conducted secretly, by the crudest of means. First, they use a sniper-rifle telescope (small enough to conceal in a coat pocket so as to minimize attention) to calculate the coordinates of the presumed location of the Romanov mass grave site. (The area of the abandoned mine is little changed from decades ago—a wooden fence still surrounds the mine shaft.) Next the stealthy crew begins probing the earth with a metal pipe until their sod soundings finally reach a blackened portion of earth in the terra-firma test tube. Avdonin and the other scientists immediately recognize this as organic matter that has been exposed to sulfuric acid. Then they excavate farther to see what will emerge. What the illegal team discovers is a wicked, blackened time capsule created by Comrade Yurovsky. First, a pelvis; next a couple of skulls. Forensic testing will eventually determine that these were once the heads of the Czar Nikolai II and Czarina Alexandra, while the pelvis belonged to the czar.

Ryabov takes the bones back to Moscow.

The year 1979 in the USSR under Comrade Brezhnev was not exactly the time to lug a couple of skulls into a lab for analysis, and especially not skulls belonging to the czar and czarina. But Ryabov manages to make molds of the skulls for the sake of history. A year later, Ryabov returns to Yekaterinburg so that he and Avdonin can reinter the bones in the original (that is, second) mass Romanov grave.

A decade passes, and it is now 1989 and the era of Gorbachev, Perestroika, and Glasnost. Ryabov, ever the showman, wants to go public. Avdonin, the empiricist, the academic, thinks it is too early. The former trumps the latter and gives a series of newspaper articles and a long interview to Soviet television, replete with details about the Romanov mass grave, but he deliberately gives false coordinates that are off by about five hundred yards from the real burial site.

The trickery is fortuitous, because within days of Ryabov's media circus, earthmoving equipment suddenly arrives at the announced location to dig enormous holes and pile the excavated earth into huge trucks, which are driven off to an unknown destination. Even if that destination might have been a top-secret forensics lab, one can only imagine the befuddlement of those tasked with finding the remains of the last czar and his family in the small mountain of late-Soviet dirt and rock. (Because that is precisely what their sifting yields, dirt and rock and nothing more.) Ironically, it would be only in early 1991—just months before the demise of the Soviet Empire—that the Kremlin would come up with the funds to begin the "official" exhumation of the Romanovs.

IT IS NOW less than forty-eight hours before the bones are to be put in caskets and moved to St. Petersburg, and I make my way back to the morgue again. Coroner Nivolin stands outside, feigning interest as he fields stock questions from journalists from everywhere: Moscow, Japan, Germany, Greece, England, and of course the gaggle of wannabe Romanov royalist hacks from my homeland, the United States. Since when did we become czarists? Is it the lingering fascination with events whose details are now being discovered eighty years later, *two* dead empires later, the Russian and now Soviet?

Nivolin looks on in barely disguised disgust as conscript soldiers hurriedly drive steamrollers to and fro, laying asphalt along the pitted road leading to his morgue. Another unit practices carrying mock coffins along the side of the same road.

"They can't rehearse and lay asphalt at the same time, so they have to take turns," he cynically tells me. "They killed him [the czar] in an inhuman way, and now he's being buried in an inhuman way."

The night before the transfer of the remains to St. Petersburg, the deceivingly soft-spoken but always determined Reuters TV producer Nino Ivanishvili manages to coax exclusive TV pictures out of one government official connected to the forensic investigation. The footage reveals that some of the bones from the czar's entourage have been kept in a cardboard box used to ship a computer printer. In exchange for the TV pictures, shot on an amateur camera, the uniformed man nervously agrees on five hundred dollars as his price for "sharing" such information, muttering a comment to Nino about supposedly using the money to buy embroidered cloths to cover some of the coffins.

The appointed time arrives and the coffins are carried out, one by one. The poorly rehearsed soldiers tilt the czarina's coffin into a precarious position, nearly dropping it, which elicits gasps. The czar's funerary motorcade makes its way to Yekaterinburg's main cathedral. The crowd is relatively small, and includes the man who took the five hundred bucks for the pictures of the bones being unpacked from the cardboard box. Tears slowly well up in his eyes. Then the Yekaterinburg duties are done, and it is time to move on to St. Petersburg.

There, things go far more smoothly. Boris Yeltsin decides to attend the reburial and delivers an eloquent speech about repentance and the need to close the door on a "bloody century."

For some of those watching, it might have seemed like bookending the birth and death of the Soviet Empire. Myself, I find succor in remembering Coroner Nivolin's words: "He [the czar] was killed in an inhuman way, and now he is being buried in an inhuman way. . . ."

But gradually the prevarications cease. The bones are finally universally acknowledged as his, and with that, reflection and closure finally becomes a possibility. . . .

A KGB CHURCH AND LATTER-DAY SAINTS

I t is a late-winter evening, 2002, and Russia's patriarch, His Holiness Alexius II, stands in front of the assemblage of icons (iconostasis). Drifting into what for most Russians is the semicomprehensible Old Church Slavonic, he leads a prayer consecrating a small cathedral in central Moscow. It has just reopened after being closed during the Soviet era and used as a warehouse.

Consecrations keep His Holiness Alexius II very busy these days. There are many churches reopening, or being newly built, to accommodate the resurgence of Orthodoxy, or at least the practice of attending services.

But this is no ordinary cathedral. After the sanctification rites are delivered for the Church of Sophia the Divine Wisdom, men dressed in long dark overcoats join His Holiness in front of the iconostasis for a photograph. They are high-ranking members of the Federal Security Service, or FSB, the renamed version of the Soviet KGB, which is itself the renamed version of Stalin's NKVD, which grew out of Lenin's Chekha, or Bolshevik Party enforcers. Among the men posing with the patriarch is the chief of the ex-KGB, Nikolai Patrushev. His Holiness and the KGB chief exchange gifts.

Was the organization that did the grunt work for the party—carrying out purges, killing millions with a shot to the back of the head, littering the country with mass graves—finding God?

Perhaps, but His Holiness the Patriarch makes it clear that even if there is an element of repentance, there is also something else: He says he hopes that the Church of Sophia the Divine Wisdom will help Russia's intelligence services "carry out the difficult work of ensuring the country's security in the face of external and internal ill-wishers, if not enemies." A partnership, in other words. The Kremlin will support the church. The church will support the Kremlin. If this is not clear enough, a plaque is placed at the entrance to St. Sophia:

> THE CHURCH OF SOPHIA THE DIVINE WISDOM WAS RE-CREATED UPON
> THE BLESSING OF THE PATRIARCH OF MOSCOW AND ALL RUSSIA AND BY
> THE ZEAL OF THE FEDERAL SECURITY SERVICE

Regardless of the fact that the Soviet state repressed religion and infiltrated the clergy with informers, there is now a new motivation for a church-state union: Unhealthy "sects" are making inroads into Russia all too quickly. The month after St. Sophia's sanctification, the heads of Russia's four Catholic dioceses—all foreigners—were effectively deported when they appeared on an FSB blacklist: Russia's intelligence services even hinted that one was a "spy." At about the same time, the late Pope John Paul II hosted a live closed-circuit television hookup between the Vatican and worshippers in one of Moscow's few Catholic churches. (Following the split between Catholicism and Orthodoxy a millennium ago, popes have not been welcome in Russia, or Rus'—the pre-Russian former Slavic incarnations that included present-day Ukraine and Belarus, among other lands.) The metropolitan of Moscow, Kirill (later to become Russia's patriarch), lambasted the electronic event and even compared it to a sixteenth-century Polish Catholic invasion of Russia.

Yet what if this new devotion on the part of the security services to somehow atone is sincere, and what if some of the post-Soviet spooks have truly turned toward God?

A GOOD PLACE to start was to attend services at Sophia the Divine. The problem of finding it was solved by a quick stop at the once notorious

FSB/KGB headquarters known as Lubyanka. My National Public Radio producer, Irina, doesn't like this at all. Anything dealing with the security services or the church gives her the creeps, she says. It's a freezing early Sunday morning and no one is out front, so we go around to the back of the Lubyanka and find a couple of sleepy guards. I bang on a heavy glass door.

"Hey!" Irina says, turning pale. "People just don't bang on the door of the KGB!"

But our sheer audacity seems to do the trick. One of the sentries even picks up an internal phone and gets us directions to the Church of Sophia the Divine Wisdom.

Tucked behind a Metro station and a gaggle of other buildings, the seventeenth-century edifice is smallish, almost miniature in size, requiring taller Congregationalists (like me) to duck slightly upon entering. Unlike a typical Orthodox church, with its odor of decades of melted candle wax and censer smoke wafting around the icons, the Divine Wisdom smells like the interior of a new car. The walls are a bright yellow; the iconostasis is glitteringly new, tarnish-free, polished to a high gloss.

The gathering on this morning is tiny—perhaps twenty, ourselves included. The priest enters, smoke lingering as he slowly waves the mysterious box filled with burning embers to and fro. Most of the worshippers are older—there are a roughly equal number of women and men. Are there KGB officers in attendance? I cannot tell.

The next stop on my quest is the Russian parliament, or Duma, where I run down the ex-head of the now-renamed KGB, Nikolai Kovalyov, in between sessions. A twenty-seven-year veteran of the "organs," Kovalyov rose all the way to the top of the security service in 1996, until being replaced by none other than Vladimir Putin two years later.

If I expect to catch him off guard with my question about the idea of the former KGB—which persecuted religion, or persecuted the religious, for so many years as the Marxist-defined "opiate of the people"—and now promoting the Orthodox Church as being somehow disingenuous, I am mistaken. Kovalyov's eyes light up with delight at my question, and the ex-head of the former KGB beamingly tells me that he was always a secret believer.

Kovalyov says that when he was growing up in then Soviet Russia, he kept a small icon in his room. The ex-FSB chief delcares to me that he had always felt Christ in his heart.

Mikhail Grishankov is another Duma member with a KGB connection who now claims a unique bond to the Orthodox Church. "I came to be a believer because I realized I couldn't live any other way. God gives my life meaning," he tells me. Over the years I interviewed Grishankov frequently, and the fact that he had essentially converted to being observant, and did not pretend to always have been a fervent "secret believer," convinces me that he is probably being honest.

Another KGB man, Lieutenant Valery Ovchinnikov, wears a gold cross, four years after being baptized. Ovchinnikov tells me that he thinks many KGB men turned to Christianity because of their brutal experiences in Chechnya. I find this plausible. If Chechens can be driven to more religiosity—or even radical Islam—because of their horrific war experiences, why can't Russian intelligence agents?

It is time to contact the current FSB leadership to find out about current operatives embracing Jesus. I make the requisite calls to the FSB headquarters to secure an interview but am told that all questions must be in writing and submitted by fax. A secretary tells us the FSB's fax machine is broken, and it takes several days before the almighty FSB replaces it. Finally I submit my questions. I wait weeks for the answers, until I get a call from the once-dreaded Lubyanka to answer my questions about religion and the heart of the intelligence man.

"It is impossible to deny that certain mistakes were made in the past involving the relationship between the church and the state . . . ," laconically reads the anonymous voice on the other end of the phone, answering one of my questions. "A moral backbone [*sterzhen'*] is desirable to instill an ethical set of values indispensable for the work of individuals involved in issues of national and international security" is the response to another.

· · ·

AND HOW DOES the church take the new alliance with its former persecu-tors? I decided to ask Father Divakov of the Moscow Patriarchate. A bespectacled, intense clergyman, he reacted sharply to my query about KGB sincerity.

"The Apostle Paul persecuted the early Christians," he seethed, his forehead burrowing as if to cast a spell. . . . "But that did not prevent Paul from becoming an apostle after he turned to Christ! The church does not cut itself off from anyone who is willing to repent."

Father Divakov's reaction made clear that the conversation was over. And in a way it would be hypocritical to judge him, or at least some of the FSB (former KGB) men. Among Americans, how many recovering something-aholics, scandal-plagued politicians, hedonists, violent con-victs, or other wayward souls have tried to ease the acceptance of their transgressions by declaring a lightning embrace of the faith?

SO THE FORMER KGB had its new church.

But many still needed a new *icon*. Not just of the painted variety, like the ones on the walls at Sophia the Divine. A flesh-and-blood symbol of good versus evil. And they would find him, or his remains, in a small town about an hour outside of Moscow.

THE TRAIN CONDUCTOR asked me, 'What are you carrying in that bag?' " said Lyubov Radionova.

It was a security measure, a typical passenger check. Perhaps the woman holding the bag held it so tightly that she evoked suspicion. Sui-cide bombers have blown up Russian trains, after all.

"I told the train conductor, my son's head is in this bag. She looked at me as if I was crazy."

She was not crazy.

The woman indeed carried the head of her son in that cotton-sewn bag. The route was Chechnya-Moscow and then a suburban train home to tiny Kurilovo, an hour from Moscow.

She held it and held it.

Her son's name was Yevgeny (Zhenya) Radionov. He was one of thousands of Russian soldiers to die during the brutal Chechen wars; in a way his fate was seemingly little different from many others, his modest goal being to become a cook after army service. Nineteen years old, he was captured by the Chechen fighters and held for a hundred days, likely as prisoner exchange material or for ransom money. And then executed.

I am sitting with his mother, Lyubov, a woman whose eyes convey exhaustion and despair. In her tiny apartment there is a mini-shrine to her son, Zhenya. There are photos of him in uniform that are indeed iconlike, his bulky frame and boyish face recast in the mystical iconic fashion, a halo above his head.

The late Zhenya's mother, Lyubov, then tells every detail: how a telegram came saying Zhenya had deserted his post. Lyubov did not believe it. "Zhenya wasn't capable of it," she tells me. Like the mothers of many missing Russian soldiers in Chechnya, she sets off for Chechnya, eventually finding the patrol post from where he supposedly "deserted." Locals there confirm the military lied; there had been a battle, and Zhenya and two other conscripts were captured by Chechen fighters after a firefight. Lyubov goes on a crusade, traveling throughout the republic and even meeting top commanders, now dead, like Aslan Maskhadov and Shamyl Basayev. Over a dozen trips in all, until the right contact is made.

A Chechen field commander, Ruslan Haihoroev, confirms it to Lyubov: He even says he personally executed Zhenya Radionov on his nineteenth birthday. The commander tells Lyubov Radionova that her son was given a choice: He could convert to Islam and join the Chechen resistance. He refused, and, moreover, refused to remove the small silver cross he always wore.

"I begged him to tell me that it wasn't true, that he had a chance to live and preferred to die," Lyubov says. "But even the Chechen commander confessed to me that he considered Zhenya had died with great dignity, a real man."

In exchange for four thousand dollars, the commander disclosed the exact site of Zhenya's grave. Lyubov and several helpers, also Russian conscripts, began digging with their hands. There was the body, decapitated, supposedly as added treatment for refusing to take off the cross, which through the clumps of dirt still hung there around what was left of Zhenya's neck. The headless body was spirited back to Moscow. Lyubov returned yet again to the Chechen commander, who gave her the bag of skull fragments. Zhenya had not only been decapitated with a rusty saw; his head had been smashed, part of a Chechen belief that if a victim is decapitated, his spirit will not come back for revenge after death.

An elaborate grave was constructed, and the story spread from tiny Kurilovo across Russia like wildfire, becoming especially popular with nationalist groups. Russian military commanders took their troops on pilgrimages to the gravesite. Songs were written about the boy saint. "Zhenya never took the cross off . . . ," go the lyrics.

Then the icons (some swore they excreted a sacred perfume, a phenomenon they maintain occurs only with icons of extremely venerated saints) started appearing in dozens of churches, as the faithful demanded canonization for "Saint Zhenya," as they referred to him. Zhenya had not been formally canonized, the hierarchy of the Russian Orthodox Church arguing that canonization is a very long process, as well as other ecclesiastical obscurities. This stopped no one. Prayers were composed and recited:

> Thy martyr Yevgeny, O Lord, in his sufferings has received an incorruptible crown from Thee, our God, for having Thy strength he has brought down his torturers, has defeated the powerless insolence of demons. Through his prayers, save our souls.

Indeed, some of the icons erected in Orthodox churches were life-size and placed next to the likes of icons of Jesus Christ. The number of times Zhenya's followers used the word "martyr" made it clear to me they had elevated this unlikely young man to practically such a status. The issue practically led to a split in the church between its mainstream leadership and elements demanding Zhenya be made a saint; an enormous debate continues to this day, with part of the church hierarchy maintaining there is yet not sufficient proof about Radionov's case, that someone killed in battle had never been canonized, and citing an obscure precept that naming "new martyrs" had ended after the Bolshevik takeover. The church and the patriarch instead formally "honored" Radionov, the real reason for the refusal to canonize the result of very understandable worries among some in the church (and doubtless the government) that such a step could lead to anti-Muslim hysteria in a country with a large Muslim minority.

AS A COLD wind blew, Radionov's mother and I walked down the few hundred meters from her house to Zhenya's grave, which she visited daily. She caressed the right side of his grave marker and whispered something to the tombstone above her son's body. I asked her if the idea of his canonization was important to her.

Her response was surprising. "I suppose it is important to some people," she said. "But for me it is not the most significant fact. I was not even a churchgoer. I was a Communist Party member for twenty-five years. All I know is that I lost my only son, and that means I have lost everything."

It is not his mother who needs her son's canonization. It is the elements within the Orthodox Church, which needs a new symbol to rouse the flock. It is elements in the state, which in turn needs the church for support, and vice versa. It is the army, which needs some sort of creed or ideology to replace Communism. It is the faithful themselves, being given back their "opiate of the masses" in exchange for the Marxist utopia that never materialized.

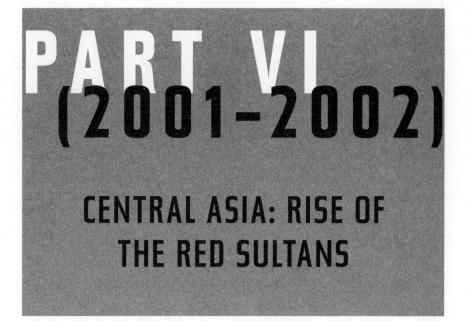

PART VI
(2001–2002)

CENTRAL ASIA: RISE OF
THE RED SULTANS

Many of them were on their way to becoming some of the most quirky countries on earth—some arguably more repressive than under the Soviets. Tajikistan, the poorest of the Central Asian countries, had torched itself in the early 1990s with a senseless civil war that killed tens of thousands. By the mid-2000s, it was little more than an opium crossing point for "exports" from Afghanistan.

Kazakhstan was building an oil powerhouse, but also a repressive dynasty dominated by the family of Communist-turned-capitalist-leader Nursultan Nazerbayev.

In Turkmenistan, one of the most flamboyant personality cults in the world was under construction. Saparmurat Niyazov—Turkmenbashi, or "Head of all Turkmen," "President for Life" of a desert country sitting on some of the largest gas reserves in the world but most of whose citizens were dirt poor—was master of the absurd. Whimsical, and in the estimation of many, demented, he renamed the days of the week after himself and his mother, outlawed opera and ballet as un-Turkmen, and even banned TV presenters from wearing makeup because he declared that the cosmetics made it difficult for him to discern between male and female anchors. In his late fifties, he dyed his hair alternately bleached blond, then soon after jet black. Billboards of Turkmenbashi coiffed in both hues competed with one another on the streets of the capital, Ashgabat. I dreamed of making it to Turkmenistan—the most bizarre corner of the former empire, its most twisted fragment. I filed for a visa, haggling over the phone with various Turkmen Foreign Ministry folks whose telephone numbers seemed to change by the week as some sort of hiding tactic. The answer was always the same: Ring back tomorrow. Finally, one call put them over the edge: The voice on the other end told us to "draw our own conclusions."

There would be no visa for me to "slander our president," and I had to settle for a happenstance incident to claim my presence in the country. My Moscow–Baku flight had been diverted to Turkmenistan because of bad weather, and we sat on the tarmac for two hours and weren't allowed to disembark. I peered out the window for any hint of what life was like, as if on an exo-planet. But at least I could say that I'd "been" in the country. Well, in a way at least.

But it was Uzbekistan, the most populous of the Central Asian "-stans," that was the most intriguing. Home to the religious citadels of Central Asian Islam—Samarkand, Bukhara, and Khiva—it had also created a brand-new ideological pseudosystem to support the continued rule of "Papa" Islam Karimov, the former Soviet Communist Uzbek chieftain turned independence leader. The reality was that by 2007, Uzbekistan ranked as one of the world's most corrupt countries, and almost half the population was scraping by, earning $1.25 a day or less.

Despite these imperfections, Uzbekistan opened up briefly owing to a warming of relations with the United States because of the war in neighboring Afghanistan. For a short while, this made it easier for foreign correspondents to visit, and I used the chance as much as I could before Papa Karimov slammed the door shut once again.

UZBEKISTAN: I CANNOT ANSWER THAT QUESTION

The red message button on the room phone was flashing. There were three messages from NPR (National Public Radio) in Washington, DC, demanding I call in. I did so.

"We have been bombing Afghanistan for two hours now and we have no reaction from you in Uzbekistan. What are you doing?"

I tried to point out that Uzbekistan was a special case to the extent that the Orwellian government could afford to ignore things like the start of an all-out international war on its border. It was a Sunday night, and all of my calls to the country's ministries went unanswered. I tried a few contacts to see if Papa Karimov's secretive machine had at least whispered an acknowledgment that the war was on. No one knew or professed to know anyone who knew anything.

There would be no public outcry over the silence. An editor sighed grudgingly and told me to keep trying.

When morning came, I descended the stairs and asked for a newspaper in the lobby and was told that there were no newspapers in the overpriced two-hundred-dollar-a-night hotel. Next I walked about a half mile down the main drag before I came to a kiosk selling the main state-run newspapers, sure there would be at least a blurb about the war having started. Instead, on the front cover I found pictures of workers being sent into the fields by the government for the annual ritual of collecting Uzbekistan's cotton crop. It was as if news simply did not exist here.

I headed back to the hotel to make some calls. Surely I could get through to at least some of the ministries by now. I started with the Foreign Ministry Press Service, asking for comment on Uzbekistan's position regarding the start of hostilities in Afghanistan.

Someone actually picked up the line!

"I'm sorry, I cannot answer your question, as I do not possess the necessary information," the voice on the other end calmly replied. This was even more worthless than a "no comment."

"Well, then can you just confirm that there is US military activity going on just over the Uzbek border with Afghanistan?"

"I'm sorry, I cannot answer your question, as I do not possess the necessary information." I wondered if I was speaking to an automated answering machine, but this was 2001 and the phones barely worked with any proficiency in Uzbekistan, let alone sporting such leaps as voice-activated technology. Nope, it was a real person, all right.

I kept dialing. Next I tried the Defense Ministry. I repeated the same question about the Uzbek reaction to the start of the war. "I am sorry, I cannot answer your question as I do not possess the necessary information." It was obvious by now that all the country's officials were reading from identical index cards.

I kept trying, this time the Interior Ministry. At first there was no answer. Then a voice at the other end. Would this be my pay dirt? This time the voice at the other end put the receiver down. You need to call the Foreign Ministry, said the voice. "I've already done that," I said. At least I got a slightly different "answer."

THREE WEEKS AFTER September 11, 2001, the day I arrived in Moscow to begin as NPR's bureau chief, my editors gave me four hours to pack before I was dispatched on an overnight flight to that never-never land of Uzbekistan. It was to be a temporary stopping-off point before going on to neighboring Afghanistan. I had not been to Uzbekistan before; knew almost no one in the country; and had no idea about how to go about reporting there, only that the place was renowned as a hotbed of terrified, stonewalling bureaucrats. Their robotic "I cannot answer your question" one-liner monologue confirmed this in short order.

I touched down early that October morning amid an endless steppe covered in those cotton fields. It felt good to be back in the warm world of Asia, despite the inevitable impending war in Afghanistan. I had left Moscow with freezing rain already falling.

Tashkent, at first sight, evoked squeaky-clean Eastern order, but with a warm, relatively cosmopolitan relaxedness. As I rode in a taxi toward the city center, old women in bright, colored head scarves emblazoned with impossibly oversized roses sold flowers at street corners, men in traditional robes yawned as they sat around on park benches, and young women in miniskirts strolled casually along wide, sun-drenched boulevards.

Uzbekistan did feel like it was still in the Soviet Union, even though the statues of Lenin had been removed. His iconic replacement on pedestal after pedestal throughout the land was Tamerlane, the fourteenth-century Turkic conqueror who ruled over most of the Middle East from his capital at Samarkand, in present-day Uzbekistan (but was not Uzbek himself). Despite this, there were statutes of him going up just about everywhere in the country. Official propaganda eulogized him despite his bloodthirsty résumé.

I checked into my overpriced, state-owned hotel and took a walk through the central pedestrian boulevard to get a feel for the town. The boulevard was lined with mom-and-pop cafés serving chicken shish kebab, rice *plov* served with chunks of fatty mutton, and spicy Korean-style carrot salad. But when I took out my long black NPR microphone and started asking questions about Uzbekistan and the possible effect of the inevitable American bombing campaign in Afghanistan, people turned their heads or silently waved me away with their hands.

"Politics, no," said one man, selling cheap cassette tapes of Turkish pop-music stars. Other rote responses to questions about Karimov, in public at least, included "Our president is golden" and "He provides everything for our country's needs."

• • •

UZBEKISTAN'S NEW, POST-SOVIET leadership was actually not new at all. It resisted most reforms of any kind, keeping a type of state command-model economy in place. There was no privatization of state-owned factories. Repetitive propaganda slogans loomed from Tashkent's major buildings—Soviet sounding, like "Uzbekistan is a country with a great future." People snuck around behind buildings to trade dollars for the Uzbek *som* at practically double the "official" rate—long after all ex-Soviet republics had abandoned artificially set exchange rates. This outmoded practice was far from ideological—it was kept in place to let cronies connected to the government of President Islam Karimov exchange their *som* into hard currency at the preferential "official rate." The rest of the population was forced to risk arrest by trading on the black market on much less profitable terms.

Karimov didn't pretend to be a democrat. He and his government had—alone among ex-Soviet republics—even invented a pseudoideology, replete with Marxist-Leninist-style volumes of unreadable psychobabble, to justify its existence. This was the "ideology of national independence," a deliberately vague synthesis of North Korean–style "Juche" (self-reliance), rigid state control over every official facet of economic and social life, and total trust in Karimov. Just as the Soviet system had supported an army of Marxist-Leninist "philosophers," the Uzbek system provided ample employment opportunities for its own theoreticians. The main elements were and are (1) distrust of the outside world and "enemies" of Uzbekistan; (2) autarky, meaning a closed economic system; and (3) most important, a justification for authoritarianism—in essence prostrating oneself to the full acceptance of the regime's ultimate wisdom in defining what is right for the nation. As one of the regime's theoreticians writes:

> The national interest is identified from the top of the pyramid of the governing of society in the process of integrating the strategic needs of national development, which often cannot be identified as distinct from the structures of power, knowledge and individuals.

Karimov was genuinely terrified of the possible spread of extremism from Taliban-run Afghanistan. Now, in exchange for his support of the US-led war and access to a key air base, Washington warmly embraced its new friend. Secretary of Defense Donald Rumsfeld made so many courtesy calls to Tashkent that I lost count. Press conference questions from journalists to Rumsfeld about the country's abominable human rights record were sidestepped or ignored. The commander of the US Central Command, General Tommy Franks, was also a regular visitor. When journalists asked questions about the wisdom of jumping in bed with one of the most repressive regimes in the world, Franks simply smiled, gently stating that the United States was always supportive of human rights everywhere.

The Karimov government's record, according to numerous reports by human rights groups, included, among other things, instances where government opponents (usually those accused of radical Islamist tendencies, but not always) had been boiled alive, raped (women and men alike), or had been forced to watch as their relatives were raped or burned with lit cigarettes, amid other forms of sickly creative barbarity.

Thus for a short time (the relationship would sour quickly and swing back and forth from good to bad to decent again depending on the circumstances) the leadership of Uzbekistan traded its status as a highly subsidized part of the Soviet Empire for a new "protector"—in the form of the United States—from Afghanistan and a possible Islamist insurgency. The US State Department continued to list a yearly litany of Uzbekistan's appalling human rights abuses, but they were subsumed under the "strategic partnership" mantra, a concession to the need to fight the war in Afghanistan first and worry about grave human rights abuses later.

SO YES, THE bombing had started, or so said the voice on the other end of the phone at the NPR foreign desk in Washington. NPR had correspondents in Pakistan, India, Tajikistan—almost every country bordering

Afghanistan—and our marching orders were simple. The second the B-52s started dropping bombs on the Taliban, we were to get reaction from the various capitals. Islamabad, New Delhi, and even Tehran issued swift if oblique responses, often couched in diplomatic-speak, and expressing various degrees of "concern" and other vacuous political verbiage.

But not Tashkent.

I switched on the TV in my hotel room, first to CNN. Secretary of Defense Rumsfeld was giving a rambling briefing about the start of the bombing campaign. Then the network turned to a slew of correspondents and analysts who rehashed every aspect of the story.

Then I switched over to Uzbekistan's state television, expecting some sort of official commentary on the nightly news. I hurriedly set up my recorder, hoping to get the official Uzbek take on the war breaking out just over its border. Instead, the broadcast concentrated on President Karimov's activities for the day, such as a visit to a new factory, a story about Uzbek tennis players (Karimov's personal obsession), some irrelevant economic statistics, and a very long weather report.

What? Nothing about the start of the bombing campaign? The start of the war in next-door Afghanistan?

I set out for the streets to try to find something more cogent; perhaps people in the few open night bars in Tashkent would know something. I struck up a few worthless conversations, learned nothing relevant because everyone was in the dark about the war that had erupted over the border, and went back to the hotel and up to my room.

It had taken the United States just three weeks to turn Uzbekistan into its biggest regional ally, with the Uzbeks agreeing to provide an air base outside the city of Karshi in the southern part of the country. The Pentagon tried to keep mum about this for some reason but had "unofficially" confirmed it as a fact. But even then, there was no admission on the part of the Uzbek authorities that the base was actually functioning. We understood the Uzbeks had legitimate security concerns about getting involved in a war with the Taliban, or with militants from the home-grown Islamic Movement of Uzbekistan, the IMU. But the entire denial game was becoming comical.

Since there was no official "confirmation" that the United States had established a major military air base on Uzbek territory, just a hundred miles or so from the Afghan frontier, my local assistant Dima and I decided to see for ourselves what was going on.

It was a long drive, mainly because of an inordinate amount of time spent at Uzbek checkpoints. By the time we reached the area near the "secret" air base, I had gone through about fifteen. At each, the questions were the same.

"Where are you going?"

"To the Khanabad airport," I answered the first time. Later I got smarter and regularly lied, saying we was going to Samarkand to see its famous blue-tiled mosques. (We did actually have plans to pass through Samarkand, but only after we were at the worst-kept "secret" air base on the face of the planet.)

The ubiquitous checkpoints meant demands to see our passports, accreditations, and gear while the police manning the stations made phone calls to some unknown bureaucrats. Unable to find anything wrong with our documents (we had been issued the necessary journalist accreditations in Tashkent), the police reluctantly would let us continue after cheerily insisting on drinking tea with them. To the Uzbek police, the friendly tea ritual seemed of far greater importance than my interest in military matters or whatever shortcomings they might perceive in my documents.

When we finally reached the vicinity of the Khanabad air base, we realized the Uzbeks had thrown a "special perimeter" around the "military secret." It was not possible to get within closer range, but we did have the opportunity to catch sight of a C-17 cargo plane making a landing. We asked one of the police officers standing nearby if there had been many such landings over previous days. "President Karimov has already answered all your questions," he grunted.

. . .

BEFORE THE AFGHAN war, foreign reporters were a rarity in Uzbekistan. But part of the improved US-Uzbek ties included loosening strict Uzbek visa requirements for foreigners. With this, a flood of reporters representing virtually every major Western newspaper outlet and TV and radio network poured in. The point was to use the area to cross into Afghanistan and not to cover Uzbekistan itself, which was convenient, as that was the last thing in the world Papa Karimov's regime wanted.

But the bridge over the Amu Darya River into Afghanistan used by Soviet troops to quit the country in 1987 had been closed for years, and the Uzbeks were resisting reopening it, even for desperately needed United Nations humanitarian supplies—and even though the Taliban were no longer in control of the area on the other side of the river.

So the TV crews and reporters bided their time with stories about little-known Uzbekistan and what life was like there. For me, this included stories of Uzbekistan's terrifying problem with drug addiction (fueled by its proximity to Afghanistan and use as a transit route for opium); a story about a young man tortured to death (cranial bruises, cigarette burns, bones broken, fingernails extracted) by police because he was suspected of being an Islamist "fundamentalist"; and the yearly forced march into the countryside of an army of state workers and school-children to collect the state cotton harvest.

Running out of story ideas, and becoming impatient in Tashkent's hotels with Uzbek's dawdling over opening the closed border, Dima and I rented a taxi and shoved off for the twelve-hour drive to Termez, a formerly closed city on the Afghan border. By midday we were getting hungry, and Dima told me he knew of a special place—an ethnic Korean collective farm that ran its own restaurant.

We sat on the floor of one of the rooms in the collective farm restaurant. Everything was as if it had been directly brought from Korea, with big pillows and a table piled high with kimchee and *bulgogi*. I casually noticed that a very loud dog had been barking behind the building when we arrived and sat down. The barking came to an abrupt end. We were then given big bowls of soup. Dima watched me slurping down the hot, slightly fatty soup a wee bit too carefully.

"Congratulations. You've just consumed your first canine cuisine," he chuckled.

The Uzbeks had sent a lower-level Foreign Ministry official named Ramazan to Termez to deal with the growing horde of journalists gathering in the city. A tiny man of around fifty, Ramazan had a great sense of humor, but absolutely no power to open the border, even though UN pressure to let humanitarian supplies in was mounting. At least we could see Afghanistan on the far bank.

The days spent in Termez were as tedious as the city was dusty beyond description. There was an open-air market selling cheap Chinese clothes and an all-night outdoor area with three or four bars with plastic chairs where old men drank vodka and ate plates piled high with fish and potatoes fried in the local cottonseed oil, which gives off a unique pungent smell that I'll never forget.

On the second day in the city, we became engulfed in a so-called "Afghan," or dust storm, kicked up across the river. The storm lasted three days and made it difficult to see your hand in front of your face, or even to open the hotel balcony door for fear of being buried under dust.

The numbers of journalists kept multiplying, and the pressure to get into Afghanistan continued to grow. Apparently in exchange for a bribe, an Uzbek official briefly took a small group of reporters on a short boat ride along the Amu Darya, docking for a few minutes on the other side in Afghanistan so that the reporters could claim an Afghanistan dateline. One of the six reporters on board then bolted, "escaping" into Afghanistani territory and leaving the rest of us seething with envy.

A group of about fifty reporters elected delegates to speak with the Uzbek officials in the city again about getting us into Afghanistan. We were seated behind a long table, one similar to those used for diplomatic discussions. The Uzbeks explained that the border was officially closed and therefore that there were no customs procedures in place for letting us cross, that it would be best if we all returned to Tashkent. I explained that we would not leave Termez unless we got into Afghanistan. I also explained that the intransigence was not good for the country's image— UN food aid to head off a predicted winter famine was being held up.

Finally, the Uzbeks offered a compromise. Rather than cross the impos-ing bridge between the two countries, they would agree on a deal to ship us all out of Uzbekistan and over into Afghanistan on a special barge. They warned us we could float away but added we might not be able to float back, no matter what happened on the other side. "You mean we might not be allowed back into the country?" I asked Ramazan. "I'm sorry, I cannot answer that question," Ramazan said, and smiled. This time I just laughed.

The next day, taciturn customs officials came armed with a card table and an array of stamps and ink pads. They set up the card table in the sand along the riverbank and sat down next to it. We were all allowed to board the barge after having our passports stamped.

We floated up to the other side, where a gaggle of Afghans was wait-ing for us. We had what we wanted—Afghanistan—within our sights. The Uzbeks had what they wanted—us out of the way. The deluge of stories by international journalists about the repressive nature of their country—torture of government opponents or suspected Islamist insur-gents, and the closed, Orwellian nature of the place—was now reduced to a trickle.

AN AFGHAN INTERLUDE

November 25, 2001

Our coughing diesel barge—captained by a Uzbek who jokingly referred to it as "our navy" (being landlocked, Uzbekistan had no "navy")—slowly chugged up the Amu Darya River toward a landing spot just under the Bridge of Friendship.

The steel rail and road link had been put up by Soviet troops in 1982. The bridge was built to send Soviet fighting men to the fraternal socialist people of the Democratic Republic of Afghanistan. But its real claim to fame was to become as a way home for the dead, injured, bedraggled, and PTSD'd out Soviet soldiers as the Kremlin exited the country.

The last Soviet soldier left Afghanistan on February 15, 1989, ten years and fifty thousand casualties after the first had entered on December 27, 1979, leaving one country, Afghanistan, bombed back to the Stone Age, and leaving the USSR so crippled economically, morally, and financially that it too would end up in the unenviable category of political entities known as "failed states."

The first Soviet commandos entered Afghanistan to aid the embattled communist ruler Hafizullah Amin, who had deposed the government of fellow Afghan communist Muhammad Taraki, who had gotten rid of the previous prime minister, Muhammad Daoud Khan, by the tried-and-true method of executing Daoud and most of his family in painful ways.

Amin thought he had called on friends, but once under Soviet "protection," he was in turn murdered by yet another Afghan communist named Babrak Karmal, who would stay in power until the security situation had so deteriorated that he was "democratically" replaced by security chief Mohammad Najibullah in 1986. This last gentleman would remain in power until murdered and mutilated in 1992 with the triumph of the (covert) Saudi/CIA-backed mujahideen, who then morphed into the al-Qaeda-friendly Taliban.

I was not there at the time, nor during the subsequent brutal inter-mujahideen power struggles that eventually resulted in the Taliban's seizure of power in Kabul and their granting safe haven to Osama bin Laden and al-Qaeda. And thus I am reluctant to comment on the decade or so between the last Soviet soldier's leaving in early 1989 and the next batch of would-be Afghan tamers when the country once again appeared on the world media radar following the attacks on the World Trade Center (and Pentagon) on September 11, 2001.

But after crossing the churning water of the Amu Darya from now-independent Uzbekistan to our muddy dock in "free" Afghanistan to observe the progress of the US/NATO response to 9/11, I was filled with foreboding that yet another glorious effort to liberate the noble Afghan people from themselves had just begun, and that I was to be a witness to it.

The date was November 25, 2001.

Operation "Enduring Freedom" had been launched on October 7, after a final ultimatum from the White House to the Taliban government in Kabul to turn over Osama bin Laden had been ignored, and bombs began to fall. Indeed, almost all the US firepower was coming from B-52s, F-15s, and other expensive toys; there had been little hand-to-hand fighting to date, and a sense of euphoria was building among the United States and its allies. After all, well into the second month of the war in Afghanistan, the United States had not suffered a single combat death. Not one.

Mazar-e-Sharif, the main city in the north, had fallen from Taliban control to the Afghan-Uzbek warlord General Abdul Rashid Dostum, and a few days later, the Taliban practically sprinted away from Kabul. Women would be throwing off the burqas! People would play music again! And as for the politics of overthrowing the repressive fundamentalist regime, we were not seeking to impose Soviet Communism on the Afghans but were determined to bring them Western democracy. And in doing so, if we met resistance, we would be careful about not harming civilians, and only kill bad guys. In essence, ours would not be the Russian experience. We would not be forced out ignominiously by a determined resistance, as had the USSR, because we were there to build, not to break. Or so went the logic. In those first weeks and months of war, this was hard to argue with, as the Taliban were barely putting up a fight. A cruel, oppressive, Islamic fundamentalist dictatorship loathed by any thinking person in the country—and indeed, the world—had been removed with extraordinary ease, and that was just plain good, and the facts plain for any eye to see.

WE DOCKED ON the Afghan side of the brownish gray Amu Darya, a color it absorbed from the area's moonscapelike relief, which spawned those nonstop dust storms. To say it was a motley crew waiting for us war pilgrims would be an understatement. The welcoming committee, such as it was, consisted of a few Northern Alliance guys wearing nonmatching uniforms and knots of would-be fixers and alleged English speakers (most of whom, as it turned out, spoke little or no English) hoping to land lucrative translating gigs.

War, as they say, is good business—and almost immediately, negotiations began, the biggest selling point seeming to be who could promise better access to General Dostum, the longtime regional strongman in the area who had come back as the Taliban fled.

"Hallo, Meester! You want talk Genril Doostum?"

It was all too easy to be cynical, watching the hustlers at work, aside from one very interesting thing: On the Afghani, southern side of the river, people actually spoke about the war; on the northern, Uzbek side, they did not.

The second thing of interest to me related to the Friendship Bridge. After trying to persuade me in broken or even often incomprehensible English to hire them as guides, it rapidly became apparent that many of the amateur translators spoke Russian—ranging from the profanity-filled street variety accrued from years of interaction and proximity to the Soviet Union, to grammatically correct Russian learned at the USSR's vast higher-education system—military institutes in Minsk to medical schools in Murmansk. Accordingly, I struck up a conversation with one Bahuladin, a barrel-chested bear of a man who seemed to have a smile permanently stretched on his face. He sported a long salt-and-pepper beard that looked like it had never been cut or combed and was filming our arrival with a cheap Sony Hi8 video camera. But after a few attempts to chat with me in broken English, Bahuladin switched into much better Russian, which caught many of the newly arrived foreign journalists by surprise.

Russian? The language of the Soviet invader? In fact, I would end up hearing much more Russian in Afghanistan than I ever anticipated, illustrative of how much the empire had penetrated the country in just a few short, bloody years.

We were next herded into an aging bus to get us off the riverbank and closer to our destination—the war, wherever that was. Now knowing that I spoke Russian, Bahuladin sat down next to me. He explained that he had been an actor in the Kabul Theater before the Taliban had banned theatre along with virtually all other forms of entertainment because such distractions were against Islam, according to the Taliban's rigorous so-called Wahhabi creed. One could have drowned in the details.

Bahuladin was boisterous to the point of being irritating about almost any subject that came to mind, rattling nonstop into my ear the entire drive to Mazar-e-Sharif, which thankfully took only an hour.

PART OF THE Uzbek claim for not letting us traverse into Afghanistan had been expressed as government "concerns over our safety." This was ridiculous, but it was the excuse that Ramazan and the other Uzbek bureaucrats had dreamt up (or more likely ordered to be repeated again and again), and so they pretended to believe in it themselves.

The irony was that on this very day, November 25, one of the bloodiest battles of the entire Afghan war had gotten under way—and just as we were arriving in Mazar-e-Sharif, a city in northern Afghanistan that the Uzbeks actually believed was safe, relatively speaking, because it was controlled by "their man" in Afghanistan, that unpredictable, ever-switching-sides ethnic Uzbek general, Abdul Rashid Dostum.

Accordingly, after crossing the Amu Darya we boarded our bus headed for Mazar-e-Sharif and the desolately flat, boulder- and sand-strewn landscape that lay between the river and the city, said to be the burial place of Ali ibn Abi Talib, the son-in-law of Muhammad and his first follower, and thus a place of lively pilgrimage in better times.

These were not better times, and the best hotel in town was a filthy five-story wreck with intermittent running water. We checked in, which meant journalists fighting for keys from an old man holding a ring of them. My room was a closet with a rusty spring for a bed—no mattress, sheets, or anything else, for that matter; at least there was a kind of balcony nearby, overlooking Mazar's blue-tiled mosque.

An odd quiet had descended over the city, so I asked Bahuladin what was happening. After conferring with some locals for a few moments, he returned with news: The day before, following an eleven-day siege by General Dostum's horseback forces (accompanied by devastating US Air Force bombings) of a place called Kunduz, thousands of Taliban and their foreign associates had surrendered to the Northern Alliance and been herded into a massive earthen fortress called Qala i-Jongi just outside Mazar-e-Sharif, where they were being interrogated by Dostum's expert handlers. The Americans, meanwhile, wanted the prisoners brought to an old airfield, possibly to make it easier to fly any big foreign fish that might be found out to Guantánamo Bay and other locations.

But the volatile General Dostum had overruled them; after all, these were his prisoners, and he would deal with them in a traditional way. First, Afghan fighters were allowed to hand in their weapons and go free; Dostum considered this an act of national reconciliation. Less explicably, the Northern Alliance troops had not disarmed all of the several hundred foreign Taliban (mainly Pakistani Pashtuns) who had been brought to the fortress. This group of four hundred or so was told that if they surrendered, they were going to be set free. But once inside the fortress, it was evident they were prisoners and that they'd been duped. On the preceding afternoon, one had pulled the pin from a grenade, killing himself and some of Dostum's fighters, and tensions were rising and spilling out of the prison and into Mazar-e-Sharif City itself.

The melee involved two very special men, who had apparently just arrived at Mazar-e-Sharif hours ahead of us.

One was Johnny Micheal Spann, a retired Marine and an agent with the ultrasecretive CIA Special Activities Division. With Spann was another CIA man, Dave Tyson. Both were tasked with weeding out the "real" foreigners from among the mass of prisoners, meaning non-Afghanstanis and Pakistanis. You might say they were looking for al-Qaeda–connected Arabs but also found the odd Turk, Uzbek, Uyghur, and Indonesian of interest too. According to accounts provided by the Northern Alliance and Taliban in attendance, Spann took a special interest in a young man who didn't seem to speak Arabic or any "Muslim" language. He was lighter skinned and stood out from the rest of the Kunduz captives and finally admitted that he was neither Arab nor Afghani, but Irish. His Taliban cohorts had told him to employ this tactic to "avoid trouble." Spann responded by asking the young man if he was a member of the Irish Republican Army and was once again met with stony silence. To intimidate the boy into talking, Tyson at one point told Spann (in the prisoner's presence) that the "Irishman" would have to decide on his own whether to live or die. Still he didn't talk.

This was John Walker Lindh, the twenty-year-old Californian convert to Islam who trekked to Afghanistan to join the Taliban after having undergone training in various Arab countries. He would eventually be spirited back to the United States and convicted. But that was later. Some of the foreign Taliban prisoners, enraged at Spann's presence and at having bought the line that they would be freed, drew out their concealed weapons. At least one threw a grenade. They quickly gained the upper hand and availed themselves of one of the many arms and ammo depots spread around the south side of the enormous fortress. They killed at least several dozen of their Northern Alliance guards and then turned on the two CIA men.

We heard shots ring out from the fortress, just a few miles away from our dumpy hotel. The shots mounted into a sustained roar and subsided sporadically. A few journalists already in the city who had entered Afghanistan via Tajikistan were already returning from the fortress, confirming that a savage battle was under way at Qala i-Jongi. We headed the other way; Bahuladin grabbed a taxi, and we set out for the fortress.

The Kabul actor-turned-war-front-translator sat in the front and extracted some opium paste wrapped in cellophane from a pocket, preparing to smoke it. He seemed entirely unconcerned about the dangers of heading toward the scene of the battle, and the continuing sounds of mortar rounds and explosions coming from that direction. He just smiled and smiled.

We soon closed on the Qala i-Jongi but were forced to stop by Northern Alliance troops, as outgoing mortar rounds were landing not far away. "Outgoing," that is, from the fortress toward us. Exercising caution, I thought it best to study the edifice from a ditch. The dimensions of the nineteenth-century mud-brick structure were still impressive. The walls were pitched at a seventy-degree angle, and the fortress seemed to be several football fields long and at least one wide. Yes, it was an impressive, if Spartan-looking, structure—and one about to be blown into rubble.

Inside the fort, according to witnesses from both sides, Spann and Tyson tried to fight off the mob with near fanaticism. Tyson fired off clip after clip from an AK-47. Spann emptied his pistol before the prisoners tore him to pieces. He thus became the first American to die in Afghanistan.

Spann's hopeless attempt to take on the hundreds of Taliban prisoners had bought Tyson time enough to run along a wall and into the northern section of the prison, where he found a German television team. "Mind if I use your satellite telephone for a moment?" said Tyson, or something to that effect. Then, on camera—how could he ask the Germans not to film him while using their phone?—Tyson dialed up someone at the US embassy in Tashkent, gave the exact coordinates of the Qala i-Jongi, and begged for reinforcements.

Bahuladin and I were oblivious to this as we huddled in our ditch along the side of the road, listening to explosions coming from the fortress and the occasional mortar round landing outside, a few dozen yards away from us. The Northern Alliance fighters chuckled at my self-preservation efforts; explosions never fazed them after so many years of war.

Whatever had happened inside the fort seemed to be dying down, anyway. Now there were only short bursts of occasional fire, and I was starting to think it was time to take a closer look when a blinding flash lit up and a shock blast shook the ground we were standing on as an explosion went off in the southern section, which the Taliban had overrun, followed by a loud whooshing noise—likely a US guided bomb or a missile of some sort.

US helicopter gunships buzzed the fort all that night, as well as central Mazar. It was difficult to make out what they were up to, as the city was pitch black and there was no electricity. But our balcony faced westward, in the direction of Qala i-Jongi. We heard occasional explosions and saw flashes of light, but so far nothing like the all-out onslaught that had been rumored to be in the offing.

The next day, we headed to the fortress again to see what truths there were to report. Not surprisingly, we found perhaps a couple dozen US and UK Special Forces in place around it, evidently there to help direct the fighting against the Taliban and to coordinate air strikes. They had made a respectable attempt to blend in with the Afghans, dressing up in traditional robes and having grown beards. But while the "purdah" had a nice style element, it was patently obvious who was who—the Americans and British had been staying at safe houses in the city, were obviously getting daily showers, and their air of cleanliness made then stand out from their unbathed Northern Alliance allies.

Northern Alliance troops perched upon the upper walls with automatic weapons and extra ammunition, shooting down into the southern area of the compound. What the cameras could not capture was the Taliban returning fire with small arms, shooting up. All other action was sporadic, such as a mortar round landing in the field next to the fortress where I was standing, doing an interview with NPR host Bob Edwards for *Morning Edition*. Then an Alliance commander stepped over to me and tapped at his watch, strongly suggesting I move myself and my equipment. Another air strike was on the way. I didn't question his authority.

We vacated the area, and bombs were soon shaking the ground as we drove back into Mazar-e-Sharif, Bahuladin laughing about the guile of the escaped Taliban prisoners all the way. *"Blyad"* ("Fuck"), he cursed in Russian. "Man, but those Chechens have balls!" The Afghans, it turned out, were referring to any Russian-speaking Taliban volunteers as "Chechens," a mistake that was to get into the vernacular of many foreign correspondents over those few days. It was a matter of confusion, not intentional. But it was wrong. Uzbeks and men from Russia's various Muslim republics were the main fighters among the Russian speakers who had joined up with the Taliban. Chechens were still busy with their own war at home, and few, if any, were ever conclusively documented as having fought in Afghanistan.

When we returned to the fortress later, we learned that one of the US air strikes had missed its target by a few dozen meters, slamming into Dostum's part of the fortress and killing more than a dozen Northern Alliance guys. An enormous part of one of the mud walls had collapsed, leaving a gaping hole in the Qala i-Jongi defenses, offering further proof—if any was needed—what modern high explosives can do to medieval-style adobe fortress walls.

And yet still the Taliban, trapped like rats in a cul-de-sac sewer, fought on.

Then, toward nightfall, we were given to understand that the Americans had run out of patience and were going to bomb Qala i-Jongi into oblivion. The best place to watch the spectacle would be from the safety of my balcony with its view toward the fortress, I decided.

Darkness fell. The odd explosion rang out; an occasional flash of light flickered. The low-intensity battle continued. Then came a different sound, a sort of *whoosh* that must have been aircraft but felt like long-range missiles coming from hell itself as the anticipated earth-shattering bombardment commenced. Huge orange balls of fire mushroomed into the sky, followed by smaller explosions when the initial blast had clearly detonated some of the tons of munitions General Dostum kept stored at the fortress. There was almost a sick beauty to it all, and flames shot into the heavens all night.

When morning came, we returned to the fortress to see what was left of it. Remarkably, there were still periodic shots coming from inside the complex, and the press was not being allowed in. That would take until the next morning.

When we were finally allowed to enter, it was a scene of absolute carnage, medieval in its choreography, gruesome beyond anything I had seen to that point in a decade of covering wars. Hundreds of bodies were strewn about in all sorts of warped poses of death, probably a spectacle Tamerlane would have delighted in. One man's chest had been splayed open with what must have been a bayonet or some sort of sword. Others lay next to some of Dostum's dead horses who had gotten caught up in the fighting. There was another group lying on the ground next to one another, hands bound and thus probably shot execution-style. Wandering around amid the sea of bodies, now attracting flies, was a small group of foreign war reporters. A battle-hardened, thick-skinned lot, some of them close to war-junkie status. I knew many of them. Even their mouths were agape at the slaughter and the sight of the bodies of the dead Taliban being tossed into flatbed trucks—four, five, and six deep, looking like livestock carcasses being loaded for processing at a meatpacking plant.

The Northern Alliance "victors"—who had just lost more than a hundred men in the battle—meanwhile, took a different approach. Many joked or laughed and posed for pictures next to the dead Taliban, putting their boots atop lifeless heads while smiling for the cameras. Another group was arguing over war booty—the bombs poured onto the fortress had blown open a storage depot containing automatic rifles with retractable coils—World War II–vintage stuff. They were still wrapped in old brown wax paper and were regarded as a real find.

Nearby there was the remainder of a staircase going into the basement of a building that had been blown away in the bombing. A couple of Northern Alliance men stood next to the hole. As I stood a few feet away recording, one held a grenade, pulled the pin and tossed it into the basement, laughing hysterically. It exploded with the predictable *kaboom*, sending the two Alliance fighters into even greater hysterical mirth. "There are still a few of them left down there," said one of the fighters.

And there were. A couple of days later, when we had left the charnel house better known as Qala i-Jongi because the battle seemed over, the Alliance forces got tired of tossing grenades and flooded the basement with water and diesel fuel, and the last starving, wounded, and dying fifty Taliban prisoners finally gave themselves up, begging for mercy.

Among those to ascend the stairs was the "Irishman" Taliban, John Walker Lindh, known to his associates by his nom de guerre, Sulayman al-Faris. (He would be taken away by CIA officials, interrogated on a navy ship, and finally be sent to the United States, where he would eventually be given a twenty-year prison sentence on a variety of charges related to his Taliban life after a plea bargain designed to save him from worse.)

Then General Dostum arrived, walking nonchalantly through the carnage and up into the terraced compound that overlooked the fortress grounds. Sipping tea and nursing what looked to be one of his common hangovers, he gave an impromptu press conference, emphasizing that the Taliban prisoners had been treated "humanely," but that his men had erred by not handcuffing the lot and even failing to check some for concealed weapons. The prisoners, he suggested, had violated a kind of unwritten Afghan trust and had only themselves to blame for the slaughter. (More serious were the allegations that the men who surrendered to Dostum had been packed into airless, scorching container trucks, and that several hundred of them had suffocated to death in the process. The general denied this, although he tried to prevent the examination of mass graves discovered years later that seemed to give credence to the ghastly story.)

Then there was the future of Taliban-free Afghanistan.

With the war ineluctably moving south toward the capital, Kabul, and the Taliban being zapped by high-tech weapons when not on the run or hiding, it was natural to assume that a major page had been turned in the history of the blighted nation, and that the American promise of bringing freedom and democracy was just a matter of weeks or at most months away.

But even before the fall of Kunduz, the slaughter at Qala i-Jongi, and the capture of John Walker Lindh, Dostum and others in the Northern Alliance had already given unsettling indications that they would come to blows over who was going to run this part of Afghanistan. There were continual rumors about tension between Dostum, the big Uzbek known to like a drink, and the more pious Mohammed Atta, leader of the local Tajiks. As for the Pashtuns, many of whom lived in the nearby ancient city of Balkh (ironically, the scene of Tamerlane's coronation in 1370), they were already complaining of ethnically based beatings and indiscriminate treatment at the hands of the Uzbeks and Tajiks. During a visit to the town, I sat on a dirt floor listening to the pleas of Pashtun town elders, who begged for an international peacekeeping force to prevent them from being exterminated.

Dostum, meanwhile, was the man of the moment and let it be known that what he wanted was any new central government in Kabul to allow a broad form of federalism, with him, Dostum, of course, at the helm in the north, just as he had been before the city fell to the Taliban. In those days Dostum was usually surrounded by provocatively dressed "assistants." Other local women spurned even head scarves, let alone burqas. Shops selling booze were not hard to find. The big Uzbek even ordered his own version of the local Afghani currency printed up—identical except for some telltale markings that shaved half of its value in comparison with the Kabul-printed variety.

The problem was, almost no one trusted Dostum as far as they could throw the gargantuan Uzbek strongman, and with good reason. His twenty-thousand-strong private militia fought on the Soviet side during their stay in Afghanistan, and he stayed loyal to the communist chieftain Najibullah until after the Russians ended financial support for Kabul as part of a "hands-off Afghanistan" deal struck with Washington in 1989. With Najib's brutal murder in 1992 and the start of the real civil war, Dostum next aligned himself with the legendary Shah Massoud, and then briefly took control of Kabul, fighting the Pakistani-installed leader Gulbuddin Hekmatyar before having a flirt with the Taliban, allowing them to enter Mazar-e-Sharif in the late 1990s, only to break with them soon thereafter.

One might say he never saw a temporary alliance he didn't like.

Thus it was not wholly surprising when Dostum and Atta hastily convened a joint press conference to dispel notions of a split. The international community was putting great pressure on the factions, including Dostum, to come to some sort of workable national agreement, and it behooved them both to make the right noises—in this case, that they were full-fledged allies, uttering platitudes about the brotherly love between the ancient and fraternal Uzbek and Tajik peoples, amid questions about how to round up the sea of weapons floating around the country. Northern Alliance fighters, with no Talibs left to fight, were busy pawning theirs. I spent a day with one group of yahoos outside of Mazar-e-Sharif who offered me everything from a worn AK-47 ($150) to a slightly used Russian T-55 tank ($5,000).

At the end of the briefing, I asked Dostum how long it would realistically take to bring a degree of order to Afghanistan. His answer was neither evasive nor glib. Rather, it was straightforward and probably prophetic:

"In my opinion, minor conflicts will continue for the next ten or fifteen years," he dourly stated. "Even before these twenty-three years of war, even during the reign of the king, Afghans always fought. If they didn't have guns, they fought with shovels and sticks."

BEFORE SETTING OFF from Moscow and heading off to Afghanistan, I had visited with dozens of Russians who shook their heads at the American decision to intervene in the so-called graveyard of empires. The United States, they predicted, would get bogged down and ultimately be forced to leave as well. In many cases, this was conveyed sincerely. In others, from former Soviet "Spetznaz" (Special Forces) types, the predictions of doom also contained a kind of smugness that the United States would ultimately fail to tame Afghanistan, just as they had, shattering the myth that the US superpower was omnipotent, just as the supposed Soviet superpower had turned out not to be.

THE BATTLE FOR Qala i-Jongi over, John Walker Lindh captured, and America having suffered its first death of the war, I was instructed by my editors at NPR to head back to Uzbekistan and then to Moscow, leaving Steve Inskeep, now the anchor for NPR's *Morning Edition,* to stay behind to cover the next developments. We spent a farewell dinner eating Afghan dumplings filled with meat, carrots, and onions in a bare-bones slop house with wallpaper featuring deer and horses with their eyes gouged out, which apparently had some sort of religious significance to the Taliban that no one was ever able to adequately explain to me. Along with this religiously motivated desecration of kitsch wall art, there was also plenty of usual graffiti, some in English.

Yes, it was time to go. I had already parted ways with the overly gregarious, dope-smoking, and fearless Bahuladin, who had latched on to a TV crew that was throwing something like five hundred dollars a day at him for his services. War can be good business for out-of-work Kabul actors, and I wonder what he is doing today.

Another Russian-speaking Mazar local drove me the hour-long drive

back up to the Bridge of Friendship with Uzbekistan, and I got my passport out as we approached the border. The interpreter turned white. "But
it's an American passport," he said. "Yes, that's because I'm American,"
I countered. He had assumed that because I spoke Russian fluently, I was
Russian. His demeanor turned from matter-of-factness and circumspec-
tion to a scramble of deference. In this part of Afghanistan, Americans
were still, at this early stage of the war, the heroes who had gotten rid of
the Taliban.

At the border, an Afghan official cheerily stamped my multiple-entry
visa, and I walked alone across the long bridge toward the Uzbek side.
When I got to the middle and showed the Uzbek guards my passport,
also with a multiple-entry Uzbek visa, the border officials look startled.
The bridge had indeed officially recently been opened with great fanfare,
they said, but there was a problem: My exit stamp from Uzbekistan was
a little ink blot in the shape of a boat, which indicated that I had left the
country by barge. Therefore, according to their logic, I would have to
reenter Uzbekistan the same way I had left—by barge. Except that no
one knew when, or even if, one would sail across the Amu Darya to the
Uzbek side again. . . .

Luckily the height of the bridge provided good cell coverage, and
I spent hours dialing US embassy numbers in Tashkent, the NPR foreign desk in Washington, and the satellite telephone of one of Dostum's Russian-speaking "colonels" back in Mazar-e-Sharif. But nothing
seemed to work—not cajoling the Uzbek border guards with kind words,
curses, or free cell phone calls to their distant families, or even proposing
special "fees" to be shared equally with all their colleagues as the border
post on the bridge. The bottom line was that they were obviously terrified of breaking anything even remotely interpreted as a rule, and they
would not budge.

My next plan was to engage in a war of psychological attrition, making them so sick of my presence outside their customs post that they
would beg me to just go through and *go*.

I lay down on the bridge in my sleeping bag. It was now December,
and an icy cold wind roared around me. A thousand stars filled the sky.

I thought again about the euphoria over the quick fall of the Taliban in Mazar-e-Sharif and Kabul, the enthusiastic reception toward Americans I had received, and the general sense that the American war to smash the Taliban for their support of al-Qaeda—unlike the many foreign interventions of the past, most recently the Soviet—would be short, sweet, and successful.

Then I thought about what the mercurial Dostum often said—essentially that Afghanistan's myriad regions were too different and unruly to be controlled by a strong central government—and that Afghans had been fighting for centuries with whatever came to hand, be it sticks or Stingers. Before I had arrived, not a single US military casualty had been recorded in Afghanistan. The first was Spann in the Qala i-Jongi uprising, him already dead on one side of the earthen walls and me hiding in a ditch on the other. But like a lone dark cloud drifting over the moon, the thought dissipated, and I was soon back in reverie. No, we were wanted here. How could one imagine that our entry into Afghanistan would result in anything but victory? Yes, lying there on the Bridge of Friendship, pondering, it seemed hard to believe that our exit from the country would ever be anything other than on our terms, and likely glorious. . . .

I woke the next morning to the gruff voice of an Uzbek military officer telling me to take my bags and head back to Afghanistan. I reminded him I was not on Uzbek soil. He angrily marched off and found his Afghan counterpart, the man who had seen me off the previous day. The Afghan was shocked I'd spent the night on the bridge and scolded a few underlings for not showing me the proper hospitality. He then offered me his own apartment in a Soviet-style bloc and sent a dozen of his young men in a halfhearted attempt to entertain me. They banged out tuneless ballads on upside-down baking sheets turned tambourines, and plied me with vodka, carefully concealed in a canvas canteen pouch. Dostum's personal stash? I was allowed to imbibe—all of this the Afghani way to atone for their fraternal Uzbek brothers having so inconvenienced their guest on the recently reopened Bridge of Friendship.

I got lucky with the barge. Many days were known to go by without one making a crossing. But the next night, the UN ferried some medical supplies across the Amu Darya into Afghanistan, and I copped a ride back to civilization, post-Soviet Uzbek style.

Behind me, the American campaign in Afghanistan seemed almost over.

It had hardly begun.

THE ISLAND OF DR. MOREAU

Having floated away from Afghanistan on the obligatory barge, I later headed for the ancient city of Bukhara. The Soviet-style Uzbek picture guide books described Bukhara as "a Museum in the Open," and that is not inaccurate. Despite a few propaganda posters praising "Papa" Islam Karimov and a new bronze Tamerlane statue, the city felt less touched by either Soviet Communism or post-Soviet commercialism than almost any other I had visited in the former USSR: a sweeping medieval expanse of one- and two-story sand-colored homes crammed together, bisected by tiny alleyways, and with minarets of six-hundred-year-old mosques towering above. Old men dressed in traditional robes and caps strolled about. Plump ladies stood outside the Ark, or fortress, in the center of the city, selling shiny pomegranates. A short distance away is the famous Jewish quarter, now reduced to a quarter or so of its original size after most of the twenty thousand Persian-speaking Bukharan Jews departed, mostly now émigrés to Brooklyn.

My stated reason to the Uzbek authorities was to visit Bukhara's Mir-i-Arab Medresseh, sometimes called the "Harvard of Islam"—one of the Muslim world's most respected centers of learning. Under Stalin and other Soviet leaders, it had been used to prepare ideologically "reliable" cadres of Muslim religious leaders—mullahs—in order to control Islam across the USSR. Now, it seemed, the venerated institution was being used for a similar purpose by the Karimov regime.

I pushed open the enormous wooden doors and was greeted by the

sounds of teenage boys running to and fro among the colonnades separating their living quarters. An older man who looked to be in charge
approached, and I was led down a long, cool, damp corridor, past some
of the rooms where the 115 future state-approved mullahs bunked, and
into a library filled with Korans and other Islamic literature (as well as a
copy of a book of the president's writings, on prominent display). A moment later, I was introduced to my host, Mukhuddin Imonov, the dean of
Mir-i-Arab. He had been expecting me.

Imonov had the air of a functionary, and it soon became apparent that
was his role: to enforce the state-approved form of Islam in Uzbekistan.

"We explain to the students there are incorrect forces . . . books
that poison people. . . . We do this so they don't go astray," Imonov
explained. "We teach them about radical groups and the mistakes they
make." Imonov then went into some detail about how this was part of
President Karimov's "National Ideology Program," a required academic
complement to any study of Islam in Uzbekistan.

I asked to speak to some students and was led into a room where
four boys were lying around on bunk beds. They had little to say when
asked about their studies and life in the medresseh, except when I asked
what they thought about radical Islam. All four began excitedly reciting
almost the same words that Imonov had said about the dangers of radical
groups and how they had everything "upside down," as one put it.

It was difficult to argue against the concept of educating budding
Muslim clerics about the undesirability and dangers of ultraradical Islam.
Karimov's desire not to see Uzbekistan succumb to the same ills that had
gripped its neighbor Afghanistan under the Taliban and al-Qaeda was
understandable. But I also had a sense that the inculcation process had
another goal—namely, that it was all part of the attempt by the Karimov
government to control everyone and everything, and all the time. Religion was simply being used as a form of control, or was being tightly
controlled for those who wanted to embrace it openly.

In fact, my visit to the Islamic Institute had been something of a ruse.

My real purpose in traveling to Bukhara was to see Yusuf Juma, a dissident poet who had only recently been released by the Uzbek authorities.

He lived on a collective farm near a place called Chovli on the border with Turkmenistan, and Bukhara was an excellent jumping-off point.

I hopped in a taxi and asked to be taken to Chovli. The destination was so obscure that the driver had to ask for directions even though he was a local and our destination only an hour away. I thought this strange, and even stranger when we had to ask for directions again. The issue was that Chovli was not a town, but a nondescript collective farm, and few who did not live there knew of its existence—nor that of the man who supposedly presented an existential threat to the Uzbek state, Juma, who was a collective farmer there.

An old man at the side of the road explained where Juma lived, and the driver, in Uzbek, inquired as to who he was. Upon learning that I was going to see a just-released political prisoner, the driver became decidedly nervous and refused to wait while I conducted my interview with Juma. I barely had enough time to hand him a wad of Uzbek *som* for the fare and get one foot out of the car before he slammed the taxi into gear and sped off, not looking back.

I was directed to a barn with a half-dismantled tractor parked outside. I knocked on the open door. A young man greeted me and led me through a hay-filled stable and up a rickety staircase to the living quarters on the second floor. There sat Yusuf Juma, banging one finger after another on the keyboard of an old mechanical Uzbek-Cyrillic typewriter. He was not expecting me, as I hadn't wanted to attract undue attention by trying to contact him beforehand, but he greeted me warmly nonetheless.

Given the government's irrational fear of his poems—unknown to almost all except a tiny group of activists left in Uzbekistan—I had expected to find a long-winded political firebrand, or possibly an implacably bitter, rambling soliloquist. Instead, I found a sturdily built farmer with an easy smile. He projected no sense of bitterness about his recent seventy days in solitary confinement for the crime of "antistate activity." Specifically, he had been caught writing "subversive poetry," as he had been all his life.

Born in 1958, Juma had started writing poetry in his teens, angering the Soviet authorities by writing verses calling for the closure of an airport used by pesticide-spraying crop dusters. Activists blamed the chemicals for a rash of unexplained cancers, miscarriages, and other assorted health problems. But in Uzbekistan, "cotton is more important than people," the collective farmer Juma told me.

The poem that got Juma in trouble he had actually written in the 1980s as a critique of the Soviet system. It was titled "Dr. Moreau" and was inspired by H. G. Wells's 1896 early sci-fi novel *The Island of Dr. Moreau*, about a failed attempt to turn animals into human beings, which in turn led to George Orwell's *Animal Farm*.

Juma recited a few lines:

Doctor Moreau, you tried to build a stairway to heaven from bales of hay. You've turned foxes into judges; They hide their eyes from injustice. You've brewed up bureaucrats from wolves; Turned rabbits into people.

  Look at our nation; They've submitted their lives to the yoke. . . .

I wondered why on earth the Uzbek government would expend such efforts to jail an obviously harmless poet-farmer.

"So what was their main complaint?" I asked.

"Officially, the authorities accused me of making fun of the president. They said I was trying to say that the president was descended from animals."

His days in solitary had not weakened Juma's poetic resolve. When I walked into his barn studio to find him banging away on his vintage typewriter (I was surprised the Uzbek authorities hadn't carted it away along with his poetry), I assumed he was crafting something new. He explained, however, that when he was arrested, the National Security Service (the Uzbek successor to the Soviet KGB) had confiscated nearly all his writings and that he was trying to retype them all from memory.

I sensed that Juma knew, and that he was indeed even proud of, the fact that his freedom was probably not permanent. There was no doubt the security services were keeping a close eye on him. We sat on the barn floor talking for several hours while his wife, Gyulnara, and several of his six children alternately joined in the discussion, laughed, or served endless rounds of tea. One of his daughters, aged twenty-one, had already been threatened with arrest for her own poetry. Uzbek Security officials had also gone to the local kindergarten and asked teachers if Yusuf's five-year-old son exhibited any "radical Islamist leanings."

Juma was no Islamist radical—that was obvious—but the government used the label to conveniently neutralize anyone deemed even a minor irritant or threat.

It started to get dark, and Juma and his family hunted down a taxi to take me back to Bukhara. We parted.

About five years later, in late 2007, Yusuf Juma and one of his sons got into their car. On the doors they had affixed handmade signs calling for the resignation of President Karimov. They put the car into gear and headed away from their home at the Chovli collective farm. They drove in the direction of Bukhara. Within minutes, squad cars forced the poet and his son off the road and pulled them out. One of the cops was allegedly injured in the fracas, and Juma was given five years in prison for "slander," as well as resisting arrest. Yusuf Juma was held in Uzbekistan's most notorious prison, Jaslyk, a word practically synonymous with torture. Initially he was allowed some family and Red Cross visits, during which he told of being chained to a ceiling, being beaten until unconscious, and forced to stand naked in a freezing room for hours. By 2010, the Uzbek authorities put a halt to visitations of all sorts, and Yusuf Juma for a period effectively disappeared from view. Human rights workers said there were reports he was near death.

Juma's poetry lived on, however, and a small group of followers— current and former inhabitants of the Island of Dr. Moreau—"Papa" Islam Karimov's Uzbekistan—kept up the pressure for his release or more information about his fate.

Just as I was completing this chapter, on May 18, 2011, the Uzbek authorities unexpectedly released Yusuf Juma—or, more properly, forced him into exile—describing the act as a humanitarian "amnesty" connected to the twentieth anniversary of Uzbekistan's independence. Juma was forced to give up his Uzbek citizenship. He was given no last glance at his homeland, which he so deeply revered. Juma was moved directly from a holding cell to Tashkent International Airport and was put on a plane for the United States, where most of his family had already been given political asylum.

PART VII
(2003–2011)

REVOLUTIONS, REINDEER, AND RADIATION

Elena Bibikova, Ulta folklore keeper, Sakhalin Island, Val, Russia, 2005.

T he facts of Georgia's 2003 "Rose Revolution" are now well documented. After years of anarchy, stagnation, and unprecedented corruption, a group of young, mostly Western-educated "reformers" plotted the regime's downfall, promising a bright new day for the Georgian state, still in shock from the ethnic and civil wars of the 1990s—as well as the reality that Georgia had gone from being the most prosperous So-viet republic to one of the most poverty-stricken ex–Soviet republics in a span of only three years or so. Their leader was a thirty-six-year-old by the name of Mikheil Saakashvili, whose boilerplate description usually included references to his educational pedigree (Columbia Law School), as well as his brash impulsiveness, seemingly boundless energy (once in power, he often hosted diplomats and journalists, including me, at meet-ings that began at three thirty a.m.). The adjective "flamboyant" has been used so many times in describing Saakashvili that it has begun to lose its meaning.

The "revolution" followed a rigged election and a couple of weeks of protests by Saakashvili's National Movement party. But it was so swift and unexpected—its active phase took only a day or so—that many for-eign correspondents had already left Georgia, their editors bored with the story and convinced that there would be no "revolution."

In the end, pundits concocted all manner of conspiracy theories to explain the Rose Revolution phenomenon—that it had been personally planned and entirely financed by the billionaire George Soros (Soros funded some NGOs, whose members ended up among the vanguard of the "revolution," but he could hardly be given credit for single-handedly bringing down the government). Another posited that the whole thing had been imported from Serbian "insurgents," overthrow-of-Milosevic-style. This was also a wild exaggeration—Saakashvili's party activists had indeed gone to Belgrade, openly, to study the tactics of that change of power, just as opposition movements and political parties study one another's strategies the world over.

The Rose Revolution was credited for inspiring other so-called color revolutions in the ex-USSR. They, however, proved to be fleeting, their leaders either deposed in farcical ways (it took only a hundred angry young men running into Kyrgyzstan's presidential palace to get rid of the increasingly authoritarian leader Askar Akayev. His successor was later overthrown in a riot, and the country descended into interethnic warfare). In Ukraine, 2004 brought the "Orange Revolution," which I lived through during its six-week-long unfolding. But what had seemed like a sea change in Ukraine withered away, as former allies—President Victor Yushchenko and Prime Minister Yulia Timoshenko—bickered themselves to death within months, eventually losing power to elements of the old authorities they had peacefully overthrown (Yushchenko, who won the high office in 2004 after an earlier vote was nullified because of massive falsification, got a miserable 6 percent of the vote in his "reelection" attempt five years later).

The Rose Revolution yielded many actual changes. One of Saakashvili's first acts was to fire the entire fifty-five-thousand-strong despised "traffic police" force—whose only competent quality was its ability to shake down drivers for bribes with astounding effectiveness. (Many were later rehired, but as regular police, and strict measures were put into place to stop bribery; the force stopped being feared and was actually trusted by most Georgians.) The electrical grid, dysfunctional for a decade, was put into order. Sweeping overhauls of the business environment meant that investments flowed in from abroad. There were also excesses, with some of Saakashvili's allies later breaking with him, often over personality clashes and ambition, and sometimes over what they saw as a concentration of too much power in his own hands. Most important, the tiny country, population 4 million or so, headed onto a collision course with giant Russia, population 140 million or so, a war of words over a host of issues culminating in a real war during 2008.

These are all the basic facts of the revolution. But I was more in-

terested in the last days in power of the titan who was toppled—
the-Man-Who-Ended-the-Cold-War, Eduard Shevardnadze—and what
had been going through his mind. A wily empire survivor, Shevardnadze had occupied political posts ranging from Soviet Georgia's
anticorruption-campaigning interior minister, to head of the Georgian
Communist Party, to Soviet foreign minister under Gorbachev, to finally
president of post-Soviet Georgia, leading the country under a banner
proclaiming the desirability of Western-style democracy.

THE FLAMING RECLINER

The throng—by now it was more like a mob—stormed into the Georgian State Chancellery, Eduard Shevardnadze's presidential palace. They raced from floor to floor of the rundown eleven-story Soviet-style building. Running like uncontrolled children do, rambunctiously, excitedly, they knew what they were looking for. In the end they found it (or at least thought they had): Shevardnadze's personal reclining chair, symbolizing his "power"—and at that adrenaline-spiked moment, symbols were everything. It mattered little to the revelers that the recliner was not actually Shevardnadze's; they had just snatched and torched the first one that looked regal enough to be the president's.

They dragged the recliner down a staircase and delivered it to the thousands assembled outside, as if the recliner were an animate object, a living, breathing incarnation of the famous Georgian leader who had just fled his office in the face of popular disgust. Someone now doused it with gasoline, and someone else threw a match; the chair exploded in flame, and the crowd roared its approval as if this were Salem, Massachusetts, and a witch was being burned at the stake.

Which all begs the obvious question: Why so much excitement in desecrating a reclining chair?

The answer is the following: In Georgian, the word *savardzeli* (literally, "chair" or "seat") also means "power" in the political sense, and "Shevy" had held it for the better part of thirty years in one guise or another. Georgians loved to quip about his attachment to "power" (*savardzeli*), the similar ring of the words s*hevardeni* (the etymological root of his last name, which means "falcon") and *savardzeli* adding an element of pun.

The final day was November 23, 2003. Ironically enough, this was the day when the nation celebrated Saint George's slaying of the dragon.

THE WRITING HAD been on the wall for several years. Aside from growing anarchy, reports were rife of members of Shevardnadze's inner circle or some relatives manipulating a growingly distant leader to enrich themselves. At one government meeting, he was reportedly forced to acknowledge this fact but slammed his fist on a table, emphasizing that in the world of close-knit Georgian families, one simply could not put one's close relatives in prison.

As the crisis deepened between demonstrators demanding that the-Man-Who-Ended-the-Cold-War quit, a nasty confrontation looked inevitable. Shevardnadze, after all, had been in positions of high power for most of the last thirty years. He wasn't going to give up power that easily, was he?

OVER HIS THIRTY-YEAR reign, Georgia's opinions of Shevy had swung back and forth wildly, almost schizophrenically. As Georgia's law-and-order-oriented interior minister from 1968 to 1972, he had been applauded by some for starting to rein in the republic's legendary levels of corruption, but was despised and widely feared by others, who resented their toes being stepped on, or as being the source of the corruption he was allegedly reining in. As its Communist leader from 1972 onward, he was generally seen as a Machiavellian schemer by average Georgians (who were always among the most anti-Communists in the entire USSR), but one who managed to obtain unthinkable concessions from Moscow for his republic. In 1978, tens of thousands dared to go into the streets and protest a proposal from Moscow to make Russian the only official language in Georgia, as in all other Soviet republics. Indeed, Georgia had been the *only* republic to have a constitution in which both Georgian and Russian were official languages—in all others, it was Russian only. Shevardnadze waded into the massive crowd and promised to do all he could to revoke the new law. The Kremlin backed down. Large demonstrations in the USSR were unheard of, never mind the Kremlin's backing down to the leader of a Soviet republic.

Then, in 1985, Shevardnadze was appointed Mikhail Gorbachev's Soviet foreign minister. A Georgian to lead the mighty Soviet foreign policy machine! And what's more, a boy from a tiny village called Mamati in the backwoods farming region of Guria.

Though many Georgians said Shevardnadze never did anything that might endanger his political career, some events suggest otherwise. His wife-to-be, Nanuli, had initially resisted his marriage proposals. Her father had been executed in the 1930s as an enemy of the state. She feared that this could either endanger Eduard's life or at least put an end to his budding political future.

Shevardnadze persisted with his marriage proposals, ignoring the risks, and they married in 1951.

While Georgians were proud that one of theirs had become the USSR's foreign minister, Communist bureaucrats in Moscow reacted with disbelief. After Stalin and Beria, another Georgian, and as foreign minister? Many scoffed at Shevardnadze's heavily accented Russian and said he wouldn't be up to the task.

He was soon to be a hate figure in Moscow among many Russian politicians as the man who "gave away" East Germany and helped bring down the Berlin Wall, and, along with Gorbachev, allegedly plotted to wreck the empire.

Then came the "Hundred Meters War" that wrecked Georgia's capital in the winter of 1991–92 as Zviad Gamsakhurdia was driven from power. Georgia's new leaders, the dramatist Ioseliani and the large-canvas painter and general hell-raiser Kitovani, however, were unable to secure international recognition, given their checkered reputations and the fact that Gamsakhurdia was ousted in a coup.

Georgia could not even secure a seat at the United Nations, practically alone among former Soviet republics. Ioseliani and Kitovani begged Shevardnadze to come back from Moscow, where he was out of politics, in order to confer a degree of legitimacy on their rule. Hundreds greeted him at the airport, tossing roses at his feet or kneeling. Again, the "Machiavellian Manipulator" as Miracle Man. With Shevardnadze's major international creds, Georgia was back on the map. Aid started to flow into the devastated country.

Even when Shevardnadze officially quit his post of head of state in 1993 in a disagreement with parliament over whether or not to sign a "peace plan" with the independence-minded Abkhaz, mediated by the Russians, thousands came into the streets and got on their knees again, asking him to reconsider. He did, and parliament agreed to sign on to the peace plan. He stayed, only to see Abkhazia fall several weeks later—the plan indeed appeared in hindsight to contain elements of a ruse.

SHEVARDNADZE WAS LAST elected in 2000, but there were more allegations of irregularities.

"The day after that election, I went into his office," one of his top aides (who I will call "The Witness") told me. "I saw emptiness in his eyes. Shevardnadze the politician died for me on that day. It was clear he had neither the desire nor the will to keep governing."

SHEVARDNADZE MADE ONE last electoral appearance, on November 2, 2003, to lead his "Citizens Union" ruling party in parliamentary polls. Most of his serious allies had deserted him, replaced by dubious characters known for corruption or bizarre behavior. Even with all the weight of the state behind it, Shevardnadze's "Citizens Union" came in only second in the elections, losing to the young Saakashvili's National Movement. Even that second-place result was pumped up by a lot of ballot stuffing.

Meanwhile, Shevardnadze was living in a Potemkin village created by the asset-stripping sycophants around him, most of whom hailed "our victory," assuring the seventy-six-year-old president that all was well. In reality, his approval ratings had fallen to a microscopic 3 percent. Only one aide, the Witness, had the guts to tell the president that if a "critical mass" of people came out into the streets to protest, he could be forced to resign. "Shevardnadze smiled and said I might turn out to be right, almost as if he wanted things to turn out that way."

A COUPLE OF nights before the day of reckoning, I went to Shevardnadze's State Chancellery. The building was empty and dark, and thousands of protesters had already assembled outside, screaming epithets like "Shevardnadze should be buried alive." Only the Witness remained in his office. All other aides had deserted. The Witness spoke in the past tense about Shevardnadze, as if it was all over. It was.

The Witness told me of how Shevardnadze, who had survived two serious assassination attempts and decades of intrigue and pressure, was simply not interested in ruling anymore. The way the "revolution" unfolded would affirm that.

The last year saw Shevardnadze spending much of his time at the side of his beloved and badly ailing wife, Nanuli, who regularly stayed up all night. He would often come to work at seven a.m., only after he was sure she was finally asleep. Essentially a lifelong teetotaler who drank sparingly and only during obligatory state functions but never showed any sign of drunkenness, he had understandably taken to sipping a bit of cognac now and then to calm his nerves.

"Of course, there have been many mistakes," said the Witness. "Much could have and should have been done differently," he said, speaking of the unbridled corruption and disorder in Georgia. "But if we speak about one man, he did his best."

Shevardnadze's biggest mistake was undoubtedly buying in to that wildly disorganized incursion into Abkhazia, a military operation that wasn't one, at least if you define it as having a clear objective. At the time, given that the art warlords Kitovani and Ioseliani were calling the shots, he perhaps thought he had no choice until he could sideline them and end the war. A riskier but perhaps more principled decision might have been to quit immediately, leaving two of the biggest, most destructive clowns in Georgian political history to fend for themselves. The fact he did not added fuel to the flames that Shevy preferred his seat of power (*savard-ʒeli*) over all else.

THE DECISIVE DAY was upon us. Shevardnadze vowed to go to parliament to open the new session, but there was no quorum—too many deputies were boycotting because of the election fraud. The Rose Revolution contingent led by Saakashvili vowed to block the session from taking place. A few fistfights broke out a few hundred meters away from the building.

That is when it became apparent that the vaunted state machine behind Shevardnadze was a fiction. Perhaps he wanted it that way.

Within minutes, the police stationed around parliament and the presidential building let the now tens of thousands of demonstrators flow through like water. (The government had not bothered to pay the police for months.) Next to parliament, army officers vowed not to intervene in what was becoming the inevitable. (The government hadn't bothered to pay them for months either.) The parliament session was to begin at four p.m. At 3:55, Shevy called the Witness. "What should I say to open parliament?" he asked. "We don't have a quorum."

"Unfortunately, we are surrounded," came the answer from the Witness, a physicist-empiricist not prone to euphemisms.

Shevardnadze answered that he understood.

As the session began, Mikheil Saakashvili, leader of the Rose Revolution, barged into the hall with hundreds of supporters, overwhelming a few guards at the door with relative ease. I was squeezed into the middle of the crowd. In his hand and in front of his bulletproof vest, Saakashvili held a bouquet of roses. He began shouting at Shevardnadze, who looked surprised and ashen. The president, after a few seconds in a trancelike state, was instantly spirited away to his residence on a hillside a few miles away.

Once back at his residence, Shevardnadze gave a rambling, nearly incomprehensible interview in which he expressed dismay and surprise, saying he had raised pensions and that the country's agriculture sector was improving. Then he announced a "State of Emergency," but because he had no loyal troops to rely on, he later admitted to me during an interview that it was more of a temporary way to cool passions than a serious measure, especially given that his army had effectively deserted him.

The next day, opposition delegates went to meet with the president. With surprising calm, Shevardnadze agreed to resign, in order to avoid bloodshed, he said. Thus, a peaceful transfer of power had taken place in a former Soviet state, a rarity.

Tens of thousands of Georgians descended on the main Rustaveli Avenue, almost everyone drinking wine and dancing, a national celebration.

Although he expressed occasional moments of bitterness, relief at having been spared the burden of his supposedly unshakable addiction to power was dominant. On the day after he resigned, Shevardnadze calmly and in high spirits went to his office and collected the memorabilia of thirty years in power: photographs with other world leaders, gifts from foreign dignitaries, and other trinkets. He and a secretary placed them in a box. Smilingly, he went home to his presidential residence high above the city, a comfort he was allowed to keep by Georgia's new rulers out of general respect.

A few dozen jeerers caught wind of his foray to retrieve his office belongings. They gathered outside the presidential building, expecting him to whisk past in his car, pretending not to notice. Instead, Shevardnadze insisted on stopping, shocking the demonstrators by getting out and engaging them in conversation.

"My time is over," he told them, smiling disarmingly. "Let's see what these young people can do with Georgia now . . . "

A few days later I went to see Shevardnadze. His eyes were clear and sharp, his voice assured. His recliner might have been destroyed in flames, but for the first time, the "Old Man" looked relaxed, and actually glad to be relieved of dealing with power.

• • •

WE MET A few more times over the years, most recently in May 2011, Shevardnadze at the time eighty-three but in remarkably strong health for a man whose life had been so shaped by upheaval.

We discussed a few main things. Shevardnadze had previously admitted that the war in Abkhazia during the early 1990s had clearly been a mistake, but said he had been powerless to stop it, as he was still at that early stage at the mercy of the warlords Kitovani and Ioseliani and was not even formally commander in chief of the "National Guard."

Then there was the subject of the Soviet Union. Could it have been reformed or dismantled less violently?

"No possibility," he said, repeating exactly the same thing he had told me fifteen years earlier.

The "Silver Fox" admitted that he had not anticipated the speed with which the empire would self-destruct. It had been he and Kremlin leader Gorbachev who on a walk along a Black Sea beach in 1985 agreed that "we cannot go on like this." What they meant was that the Soviet system was an untenable entity.

"I was convinced the Soviet Union would disintegrate. But to be honest, I was off by ten or fifteen years," reflected Shevardnadze, the former Soviet Politburo member. "I did not at all anticipate the USSR would fall apart so quickly."

Shevardnadze made another prediction he had made before: that Russia itself would break down further, along ethnic lines, especially in the hopelessly corrupt Islamist insurrection–troubled regions of Chechnya, Dagestan, and some others—all of which are almost totally dependent on billions of dollars, most of it used corruptly, to prop up local chieftains, like the technically pro-Moscow chieftain, Ramzan Kadyrov.

Enough politics.

SHEVARDNADZE, THE MAN so thoroughly associated with his supposed love of power above all else, had married a woman who tried her utmost to dissuade him—out of a fear that he would destroy his life because of her father's "enemy of the people" reputation.

And when Shevardnadze's wife, Nanuli, died, the now-president Saa-kashvili made an emotional call to Shevardnadze's aides, passing along a message that the government would help with her burial anywhere in Georgia.

Eduard Shevardnadze, the supposed political power-junkie, stated quietly that he and his wife had agreed they would be close together, whoever died first. "She said, 'We will be together,' " he told me. She insisted on being buried as close as possible to her still-living husband.

"So I had her buried right outside my door here, for us to be close to each other. It is what she wanted."

Georgia's patriarch, Ilya II, strongly advised against this; it was a violation of Orthodox practices. "Our patriarch told me that those not buried in family cemetery plots, and too close to their loved ones, were fated to a restless, nonstop suffering after their passing," Shevardnadze said.

"But we buried her here, right outside my door, and I am so gratified that we did."

LAST SONG OF THE ULTAS

It was March 2005. I set off on a five-thousand-mile trek and nine time zones to find them.

And while this is not the absolute maximum distance one can travel from Moscow and still be in Russia, it is very close. I wanted to know *how* they had survived, all 350-odd of them. Why were there so few of them? More important, I wanted to know whether they *would* survive. They were the Ulta people, their self-designation meaning "reindeer herder." They had been reindeer herders for centuries, as nomads, then had been forced into state collectives during Communism, and now were on their own again, living a post-Communist village life, neither nomadic nor collectivized.

I first read about the Ultas (called Oroks in Russian) while research-ing a trip to Sakhalin Island, the massive Russian island within sight of Japan. The actual intent was to get as far away from Moscow as possible, to again feel the incredible breadth of Russia, even after it had lost its fourteen former "colonies," or Soviet republics. There was plenty to re-port on. The island had a complicated history—until World War II the southern part was controlled by Japan and the north by Russia, which established a penal colony there for hard convicts. Chekhov had taken an arduous, more than two-month journey to Sakhalin from European Russia in which he lamented the inhuman state the prisoners were kept in. Now, in the mid-2000s, Sakhalin was again on the map, this time in the midst of an oil-drilling boom, with Western companies and ones controlled by the Kremlin squabbling over the spoils.

Crude-oil contracts were not what attracted me to Sakhalin. It was the natives who drew me—among them the Nivkhs and the Ainu, numbering just over a few thousand, living amid more than 200,000 ethnic Russian residents. And then there were the 350-odd Ultas, about whom I could find very little information.

So big is Sakhalin that it takes an overnight train ride from the pseudo-Western oil-boom regional capital of Yuzhno-Sakhalinsk just to get to the middle of the island, to the last depot in the town of Nogliki. Many anomalies of Sakhalin's curious history remain. The railway is not according to Russian standards: It was set up by the Japanese, who used a 3.6-foot wide-gauge track, as opposed to the 5.0 feet standard in Russia.

The train lurched forward and sideways, snow squalls buffeting us all night on the way up the island. We finally ground to a halt at Nogliki, a tiny town and kind of "capital" for the remaining native peoples.

I woke up, got out, and was met by Alexei Limanzo, a diminutive, quiet, but determined man, the head of the Sakhalin native peoples association. We drove to the house of a friend of his, where despite the early hour we were served rounds of vodka. When I went to empty my bladder, there was a slaughtered reindeer lying in the bloody bathtub.

I had arrived at my destination.

Limanzo explained the intricacies of the discipline: A reindeer's everything is edible, down to the intestines and other organs; the antlers are treasured, especially in Asia, as an aphrodisiac when ground to a fine powder. Limanzo arranged for me to meet with some of the local activists from among the Nivkhs, the largest of the native groups—but still numbering just a few thousand souls. Most of them were women. They seemed genuinely surprised that someone would be interested in their culture. I asked a lot of questions about the Nivkh language. The women explained that in addition to the neuter, female, and masculine genders found in Russian, for instance, there were specific genders for "round things" and, more interesting, for dogs—dogs being central to the native existence of sledding and herding.

The next day, a perfect sunny Sunday morning, I headed farther north to seek out my goal, the Ultas. About half of them live in the village of Val, a down-at-the-heels-looking hamlet, more Russian-style *izbushkas*, simple wood-frame houses. Pristine snow reached their rooftops. My taxi driver let me out of his car at eight a.m. Except for the incessant barking of dogs, there was not a soul stirring, and amid the silence, the crackling of my feet in the snow sounded like glass being smashed. I knew no one in Val and had no leads, save for the name of the head of a local reindeer collective that Limanzo had given me. Even then, I didn't have his address. I knocked on the first door that I saw.

A woman in a flowery robe opened it gradually, for some reason laughing that someone would knock on the door at eight a.m. on a Sunday morning in the middle of a subarctic, bone-chilling winter. She invited me in for tea. I declined, telling her I needed to find the reindeer herd man, Borisov. She made a motion to the left and then said turn right and then straight and to the left at the end of the road again. I got lost, and repeated this exercise at several other houses, until I finally found Alexander Borisov's humble abode.

I walked into the yard, which was guarded by a half-feral yapping dog. I knocked a few times. A scruffy-looking man, an acquaintance of Borisov's, opened the door and invited me in.

Borisov was still asleep, it turned out. There were the remnants of a birthday party from the previous night on a wooden table—nearly empty bottles of vodka and some half-eaten cake. Borisov had not been warned of my arrival. His friend roused him, and Borisov emerged, his hair tousled, eyes glued half shut, the remainder of his face inviting and warm. His first question was to ask me what the hell I was doing in Val on a Sunday morning. It seemed not too many outsiders visited.

Before the advent of Soviet rule, the Ultas had for centuries lived on nomadic reindeer herding, passing the winter months grazing them, and trading their meat or deriving sustenance from it during the summer. But the freedom to move about at will ended with forced collectivization. The reindeer herding continued, but in a more regimented form.

It was one of the ironies of the empire that although the Ultas were subject to collectivization (and the repression of their native language), state subsidies kept the reindeer business alive, even thriving.

Before the Soviet breakup, there had been fifteen thousand head of reindeer tended by hundreds of herders. Now, Borisov said, there were just a few hundred head looked after by a mere fifteen men or so. On the day I visited, they were somewhere out in the frozen lands on snow-mobiles, plying their trade, perhaps dozens, perhaps more than a hundred miles away.

Borisov got dressed and started telling me about the post-Soviet fate of the collective. Our interview started with the obligatory morning shot of vodka.

"We are a dying people," he told me, without any sense of regret or overemphasis, as if speaking of an empirical inevitability. "Without reindeer herding, Ultas will cease being Ultas," he said. When I asked about what his forebears had done for a living, he almost fell off his chair in laughter. "We are *Ultas*," he said.

I eyed a few reading items on a bookshelf. There was a magazine about race car driving, which Borisov was eager to talk about, although he conceded he'd never been close to a race car and the only road in the town was a dirt one. There was also an Ulta-Russian dictionary. I picked it up and started leafing through it. Borisov expressed the same sort of amusement that the Nivkhs had about my interest in their language. He gave me a few rough translations from Ulta into Russian. He conceded that only one thousand of the dictionaries had been printed—the work of a quixotic Russian linguist. Despite its rarity, Borisov insisted I take it as a gift—he had no real need for it, he insisted. That was clear—it looked as if it had never been cracked open. He signed it and eagerly put it into my hands.

I had more questions about Ulta traditions, folklore, and the language of the Ultas. Borisov admitted he was no folklore expert. He was a reindeer collective boss, and his mission was to resurrect the trade. Then he directed me to a house nearby, where he said I'd find a woman who was the local expert on the Ulta language and folklore. He warmly escorted me to the door and insisted I return during the summer, when he said the wildflowers were in bloom, the berries would be ripe for picking, and the nights were long and full of partying.

Borisov's dog was a poodle compared to the one I encountered at the house of Elena Bibikova, which was so large and ferocious it looked like it had been feasting on reindeer carcasses 24/7.

Bibikova, a slight woman with characteristic Asiatic features and a face etched with deep age lines, opened the door a crack. Without asking who I was, she invited me into her home, decorated with handmade curtains and dominated by the hiss of a natural gas heater. She explained that out of the people living in the village, only a dozen or so still spoke Ulta fluently, all of them elderly. She was the expert among them: the keeper of the language, so to speak.

Bibikova was incredibly patient, as evidenced by her gentle methods of dealing with her husband, Vanya. By now it was ten a.m., and Vanya was already smashed on cheap vodka, a remedy for unemployment and resignation. He called the rotgut *asetonka*—acetone, or paint thinner, and just such an aroma filled the house. Vanya invited me to join him in a round of his paint-thinner stash, but I was already staggering from the chief reindeer herder's toasts. I told Bibikova that I preferred some green tea.

We finished our tea (Vanya declined, calling green tea "atrocious stuff"), and Elena said she needed to go to her sister's house, across the street. She volunteered, with a bit of resignation, that "somebody has to take care of him [Vanya]. He has this mania—he doesn't sleep at night— only in the mornings. So I turn the gas off at night. I had to visit a relative in another town a few weeks ago, and I called the house to check on him. Vanya didn't answer." She thought perhaps he'd burnt the place to the ground. When she returned the house was intact, but the door was open— Vanya had simply wandered off to a buddy's house to find another bottle.

"When they get up in the morning here, they think only about one thing: where to go and drink—nothing else," said Bibikova. Again, it was the paradox of the Soviet system. Without the state subsidies that had kept the reindeer trade going—or at least made it dependent on the government—the Ultas' way of life had been ravaged. In this unforgiving, monotone climate, alcohol was the natural way of self-medication, and the parallels with disproportionately high levels of alcoholism among US Native Americans, equally displaced, were obvious.

Elena Bibikova was the only one in the village I met who seemed to recognize the significance of the impending loss of the language and identity of the Ultas. There were so many paradoxes at work. The development of energy-rich Sakhalin Island was as inevitable as the Ultas' inevitable abandonment of their nomad culture. Then again, the empire, with its mass of subsidies, had kept the Ulta way of life alive, by subsidizing their otherwise unprofitable reindeer-herding industry. Now those subsidies and preferences were gone, and the only ones left who cared were fighting a losing battle.

"I try to organize classes to teach Ulta to our young people, but most parents here say 'what's the point?' They'd rather their kids learn English than Ulta. We don't even have a system for teaching our language. Our language is dying. Nobody needs it."

Bibikova struggled on nonetheless. She composed simple ballads about Ulta life, reflecting on their customs of berry picking, and the precollectivization era of the months away from the village roaming the taiga forests, keeping camp while the Ulta men herded, and, of course, her singing of ballads.

"When our people rode in the sleds or the men would sit around, we would sing these songs. They were called 'ya-ya.' . . . I even made some up myself. I'd sing them to my sisters. When I was naughty, my mom told me: 'You don't want to do anything but sing!' "

Bibikova sang a song she had written herself, one she taught to the Ulta children in the village, or at least to those whose attention she could hold:

Ultay die risu
Ultay die risu
Ultay die rikhu
Ge-aya!

"We the Ulta people have lost our language. . . . People, do not lose your language. Speak it."

Bibikova betrayed no resentment that she was among only a handful of people still speaking Ulta fluently, all of them over sixty. "When we die, the Ulta language will die with us," she said.

Given her sense of conviction, I did not believe her.

HOME, SWEET CHERNOBYL

It was a bitterly cold, crisp December day, but Nina Melnik was determined to show me her snow-covered rose backyard garden, her new shed made of cedar, her Russian-style *banya* ("your skin will feel like a newborn's"), and her prized peach trees. It could have been anywhere in the vastness of pristine, pine-covered northern Ukraine.

Except that we were deep in the heart of the "restricted zone," the area around the Chernobyl nuclear disaster of 1986. The entire zone was evacuated after the accident—one hundred thousand residents hurriedly sent away to temporary shelters or to live with relatives and eventually given new, often shoddily built apartments in distant cities. So Nina was effectively an illegal, one of just four hundred defiant residents who had trickled back in recent years, their determination to stay and their ties to the land so deep that the authorities grudgingly acquiesced to their presence.

After all, it's tough to argue with people hell-bent on living in a declared "radiation belt."

Melnik is a Chernobyl icon. Irrepressive in her optimism, she preferred to talk about everything *but* the possible dangers of lingering radiation in the zone, from music to astrology. We sat in her home in the town of Chernobyl itself, drinking tea, just six miles from the now-shuttered plant covered by that giant concrete sarcophagus like a hastily erected tomb designed to prevent evil spirits, or in this case radiation, from leaking.

Everything about Melnik seemed in fact designed to project normalcy. Now around fifty, she lived alone on her street in the heart of the once-bustling town, the rest of the wooden-style Slavic houses gradually falling down, paint peeling, windows cracking, shingles falling off, beginning to lean to one side. Hers was immaculate, the floors buffed to a high gloss, the paint fresh. She talked about the other projects she was planning for the house and how the town was far from beyond repair, as if expecting an impending real estate boom in the deserted area.

She prided herself on running an organization that defended the rights of those who dared live inside the zone against warnings and official prohibitions.

It was not that Nina was a fatalist or had a death wish. She believed fervently that the emotional stress of the forced evacuation, even from areas not documented as dangerously contaminated—and the continuing prohibition from living in the zone—killed many more people than did the actual effects of radiation, which were also significant. And now she had been partially vindicated: A United Nations study in 2002 concluded that the emotional stress of resettlement, hypochondria, shattered communities, and unemployment killed or sickened many more people over the following years than the actual radiation, although it still remains to be seen what the long-term effects of the disaster will be.

Melnik exuded fearlessness about potential radiation poisoning, but also a beaming pride shared by the few residents who had trickled back to the zone.

"No one even thinks about radiation anymore," she told me, as if I'd asked a silly question. "It's gone out of our vocabulary."

It was Nina Melnik, a local radio announcer, whose fate it had been to make a broadcast on that fateful April 1986 day at about one p.m., some thirty-six hours after the explosion in Chernobyl Reactor Number Four sent chunks of highly radioactive graphite shooting out of the core, resulting in a fireball and mushroom cloud nearly one thousand feet high into the air above the plant. An old-style RBMK ("High-Power Channel-Type") Soviet reactor, Chernobyl lacked the basic disaster containment facilities that were obligatory in the West. Because of shortages, inferior materials had sometimes been used in construction. Officials put on trial for approving the use of inferior construction materials said they had been forced to, told by higher-ups that if they did not approve their use, someone else would.

It was simple. Nina Melnik was handed a piece of paper to read over the airwaves, from a studio in the now completely abandoned town of Pripyat, less than a kilometer from the plant itself and the most contaminated area in the zone.

"Citizens of Pripyat," she had read. *"There has been an accident at our nuclear power station. Collect enough food and clothes for three days. Buses will be arriving at two p.m. to collect you."*

"My voice was shaking," she told me. "I told people they would be coming back in a few days."

It's now been over a quarter of a century.

Scientists say people will someday be able to safely return to Pripyat, formerly home to fifty thousand people and just downwind of the plant, once the strontium-90 and cesium-137 and other radionuclides littering the soil break down enough to allow human habitation again—in an estimated thirty thousand years or so.

AS IS NOW well established, Soviet officials, once they began to understand the gravity of the calamity, organized a herculean effort to evacuate a hundred thousand people. Yet they also took days to admit the seriousness of the meltdown at Chernobyl, as a radiation cloud spewed contamination over Belarus, other parts of Ukraine, and Europe. The Communist authorities even ordered the annual May Day parade to go ahead in nearby Kiev a few days after the disaster.

Like the fiasco in Afghanistan that showed the limits of Soviet military power, Chernobyl became the symbol of a closed system of secretiveness and the brushing-aside of safety concerns in the name of meeting arbitrary state-set targets. Chernobyl forced the government to be more candid. Both Afghanistan and Chernobyl were factors in hastening the USSR's breakup. Indeed, one of the most lurid details of the accident was that even while Reactor Number Four was spewing radiation all the way to Sweden, the authorities kept Reactors Number One and Two running for another day, fearing political repercussions caused by power outages.

As the reactor burned, some Pripyat residents stood on a bridge nearby, mesmerized by the glow of the bright orange flames, as if watching a fireworks display. Many of them would be dead or sick within weeks or months, victims of massive radiation poisoning that would literally peel off their skin.

THOSE WHO WANT to visit the "exclusion zone" must make formal advance arrangements with the Ukrainian authorities. The road leading north from Kiev is deceivingly serene. Snow-covered forests dominate the drive, and we barely met another car. At the entrance to the "zone," men with Geiger counters bent around cars coming out, checking every rocker panel, bumper, and tailpipe.

"Sometimes cars go off onto the shoulder or back roads, and they can kick up radiation," said one. He was standing next to a sign with a symbol resembling those of the fallout shelters of my Cold War American youth.

I was met at the checkpoint by Rimma Kiselitsa, a curly-haired Chernobyl "guide" who worked fifteen-day shifts and spent the remaining fifteen of each month at her home outside the zone. "It's forbidden to work here constantly because of the radiation risk," she told me with obvious pride.

At the ten-kilometer circle drawn around the plant, we encountered a second, stricter checkpoint, where guards examined our papers like FBI officers checking for counterfeit currency. "This is the zone of strict control," whispered Rimma. There was the odd falling-down building here and there, more Slavic-style wooden *izbushkas,* seemingly quickly abandoned, as if the owners had fled in the middle of the night like fugitives.

Our first stop was a special "information center" where workers who man the decommissioned plant are housed—along with the guides like

Rimma, who mostly handle scientists and researchers. Then we headed to meet Nina Melnik.

Part of Nina's explanations about much of the zone being relatively safe soon became clearer. At the information center, Rimma had introduced me to a Ukrainian scientist brandishing a pointer and gesturing toward a map of Ukraine and Belarus. He pointed out that the original "exclusion zone" did not conform to the actual dispersion of radiation carried by winds in the days and weeks after the explosion.

"There are areas of central Ukraine where the radiation levels measured in the soil are far higher than some areas in the actual exclusion zone. The situation in southern Belarus is even worse," he remarked, pointing to a map area highlighted in deep red.

In other words, the idea of the original exclusion zones, including the thirty-kilometer "zone of alienation," had been more emotional than scientific constructs—clean, semiconcentric, and perhaps comforting politically, but having little to do with the actual spread of the radiation from Chernobyl. Years later, scientists redrew the zones to reflect that the area was affected unevenly and that closer proximity to the Chernobyl plant did not necessarily mean higher contamination.

Indeed—in some cases, authorities gave evacuees new housing in towns and areas that were later documented as being more contaminated than the official radiation zone around the plant.

WE LEFT FOR Pripyat, the eerie, empty city once home to fifty thousand, just down the road from the reactor. There is none like it on earth; if a neutron bomb is ever detonated, Pripyat gives a good idea of what it would look like afterward.

Almost the entire Chernobyl community of workers, from control room engineers to workers in the reactor core to cleaners to bookkeepers, lived in Pripyat—a fairly typical Soviet-style town of high-rise prefabs, a central square, and the requisite Soviet House of Culture—until Nina Melnik's announcement that the entire population had an hour to pack and get out.

A Ferris wheel stands in the center, finished so soon before the accident that it was never switched on. Rimma and our driver allowed me to wander around alone in the silence of the city. I walked up to the "new" cinema near the central square, as if still waiting for showings of the latest 1986 Hollywood knockoffs. I peeked into the local post office, where someone had rifled through piles of undelivered letters. Inexplicably, a dusty but glowing lightbulb hung from the ceiling, evidently never switched off or having burned out. There was not a single human being in the city, and a total silence prevailed.

"People are allowed to come back once a year to visit their old apartments, and it's very emotional," Nina said to me. She pointed out that scavengers had stripped out many of the appliances, even though they were likely contaminated with all manner of radiation. Thieves had even scavenged parts from cars that had been hastily buried in pits around the city after the disaster, stripping out everything from seats to engines to presumably contaminated wiring harnesses.

We visited the mini-museum at the power plant dedicated to the history of the calamity—a shrine to the heroes, from technicians to hundreds of firefighters—who fought the radiation fire after it broke out on the morning of April 26, 1986. Those at the plant during the explosion or others first on the scene were the first to die of radiation sickness.

"Why do you do this?" I asked Rimma, regarding her life choice as a Chernobyl guide. Her English and her intuition were so sharp that she probably could have landed work anywhere.

"I wouldn't trade it for anything in the world," she said. "We are a tight community, and those who are here *want* to be here."

WE DEPARTED THE information center and picked up Nina Melnik at her pristine house. We set off again, this time for a village in the zone named Opachichi. We passed over rolling hills in the twilight, meeting not a single car, not a single pedestrian, not a single sign of life until we reached a house where dim light shone through the windows. There were chickens pecking about in the icy yard.

Ninety-year-old Anastasia Chikolovets and her eighty-nine-year-old husband, Kolya, met us at the door like long-lost friends. We entered a single room, where some soup was warming on an old stove, and the elderly couple began the ritual of taking care of a rare guest to the now practically abandoned village.

Anastasia asked me to help her, motioning toward a shed outside in the cold. We opened an enormous old steam trunk. Inside was a huge glass jug that looked as if it could hold ten to twenty gallons of liquid. It was Anastasia's homemade moonshine, made from fermented leftover bread. I lifted the thing out of the steam trunk, and we laid it on the frozen ground, pouring the hooch into a smaller jug that we took back inside the house. I quipped about imbibing potentially radioactive moonshine, and both she and her husband laughed at me. "At our age, who cares about radiation?" Anastasia piped up happily. "It doesn't matter. We'd rather die here on our own land, whatever the reason."

She poured the bread moonshine into small shot glasses and the toasts began.

Anastasia recalled the recent history of Opachichi, where they had lived since 1946, seven years before the death of Stalin. Before "the accident," as everyone called it, there had been twenty thousand people living here. Now there were twenty. No post office, no stores.

She talked endlessly, and joyously, of their decision to return from the antiseptic apartment they'd been given in another Ukrainian city after being forced to leave the "forbidden zone" around Chernobyl, despite the total lack of services and the abandoned aura of the place.

As she ruminated about their choice to live in practically complete isolation in Opachichi, Anastasia continued to pile the table with *salo* (cured Ukrainian pork fat), pickles, and fish.

"How do you know what's safe to eat and what's not?" I asked.

Anastasia ignored the question, but Rimma answered for her: Nothing was allowed to leave the exclusion zone, period. For the workers like her, everything was required to be shipped in from the outside—from bottled water to canned tuna to ice cream.

"The fish in the rivers here have all been studied. Certain types, depending on their fat composition and physiological characteristics, don't show any evidence of radionuclide accumulation," she explained. "Others do. We know precisely which ones are safe and which are not. Berries and mushroom picking—that's strictly forbidden."

For me, it was surreal, watching humans adapt to the consequences of how their own technology had poisoned the land for generations. I tried to come up with a picture and ended up thinking of fish trying to discern which worms concealed a fisherman's lethal hook and which were harmless.

Anastasia, wearing an old cooking apron and a tattered blouse, stirred the soup in a big pot. She was tired of talking radiation. Kolya turned the knobs on an old radio and finally found some Ukrainian pop music to add some entertainment.

We downed shot after shot of the bread moonshine, making toasts to the delights of the semilegal life in the radiation zone. Anastasia showed practically no signs of inebriation; Kolya, in contrast, slowly moved over to the metal-framed bed and slumped up against the wall after his sixth shot, which must have been close to 120 proof.

"I've always been able to outdrink him," she said, laughing.

Nina Melnik, meanwhile, had gone to visit acquaintances in one of the only other inhabited houses in the village. Now she was back, taking off her boots just outside the door, slapping them together to shake off the perfectly pristine snow, and rejoining the party.

Nina, the woman who had announced the 1986 disaster to her townsfolk in Pripyat, now led us in the singing of traditional Ukrainian folk songs, the content of which I could not precisely understand because of the differences between their Ukrainian and my Russian. Then, after a long, last toast of the bread-based moonshine, we parted company with Anastasia and Kolya. Given their ages, I knew I'd never see them again.

As we drove along eerily deserted roads, Nina sang the entire way back to her house, through the blackness along the zone's snow-covered roads. She continued to explain her decision to live in Chernobyl, and to lead the effort to protect the rights of those who wanted to do the same.

"Without land under his feet, a person has no essence. Here there is everything. A forest, a river. My great-grandfather lived on this land," she said proudly.

A child was born in the forbidden zone that year, and everyone living there celebrated, without a thought about cesium, plutonium, or strontium.

THE ROAD TO THE SCHOOLHOUSE

2004

It was early morning on September 1, 2004. I had come back after one a.m. the previous night from covering a suicide bombing by a pro-Islamist insurgent at a Moscow Metro station. A woman had blown herself up in the entranceway of the busy Rizhky (Riga) station near the city center, taking the lives of nine others with her. A week earlier, two more "Shahidki," aka "Black Widows" (female suicide bombers), boarded two separate southbound planes in Moscow's most elegant, newest, and supposedly safest airport, Domodedovo. Their large, fluffy dresses concealed powerful suicide bombs. They detonated them only minutes apart, blowing the Tupelev-134 planes into pieces as they disintegrated on air traffic controllers' screens. I got the obligatory two-thirty a.m. phone call from Washington to try to explain it all live on NPR's *All Things Considered* to host Robert Siegel, and although to me it was obvious what had occurred—midair suicide bombings—we had few details to go on at such an early stage. Three weeks before that, another suicide bomber had attacked a Russian military hospital outside Chechnya, killing thirty-five. Another three weeks prior, a Chechen woman had detonated herself at an outdoor rock concert, killing another fourteen. (The organizers kept the rock concert going for several hours more despite the carnage, either because of the fact that some of the revelers were too oblivious—thanks to inebriation, the earsplitting sound of the music, or the enormous size of the venue—or because of a kind of classic Russian fatalism.)

So we knew something terribly ominous was up when the sketchy news came through on Russian state TV, early on September 1, that gunmen with some connection to the Islamist insurgency had entered a school in southern Russia, close to Chechnya.

September 1 is a special day, a festive holiday marking the first day of the academic calendar, when children dress up in their Sunday finest and parents accompany them for song, pictures, and celebration.

I was scheduled to leave that evening on a vacation to the United States and had been up packing a suitcase. It was the middle of the night in DC; no one would be answering the telephone. But it was obvious that this was something extremely serious, so without consulting with DC, I decided to stay behind and get to the town, now forever freighted with that infamous name Beslan, in Russia's North Caucasus region.

After a three-hour drive from Nalchik, I arrived with Boris Ryzhak, our NPR office manager, who helped me lug our gear around and guard it and who would double as an additional soundman. We arrived in the town of low-slung homes just before midnight. Beslan School Number 1 was not even visible through the swell of police and terrified towns-folk, whose relatives, friends, or children were trapped inside with the gunmen. After hastily attaching a car battery to our satellite telephone and going on the air live, we spent a couple of hours slumped over in the backseat of the car, waiting.

When morning came, it was clear that little *was* clear. Russian officials claimed that in addition to around two dozen gunmen, there were 354 people inside the school. And because Russian government media outlets were reporting that disinformation, many world media outlets were simply repeating it. Although something was very wrong with this depiction, the government was able to sustain that lie for another day or so before the real numbers of hostages became clearer.

Near the back of a city administration building, angered relatives confronted defensive local government officials. I listened carefully as the relatives insisted there were more than 1,000 hostages inside, not the 354 the officials were claiming.

The government gave very little away in terms of information. It was said most of the terrorists were from Chechnya—as well as a group of Ingush. It later turned out that there were also two Ossetians and, somewhat ironically, three Russians. The government claimed that the terrorists were making no coherent demands, though that also turned out to be a blatant lie. The demand had in fact been much the same as in previous terror attacks masterminded by chief terrorist Shamyl Basayev, who would later take credit for this one as well: that Russia fully withdraw from Chechnya and accept it as a neutral, independent state. This had been the case with previous major hostage takings in Russia—at Moscow's House of Culture of State Ball-Bearing Plant Number 1 theater in 2002—which I had also covered, as well as the 1995 Buddyonovsk hospital raid, which I detailed earlier in this book.

After herding the over 1,000 hostages into a sweltering gymnasium, the terrorists immediately executed several male hostages—either deemed physically fit enough to put up resistance, or ones they somehow identified as members of the Russian armed forces, former or current, perceived or not.

Time seemed to stand still throughout the next day, September 2. By this time the truth stated to emerge that more than 1,100—not 354—hostages were inside the schoolhouse. Relatives of those inside, some of whom I knew personally from years of working in the region, continued to descend on the scene, inconsolable. Russian Special Forces units, poorly disguised, moved in, going back and forth around some of the high walls leading to the school, along with young Interior Ministry troops, who were busy building sandbag barriers outside.

It was confirmed that the hostage takers were denying food—but much more important, water—to their captives, and that the young children inside the sweltering gym, who were desperately thirsty in the one-hundred-plus-degree Fahrenheit temperatures, were urinating into plastic bottles and passing them about to share.

• • •

ON SEPTEMBER 3 at about one p.m., the end commenced. In need of more minidiscs to record with, I had just started to walk back to the house where we were renting rooms from a local family when an enormous explosion shook the ground. To this day, theories abound: that either the Russians fired on the building with rockets or grenade launchers to end the siege; that the terrorists had accidentally detonated the booby-trapped bombs they had rigged up in the school gymnasium; that some armed local partisans started shooting in the direction of the school, and that the hostage takers, sensing the building was being stormed, began shooting back. A long gun-battle broke out between the terrorists inside and Russian forces, who investigations later confirmed had used tanks and flamethrowers in the assault. The rooftop of the school caught fire, the flaming beams eventually caving in, incinerating dozens of children, their parents, and teachers—together with some of the terrorists—still being forced to lie prone or stand in the gymnasium.*

By now the relatives had gone from inconsolability to hysteria, left to only wonder and hope their loved ones would survive. Ambulances inched toward the smoking school, but there were not enough of them, and the "rescue" was chaotic. I ran across a street to get closer. We started seeing injured, dead, or dying people being hauled away in the backseats of regular passenger cars. The firing between the Russians and the terrorists became more intense, bullets now flying inches above our heads. I lay flat to the ground with Natalie Nougayrède of *Le Monde,* and Paul Quinn-Judge, then of *Time* magazine. I was slightly elevated above Paul, and as the bullets whisked about, he calmly looked me in the eyes and said: *"Not many people are going to get out of there alive."*

During a lull, we moved toward the perimeter wall in front of the school. We were pinned down again as nonstop volleys of AK fire rang out from the building, bullets again whizzing over our heads or rico-cheting wildly between the walls and adjacent buildings. Then the dead

---

* For an excellent full investigative account of the Beslan School Massacre, please read Chris Chivers's outstanding article in the June 2006 edition of *Esquire.*

and injured started to flow out. A teenage girl, delirious but seemingly physically uninjured, ran to the safety of the crowd of relatives around the administration building near the school, oblivious to the back of her hair—mashed down with the brain matter of another hostage who had obviously not gotten out alive.

Slowly the shooting slowed. Then it gradually stopped. It was clear that most of the terrorists had been killed or, as some theories have it, escaped. Former hostages who had escaped the carnage ran from the still-smoldering building or were carried away, many in evident shock.

I approached one disoriented and wailing teenage boy, who asked to use my cell phone. He was filthy. He had been a hostage, as was his sister, but in the chaos he had lost track of her. She had still been somewhere in the gym as it erupted in flames, and he was sure she had died. Using my phone, he called her, punching the buttons on my cell phone repeatedly. He hit the redial button over and over, each time getting the same message: *"This number is either switched off or out of service."*

I felt inhuman with my large reporting microphone, not able to find the words to ask him to describe what life in the hell he'd escaped from had been like. Feeling at best an interloper and at worst a tragedy speculator, I put my equipment away. There was no prospect of comforting him with anything I could say or do, and any news value to be derived was either too callous or too voyeuristic for me to gather or to be interested in. After a few more fruitless cell phone calls, he sprinted away in tears.

I went back to my transmission gear, which was lying on the ground in front of the local administration building. An editor from NPR in Washington called saying there were reports that dozens of bodies were lying outside the school, victims, evidently killed on the first day of the siege, when the terrorists had executed a number of young men, most of whom they believed to be Russian servicemen. *"Go and check,"* he said.

It was not that quite that easy—near-delirious Russian Special Forces surrounded the school, letting almost no one pass. New reports of victims and myriad gory details were coming in faster than water pouring over a dam. Moreover, the phone was ringing off the hook with requests from various NPR desks demanding news.

"Get to the morgue" was the next set of instructions from the NPR foreign desk. I didn't actually need such directives; it was a natural next place to go and I was already on my way.

There was not much of an actual morgue in Beslan, simply a hospital where the small basement morgue had overflowed as the first bodies were brought in. The rest were laid down in a courtyard, mostly children, who would turn out to be 186 out of the at least 334 victims, many badly burned. Relatives searched frantically. On one plastic sheet the bodies of two boys lay together, looking like twins, their father or a relative embracing each one by one and putting them down again. I asked no one any questions, just listened. Many of them screeched uncontrollably, livid with President Vladimir Putin, whom they accused of not having done enough to avert bloodshed.

My office manager, Boris, a deep, emotive six-foot-two man with three children, broke down and wept openly as we exited the makeshift morgue. I bit my lip and walked on.

The electrical power in Beslan went out that night, and we were barely able to assemble our story for *All Things Considered* on car batteries before transferring the sound and tracks to Washington. I then downed about seven beers and pretended to sleep, eyes wide open.

The next day was a Saturday; it was not until Sunday that we were allowed into the school. Once inside, we found bone fragments everywhere, and in one room, a skull fragment, hair follicles intact, stuck to a wall belonging to a female suicide bomber who had blown herself up or set off her explosives by mistake.

Relatives of those still missing, and almost certainly dead, milled about the reeking-of-death gymnasium, grasping photographs and asking anyone who would listen if they had seen their people.

The thing that struck me more than anything is that hundreds of us—journalists, relatives of victims, and townspeople—were allowed to roam freely about the mostly burned-down school.

There was no attempt to stop anyone from picking up, kicking, or moving evidence in what was, after all, a crime scene. There were no police. It certainly seemed like a calculated effort to let as much evidence as possible be destroyed.

One of my most serious questions involved a gaping hole in the lower brick outer wall of the school. It had obviously been created by some sort of high-caliber weapon fired from outside the school.

Later, I interviewed a teacher who had been held hostage inside. She had been hiding behind a locker-sized safe in the gymnasium when she said the Russian Special Forces fired a rocket or other high-powered weapon, opening that gaping hole in the side of the school. Many other hostages recalled the same account.

This, they maintained, allowed some of the captives to escape but also set off the furious battle that would end in the school's being turned into an inferno, taking more than three hundred lives with it.

By the end of the day, what clearly was a gaping hole had been walked through by so many people that only a pile of bricks was left, evidence destroyed.

Mass funerals were planned for Monday, September 6. Nearby, entire farm fields had to be quickly converted into cemeteries. A crowd gathered just outside of the school, many hoisting coffins.

Reporters rushed behind the coffin carriers, but I felt a kind of sickness and sense of selfish voyeurism that I had never quite experienced in so many years of reporting on senseless violence and killing.

SO I DECIDED not to go to the Beslan funerals. I'd had enough in so many years of covering carnage, and Beslan was beyond the pale. I told myself not to go. I swore I would not go. I could be of no help to anyone there; I'd only get in the way, a vulture pecking away at the sacred right to grieve. My office manager, Boris, swore that he would not be one of the "vultures" at the mass funeral either.

In the end, however, my news instincts won the day; we proceeded, somehow automatically, following the procession to the muddy former farm field, a wailing ground, women and men screaming uncontrollably as coffins were lowered into the ground. Ashamed, I did my story and left, at least somewhat relieved that a few of the mourners actually felt a need to tell their stories to me without being asked, describing the lives that had belonged to their relatives. Maybe I hadn't gone completely in vain.

I'LL BROACH A subject that I intentionally avoided during the writing of most of this book, not having wanted to distract from the stories I was relating. Covering war and scores of human tragedies, which is what I did for nearly twenty years, is a bit like exposing oneself to radiation. In carefully measured doses, it often poses few well-established health risks, as for those who continue to work limited shifts in the most contaminated areas of Chernobyl—although journalists can also suffer devastating psychological effects from even a single traumatic event, just as soldiers and emergency workers can.

Unlimited exposure over very long periods, however, is unwise for the mind and soul, and I've seen the deadly effects on many a fellow reporter, from relationship problems to irritability to self-medication and various forms of depression, including a higher than normal rate of suicide among those who specialize in covering such stories. In many cases, denial precedes acknowledgment, often in the form of justification that any ill effects we suffer are minuscule compared with those of the victims we write about. All of this exacerbates the symptoms. It can also take over a decade for symptoms to suddenly appear, even if the traumatic experiences were limited in duration or involved only single events.

There are also special risks in covering essentially one interconnected area, as I did, for highly extended periods—in my opinion, because of the personal relationships and emotional bonds that develop with the people and their respective countries that one writes about over such a long period of time and the difficulty of combining these bonds with the journalistic need to stay somewhat removed from the situation. Many correspondents who end up spending more than their fair share in a single war-affected region pay an especially high price in this regard.

I CAME TO no quick conclusions on that September day in Beslan, but I did increasingly start to question the nature of my work. It was a combination of factors—my adult life mostly spent on writing about people killing each other out of the most primitive motivations; the fact that I knew many of the victims either personally or through their extended families; the sense of denial that I could report on all of it without any effect on my psyche or those close to me; and in the case of Beslan, the fact that most of the dead were children, deprived of the natural, celebratory rites of passage in this life, just as thousands of children in Chechnya had been by the war there.

PART VIII

AN EMPIRE EPILOGUE

I n 2006 I took a trip to St. Petersburg. I dialed the same number, 233-4832, and Nina Nikolaevna answered what I imagined in my head was that same indestructible East German–made rotary phone. She insisted I head off on the Metro to her communal, where she was still living and where I had stayed during that summer of 1989. It was around dusk, and I walked along in one of the classic mists that often envelop the city in a sometimes annoying but always elegant haze.

Talalikhina Lane had been spiffed up with new shops and repainted buildings. I stopped to watch the worshippers trickling into St. Vladimir's Cathedral, which looked exactly as it had almost two decades earlier. The cheap beer stand was long gone, along with the drunks and their skirmishes with the churchgoers. As a sign of the times, an upscale wine store had opened in a building across the street. I remembered it as a place where a state worker used to sit outside from time to time, selling single eggs for few kopecks each. The wine store was now selling a bottle of 2005 Dom Perignon priced at more than three hundred dollars.

I ascended the stairs to Nina Nikolaevna's. Despite the exterior repairs, the stairwell was as dark as ever, its iron railings and broken tiles a throwback to pre–Bolshevik Revolution days. The old mechanical bell had been replaced by plastic doorbell buttons. When pressed, they made sound reproductions of birdcalls.

She was still there after all these years, a few more silver teeth, a slightly larger limp, but smiling and seemingly strong. No less commanding than before, she quickly assembled a pair of ill-fitting *topochki* (slippers) and ordered me to doff my shoes and come in.

She looked surprisingly well for a woman of eighty-one who had some sixty-two years ago barely avoided starving to death. Most of the former inhabitants of the communal were gone, she said, explaining that either this one had died or that one had moved away to some unknown destination. All of them except the Widow, who emerged from her two-room spread and greeted me warmly.

Ever the matriarch of the communal, Nina Nikolaevna ordered me to sit down. An old TV blared out the evening staple of the Russian state-run news program, the content dominated by the daily activities of President Vladimir Putin. Inevitably, as a woman who had initially lamented the empire's demise, she generally supported Putin, despite his authoritarian reputation. The reasons for this were not difficult to understand.

Like many Russians, Nina Nikolaevna was not a political person. Her material life had improved considerably. *It had become predictable again.* She and her husband received their pensions on time, and at about $250 a month total, with no rent to pay, the money was enough to get by on. The city authorities had repaired her leaky ceiling and replaced the dusty orb hanging from the hallway ceiling with progressive-looking, if antiseptic, fluorescent lights. Every week she handed a state social worker a list of needed groceries. The worker delivered the groceries to her communal room for a nominal fee, the equivalent of about $1.50.

"These may be little things to you, but they make it a lot easier for us. Under Yeltsin our pensions were never paid on time and no one could have been bothered to patch up the ceiling," she said.

Nina Nikolaevna argued that Putin had instilled some sense of order with his heavy-handed ways.

"Now people respect Russia in the world again," she said with a confident smile. Her husband, Igor, quiet as ever, nodded in affirmation. Perhaps Putin had not been able to resurrect the empire, but according to Nina, Russia was once again a country to be taken seriously, according to the newspaper accounts she was reading.

She did have one main qualm with Vladimir Vladimirovich Putin:

"His main problem is that he is not tough enough," she told me.

It was the kind of feeling backed up by other Russians, particularly older ones, who had lived through the chaos and economic meltdown of the 1990s. The transition was still shaky; corruption still rife; but petrodollars were just starting to flow into the economy. Tellingly, surveys of all kinds show that although few would prefer a return to communism, contemporary attitudes to, for instance, former dictator Joseph Stalin are mixed. In 2003 a majority regarded Stalin's bloody reign more positively than negatively, and in 2010 another survey showed that while approximately half of Russians expressed "indifference" to Stalin, a substantial minority still revered him as a great leader.

I was not about to get into a pointless polemic with an octogenarian woman who had lived through multitudes more than I, and whom I had come to see, perhaps for the last time.

We sat around the same battered wooden dinner table in that lone communal room with the sheet hiding the bed in the corner, and, together with her trademark soup and mashed potatoes, we downed a bottle of Moldovan wine.

I asked why she and her husband, Igor, who again sat at the table but said little as I conversed with his wife, continued to live in the communal. History was repeating itself; just as rich barons owned the stately building before the Bolsheviks carved it up, now rich businessmen were buying up communals and reincarnating their regality. Often there was a tenant or two holding out for more money, so real estate movers and shakers gradually bought the individual rooms from them, in which turn the residents could buy a comfortable, private flat in the farther-flung but quiet bedroom district of St. Petersburg—devoid of all the distractions of the communal.

Nina Nikolaevna laughed.

"Yes, we could have moved many times. But at our age? We've been here for forty years. They offered us apartments far away, but here we can walk out and see the Winter Palace." (The former czarist residence, which now houses the Hermitage Museum.) "They'll sort it out when we die anyway, so what's the rush," she said, laughing again.

WE FINISHED DINNER and said our good-byes. I called Nina Nikolaevna several times over the next three years or so, rechecking the details of her eventful life, which she reiterated in razor-sharp recollections.

Nina Nikolaevna, born on September 11, 1925, finally suffered a stroke, and died on December 10, 2010, at the age of eighty-six.

A BOOK ABOUT the implosion of the Soviet Empire doesn't really have an ending; for the fragmentation from that supernova continues to this day and will continue for years and probably decades.

Immense changes have taken place over the years this book covers. Few of these changes fit into clean categories or embrace the neat story lines that lend themselves to the traditional nonfiction literary "arc"; and while all involve more fragmentation—personal, social, or otherwise—each has its distinct features.

The visitor to many of the states of the former empire—from now-oil-rich Kazakhstan to Moscow or St. Petersburg—would be hard pressed to recognize them from what they looked like, at least on the surface, in the anarchic 1990s. Enormous supermarkets and every conceivable type of creature comfort are available just about everywhere. A middle class, in many cases fueled by oil wealth, has emerged in many former Soviet republics. In Georgia, the years of electrical blackouts are history, and the capital, Tbilisi, has been transformed into an orderly place, decorated with new buildings and beautification projects. Poverty, however, remains a serious problem in Georgia, as in many former Soviet republics, especially in rural areas.

And the former empire is dotted with unresolved conflicts. Witness the slow buildup to a war between Russia and Georgia over the tiny region of South Ossetia—a smoldering conflict few paid any attention to until it exploded on an August night in 2008—a deeply complex combination of geopolitics (namely, Russia's efforts to reestablish itself as a power to be reckoned with in the world coupled with its desire to carve out a zone of influence in the former Soviet space, especially in coveted Georgia), ethnic discord, and a lack of careful contemplation on the Georgians' part as to the consequences of getting involved in a full-blown war with their giant northern neighbor. To simplify the demographic problem of a population split between twenty-five thousand or so Ossetians and a roughly equal number of Georgians, most ethnic Georgians were forced to leave South Ossetia, their homes burned and then bulldozed. Following the short war, Russia nearly alone recognized South Ossetia and Abkhazia as "independent countries," and established military bases in both, in violation of an internationally backed agreement that ended the short war. And Georgia still has yet to fully acknowledge that it faces real disputes with ethnic minorities like the Abkhaz or the Ossetians, as small as their numbers may be.

The conflict between Azerbaijan and Armenia remained at a deadlock as of this writing, bogged down in details, both sides continuing to arm themselves to the teeth with more and more sophisticated weapons, bringing closer the prospect of another, and far more dangerous, war.

The republics of Central Asia for the most part have continued to grow more authoritarian. In Kyrgyzstan, 2010 brought an out-of-control blowup between ethnic Kyrgyz and ethnic Uzbeks in the south of the country. Neighboring Tajikistan's economy found its only economic comparative advantage, in acting as a narco-traffic state for heroin or opium coming through from Afghanistan. The bizarre "Head of All Turkmen," Saparmurat Niyazov, passed away in late 2006, replaced by a less eccentric but only slightly less repressive leader, a former dentist with the challenging name (at least for English speakers) of Kurbanguly Berdymukhamedov.

Uzbekistan remains practically unreformed and mostly closed to the outside world, and Belarus, which never really wanted independence from the empire, given its close cultural and linguistic links to Russia, is alone in having retained a truly planned economy.

But it is Russia, of course, the former empire metropole, that remains the biggest question. With its eighty-eight regions and dozens of languages and ethnicities, Russia is still an empire in many ways, albeit a smaller one today. The biggest issue is what will happen with the country's predominantly Muslim North Caucasus region. Russian spent billions to rebuild the Chechen capital, Grozny, but the trade-off was to hand power to Ramzan Kadyrov, the son of the country's former separatist chief mufti. Kadyrov has an unbridled taste for luxury and excess, including expensive cars and a personal zoo. He's also accused of personal brutality, opponents and critics having disappeared or been killed in brazen ways, most notably the brave journalist Anna Politkovskaya and the fearless human rights defender Natalya Estimirova.

Ironically, Kadyrov has achieved a level of independence from Moscow that even former "real" separatists might envy, replete with the trappings of Sharia law. As long as Moscow keeps the cash flowing, Kadyrov keeps the Russian flag flying. The Kremlin, in most other ways, leaves its hands off Kadyrov to run Chechnya as he sees fit. Kadyrov has nonetheless made many enemies, and it remains to be seen how long he will hold on to power.

Meanwhile, the once-secular Chechen independence movement morphed—thanks in no small part to the brutality of Moscow's Chechen campaigns—into a violent regionwide insurrection by varied Islamist radicals who want to set up a "caliphate" across the southern parts of Russia populated mostly by Muslims. The insurgency is an increasingly bloody one, and Moscow has paid billions to support regional governments there, including that of the handpicked Chechen leader Kadyrov and his personal militia—many of them former separatist fighters. It paid billions more to rebuild shattered Grozny. There is every chance the Russian public may grow tired of holding on to Chechnya and the broader region around it, whose population is growing at a much faster rate than the Slavic, Orthodox Christian part of the country. One recent survey found that nearly two-thirds of Slavic Russians no longer wanted the Muslim republics of the North Caucasus region to be a part of the Russian Federation.

The process of a further fragmentation of Russia itself is entirely possible, though few but the most addicted Russia watchers seem ready to consider the consequences, another symptom of the simple truth that the concept of empire—and life itself—are fleeting, we humans rarely able to react until after the facts have seared themselves into history.

Lawrence Scott Sheets
July 2011

ACKNOWLEDGMENTS

For more than twenty years, so many people have contributed to making this book a reality, both consciously and casually, through their generosity, time, and patience.

First, there are those, described in the book—we traveled, reported, lived, celebrated, and mourned together—whose lives ended prematurely in reporting the events described herein. They were my friends. They include the late Adil Bunyatov, Farkhad Kerimov, Taras Protsyuk, and Adlan Khasanov, with whom I worked at Reuters. Galina Nizhelkskaya was not a reporter but a friend, and all of these brave individuals never wavered in their understanding of the dangers of living where they did and doing what they did, and the potential consequences—and paid the ultimate price far before their time.

My three younger sisters served as hands-off, no-pressure muse inspirationalists: Annie-Laurie Sheets Jankowski and her husband, Dr. Marcin Jankowski; Kristin Nicholson and her husband, Tom; and Valerie Robichaud and her husband, Dr. Jeffrey Robichaud; as well as my niece, Kristin-Annie Espinoza.

I am deeply grateful to Gillian MacKenzie of the Gillian MacKenzie Agency, who was absolutely unbridled in her belief, even when mine wavered.

Vanessa Mobley, my editor at Crown worked under great pressure and offered constant reassurance and support, as did her assistant, Stephanie Chan.

Rachel Klayman of Crown understood from the start the time needed to complete the book.

Michigan State University and Dr. Sherman Garnett, Dr. Folke Lindahl and his wife, Dr. Oumatie Marajh, Dr. Michael Schechter, and Dr. Norman Graham allowed me a degree of freedom that gave me time, space, and support to think and write.

Author Thomas Goltz was good-humored with his five-a.m. phone calls to make sure I was up and working on the book; he was a well-needed war travel companion, possessing a keen eye as a brutally honest (even if rightfully opinionated) reader and adviser.

Dr. Ronald Suny of the University of Michigan provided companionship, support, and advice. Dr. Andrew March of Yale University provided guideposts on the nature of, among other things, Uzbekistan.

Thomas Dworzak of Magnum Photography offered great friendship, resilience, humor, help, and photo advice.

Dr. Frank Ochberg provided immense personal support, as did Dr. John Funkhouser and the entire Funkhouser clan: Andrea, Sarah, Lisa, and Peter Funkhouser.

Dr. Viktor Dmitriev and Mila Dmitriev helped in ways only they are capable of imagining, and supplied many details about their Leningrad lives that helped fill in missing fragments.

James Bettinger and Dawn Garcia of Stanford University were always there to help. Thomas Dumstorf, John Karren, Thomas Jackson, Ariela Shapiro, and Masha Savchuk generously offered their time to review the manuscript and offer words of encouragement.

Dr. Louise Arbour, Dr. Sabine Freizer, Alain Deletroz, Andrew Stroehlein, and Iskra Kirova of the International Crisis Group were gracious and patient through it all.

From National Public Radio I wish to especially thank Irina Mikhailova, Boris Ryzhak, Kevin Beesley, Ivan Watson, Michael Sullivan, Bob Duncan, Steve Inskeep, Renee Montagne, Martha Wexler, Melissa Block, Lisa Simeone, Richard Gonzales, Michelle Keleman, Kitty Elsele, and Paul Brown.

Eteri Chkadua offered patience, humor, and insistence during the last difficult months of writing. Many friends contributed in all sorts of ways, from knowledge to wisdom to camaraderie and support, including John Pollack, Lana and Dr. Henry Pollack, Dr. Alexander Rondeli, Dr. Aslan Dukayev, Dr. Robert Parsons, Nino Kirtadze, Mika Khruashvili, Richard Giragosian, Esma Khunchulia, Mike Payne, Nestan Nejiradze, Ninka Nejiradze, Sergiy Karazy, Eve Elden, Ekaterina Kuba, Magdalena Frichova, Sophia Elza, Alexis Rowell, Liam McDowall, Nino Ivanish-vili, Martin Nesirky, George (Zhorra) Vardzelashvili, Mark Mullen, Dato Chikhvishili, Margarita Antidze, Petre Mamradze, Karina Khodikyan, Khalid Askerov, Hugh Pope, Natalia Amirejibi, Tom de Waal, Michael Ochs, Lado Pochkhua, Hasmik Mkrtchyan, Victoria Belyavskaya, David Mikautadze, Jan Lopatka, Nino Maglakelidze, Shahin Hajiyev, Richard Wallis, Dr. Asim Mollzade, Ada Trapsh, Zurab Smyr, Helena Bedwell, Vanora Bennett, Manon L'Oiseau, Natalie Nougayrède, Boris Eisen-baum, Nana Talakvadze, Georgina Prodhan, Seda Muradyan, Hussniye Babaeva, Terezie Taubelova, James Hill, Magda Nowakowska, Matthew Collin, Varvara Pakhomenko, Arkady Ostrovsky, Sergei Lazaruk, Gini Sikes, Robert D. Kaplan, Misha Glenny, Robert Finn, James Weimann, Helena Bedwell, Nick Ivanishvili, Natia Koiava and Tea Koiava, Steve LeVine, and Elizabeth Eagen.

SELECTED BIBLIOGRAPHY

Altstadt, Audrey. *The Azerbaijani Turks*. Stanford, CA: Hoover Institution Press, 1992.

Areshidze, Irakly. *Democracy and Autocracy in Eurasia: Georgia in Transition*. East Lansing, MI: Michigan State University Press, 2007.

Astourian, Stephan. "Armenian Migration Crisis in the South Caucasus, 1988–2000." *Contemporary Caucasus Newsletter*, Issue 10 (Fall, 2000). Berkeley, CA: Program in Soviet and Post-Soviet Studies.

Baiev, Khassan. *The Oath*. New York: Simon & Schuster, 2003.

Barfield, Thomas. *Afghanistan: A Cultural and Political History*. Princeton: Princeton University Press, 2010.

Bissell, Tom. *Chasing the Sea*. New York: Pantheon, 2003.

Blanch, Lesley. *The Sabres of Paradise*. New York: Carroll and Graf, 1960.

Brodsky, Joseph. *Less Than One*. New York: Farrar, Straus and Giroux, 1986.

Brook, Kevin A: *The Jews of Khazaria*. Lanham, MD: Rowman & Littlefield, 2006.

Bullough, Oliver. *Let Our Fame Be Great*. London: Basic Books, 2010.

Chernyaev, Anatoly. *Shest' let s Gorbachevym; po dnevnikovym zampisam*. Moscow: Progress Kurtura, 1993.

Chorbajian, Levon (et al.). *The Caucasian Knot*. London: Zed Books, 1994.

Derluguian, Giori. *Bourdieu's Secret Admirer in the Caucasus*. Chicago: University of Chicago Press, 2005.

———."How Adjaria Did Not Become Another Bosnia," in *After the Fall*, London: Routledge, 2001.

———. "The Forgotten Abkhazia." Working Paper No.18 for Program on New Approaches to Russian Security. Council on Foreign Relations, 2001.

————. "Recasting Russia." *New Left Review* (November–December 2001).

De Waal, Thomas. *The Black Garden*. New York: NYU Press, 2003.

De Waal, Thomas, and Carlotta Gall. *Calamity in the Caucasus*. New York: NYU Press, 1998.

————. *Chechnya: A Small Victorious War*. London: Pan Books, 1997.

Eismont, Maria. *The Chechen War: How It All Began*. Washington, DC: Jamestown Foundation, March 1996.

Feifer, George: *Moscow Farewell*. Backinprint.com, 2000.

Fairbanks, Charles Jr. "The Post-Communist Wars." *Journal of Democracy*, Vol. 6, No. 4, 1995.

Gellner, Ernest. *Nations and Nationalism*. London: Blackwell, 2000.

Ginzburg, Eugenia. *Journey into the Whirlwind*. Philadelphia: Harvest/HBJ, 1967.

Goltz, Thomas. *Azerbaijan Diary*. Armonk, NY: M. E. Sharpe, 1998.

————.*Chechnya Diary*. New York: St. Martin's Press, 2003.

————. "Russia's Hidden Hand." *Foreign Policy*, No. 92, Fall 1993.

Graham, Norman A. and Lindahl, Folke, eds. *The Political Economy of Transition in Eurasia: Democratization and Economic Liberalization in a Global Economy*. East Lansing, MI: Michigan State University Press, 2008.

Henze, Paul. *Islam in the North Caucasus*. Washington, DC: RAND Publication, 1995 (P-7935).

Hewitt, George. *The Abkhazians*. New York: St. Martin's Press, 1998.

Hildinger, Erik. *Warriors of the Steppe—A Military History of Central Asia*. New York: De Capo Press, 1997.

Hirsch, Francine. *Empire of Nations*. Ithaca, NY: Cornell University Press, 2005.

Hobsbawm, Eric. *Nations and Nationalism Since 1780*. Cambridge University Press, 1990.

Human Rights Watch. *Azerbaijan, Seven Years of Conflict*. Helsinki: Human Rights Watch, 1994.

Jones, Stephen: *Socialism in Georgian Colors*. Boston: Harvard University Press, 2005.

Karny, Yo'av. *The Highlanders*. New York: Farrar, Straus and Giroux, 2000.

Kramer, Mark. *Travels with a Hungry Bear*. Boston: Houghton Mifflin Harcourt, 1996.

Kuprava, A. E. *Traditionnaya Kul'tura Abkhazov* (Traditional Culture of the Abkhaz). Krasnodar: Abkhaz Gosudarstvenniy Universitet, 2002.

LeVine, Steve: *The Oil and the Glory*. New York: Random House, 2007.

Lieven, Anatol. *Chechnya—Tombstone of Russian Power*. New Haven: Yale University Press, 1998.

March, Andrew F. "State Ideology and the Legitimization of Authoritarianism: The Case of Post-Soviet Uzbekistan." *Journal of Political Ideologies* (2003), 8(2), 209–232, St. John's College, Oxford, UK, 2003.

———. "The Use and Abuse of History: 'National Ideology' as Transcendental Object in Islam"; "Karimov's 'Ideology of National Independence'." *Central Asian Survey* (2002) 21(4), 371–384.

———. "From Leninism to Karimovism: Hegemony, Ideology, and Authoritarian Legitimization." *Post-Soviet Affairs*, (2003), 19, 4, pp. 307–336.

Martin, Terry. *The Affirmative Action Empire*. Ithaca, NY: Cornell University Press, 2001.

McCarthy, Justin. *Death and Exile—The Ethnic Cleansing of Ottoman Muslims, 1821–1922*. London: Darwin Press, 1995.

Melkonian, Markar. *The Right to Struggle*. San Francisco: Sardarabad Press, 2006.

Melkonian, Monte: *My Brother's Road*. London: I. B. Tauris, 2005.

Montefiore, Simon Sebag. *Stalin: In the Court of the Red Czar*. New York: Alfred A. Knopf, 2004.

———. *The Young Stalin*. New York: Alfred A. Knopf, 2007.

Motyl, Alexander: *Imperial Ends: The Decay, Collapse, and Revival of Empire*. New York: Columbia University Press, 2001.

Pope, Hugh. *Sons of the Conquerors: The Rise of the Turkic World*. New York: Overlook, 2005.

Radzinsky, Edvard. *The Last Tsar*. New York: Doubleday, 1992.

Reid, Anna. *Borderland: A Journey Through the History of Ukraine*. Boulder, CO: University of Colorado Press, 2000.

Reiss, Tom. *The Orientalist*. New York: Random House, 2005.

Riddell, John, ed. *To See the Dawn, Baku, 1920: First Congress of the Peoples of the East*. Pathfinder, 1993.

Saikal, Amin. *Modern Afghanistan: A History of Struggle and Survival*. London: I. B. Tauris, 2006.

Shevardnadze, Eduard. *Moj Vybor v zashchitu demokratii i svobody*. Moscow: Novosti, 1991.

Smith, Sebastian: *Allah's Mountains: Politics and War in the Russian Caucasus*. New York: St. Martin's Press, 1998.

Suny, Ronald. *The Baku Commune, 1917–1918*. Princeton, NJ: Princeton University Press, 1972.

————. *Looking at Ararat: Armenia in Modern History*. Bloomington: Indiana University Press, 1993.

————. *The Making of the Georgian Nation*. London: I. B. Tauris, 1989.

Talbot, Strobe. "Self-Determination." *Foreign Policy*, Spring 2000.

Thomas, D. M. *Ararat*. New York: Viking Press, 1983.

Tishkov, Valery. *Ethnicity, Nationalism, and Conflict in and After the Soviet Union: The Mind Aflame*. London: Sage Publications, 1997.

Volkov, Vadim. "The Political Economy of Protection Rackets." *Social Research*, Vol. 67, No. 3 (Fall 2000).

Walker, Christopher. *Armenia: The Survival of a Nation*. London: Routledge, 1980.

————. *Visions of Ararat Writings on Armenia*. London: I. B. Tauris, 1997.

Wilhelmsen, Julie. *Between a Rock and a Hard Place (Islam in Chechnya)*, Norwegian Institute of International Studies, 2005.

Yandarbiev, Zelimkha. *Checheniya — Bitva za svobodu*. Lvov: n.p., 1996.

Yergin, Daniel. *The Prize*. New York: Simon & Schuster, 1991.

ABOUT THE AUTHOR

LAWRENCE SCOTT SHEETS reported for National Public Radio for seven years and was NPR's Moscow bureau chief from 2001 to 2005, covering the entire former USSR. He was Caucasus region bureau chief for Reuters from 1992 to 2000 and a Knight Journalism Fellow at Stanford University from 2000 to 2001. His work has been published in the *Atlantic Monthly* and the *New York Times* and has been heard on the BBC World Service, Public Radio International, and other news outlets. Sheets is currently South Caucasus project director of the International Crisis Group, focusing on Georgia, Azerbaijan, and Armenia.